Organised Sexual Abuse

90 0949470 0

D0303757

Organised Sexual Abuse offers a comprehensive, interdisciplinary investigation of the phenomenon of multi-perpetrator, multi-victim sexual abuse. Since the early 1980s, social workers and mental health professionals around the globe have encountered clients reporting sexual abuse by organised groups or networks. These allegations have been amongst the most controversial in debates over child sexual abuse, raising many unanswered questions. Are reports of organised abuse factual or the product of moral panic and false ppropriate response? The n polarised over the issue. be uncovered, a reasoned overdue. Examining the er qualitative research, in between sexual abuse and abuse cases; the historical over the veracity of testi develop and operate; the rpetrator sexual abuse; as stories of organised abuse *ganised Sexual Abuse* thus nse value to those with

Michael Salter is lecturer in Criminology at the University of Western Sydney. His work is focused on the intersections of gendered violence, health and culture, and the significance of violence in the formation of culture and identity.

Organised Sexual Abuse

Michael Salter

Routledge
Taylor & Francis Group
a GlassHouse Book

First published 2013
by Routledge
2 Park Square, Milton Park, Abingdon, Oxfordshire OX14 4RN

Simultaneously published in the USA and Canada
by Routledge
711 Third Avenue, New York, NY 10017

First issued in paperback 2014
Routledge is an imprint of the Taylor & Francis Group, an informa company

A GlassHouse Book

British Library Cataloguing in Publication Data
A catalogue record for this book is available from the British Library

Library of Congress Cataloging-in-Publication Data
Salter, Michael, 1957–
Organised child sexual abuse / Michael Salter.
p. cm.
"Simultaneously published in the USA and Canada."
1. Child sexual abuse. 2. Child abuse—Law and legislation.
3. Sexually abused children—Legal status, laws, etc. I. Title.
K5189.S25 2013
362.76—dc23   2012018406

ISBN 13: 978-0-415-68977-9 (hbk)
ISBN 13: 978-1-138-78915-9 (pbk)

Typeset in Garamond
by Cenveo Publisher Services

Contents

Acknowledgements

This book was written for 'Sarah' and for the other brave survivors who came forward and trusted me with their stories. Thanks are also due to the many people who have provided valuable feedback on the material presented here, including: Jan Breckenridge, Juliet Richters, Anne Cossins, Stephen Tomsen, Sanja Milivejovic, Walter DeKeseredy, Molly Dragiewicz, Fran Gale, Mary Hawkins and Charles Barbour. The research upon which this book is based was made possible by an Australian Postgraduate Award and the support of the School of Public Health and Community Medicine and the School of Law at the University of New South Wales. I am also appreciative for the support shown by the School of Social Sciences and Psychology at the University of Western Sydney. Most of all I would like to thank Paul Brace whose support has meant so much throughout the research and writing process.

Introduction

Batley insisted that no cult existed but the jury found him guilty of 35 offences including 11 rapes, three indecent assaults, causing prostitution for personal gain, causing a child to have sex and inciting a child to have sex. The three women, who got Egyptian Eye of Horus tattoos apparently to show their allegiance to the organisation, were found guilty of sex-related charges.

Young boys and girls were procured by cult members to take part in sex sessions, the trial heard. The group preyed on vulnerable youngsters, impelling them to join with veiled death threats. Batley was accused of forcing a number of his victims into prostitution.

(Morris 2011)

There are, after all, no paedophile rings; there is no ritual abuse; recovered memories cannot be trusted; not all victimization claims are legitimate.

(Pratt 2009: 70)

Allegations of multi-perpetrator and multi-victim sexual abuse emerged to public awareness in the early 1980s contemporaneously with the denials of the accused and their supporters. Multi-perpetrator sexual offences are typically more sadistic than solo offences and organised sexual abuse is no exception. Adults and children with histories of organised abuse have described lives marked by torturous and sometimes ritualistic sexual abuse arranged by family members and other care-givers and authority figures. It is widely acknowledged, at least in theory, that sexual abuse can take severe forms, but when disclosures of such abuse occur, they are routinely subject to contestation and challenge. People accused of organised, sadistic or ritualistic abuse have protested that their accusers are liars and fantasists, or else innocents led astray by overly zealous investigators. This was an argument that many journalists and academics have found more convincing than the testimony of alleged victims. Today, acknowledgement of the prevalence and harms of child sexual abuse is counterbalanced with cautionary tales about children and women who, under pressure from social workers and therapists, produce false allegations of 'paedophile rings', 'cult abuse' and 'ritual abuse'. Child protection investigations or legal cases involving allegations of organised child sexual abuse are regularly invoked to illustrate the dangers of 'false memories', 'moral panic' and 'community hysteria'. These cautionary tales effectively delimit the bounds of acceptable knowledge in relation to sexual abuse. They are circulated by those who locate themselves firmly within those bounds, characterising those beyond as ideologues and conspiracy theorists.

However firmly these boundaries have been drawn, they have been persistently transgressed by substantiated disclosures of organised abuse that have led to child protection interventions and prosecutions. Throughout the 1990s, in a sustained effort to redraw these boundaries, investigations and prosecutions for organised abuse were widely labelled 'miscarriages of justice' and workers and therapists confronted with incidents of organised abuse were accused of fabricating or exaggerating the available evidence. These accusations have faded over time as evidence of organised abuse has accumulated, while investigatory procedures have become more standardised and less vulnerable to discrediting attacks. However, as the opening quotes to this introduction illustrate, the contemporary situation in relation to organised abuse is one of considerable ambiguity in which journalists and academics claim that organised abuse is a discredited 'moral panic' even as cases are being investigated and prosecuted.

This vacillation between assertion and denial in discussions about organised abuse can be understood as functional, in that it serves to contain the traumatic kernel at the heart of allegations of organised abuse. In his influential 'just world' theory, Lerner (1980) argued that emotional wellbeing is predicated on the assumption that the world is an orderly, predictable and just place in which people get what they deserve. Whilst such assumptions are objectively false, Lerner argued that individuals have considerable investment in maintaining them since they are conducive to feelings of self-efficacy and trust in others. When they encounter evidence contradicting the view that the world is just, individuals are motivated to defend this belief either by helping the victim (and thus restoring a sense of justice) or by persuading themselves that no injustice has occurred. Lerner (1980) focused on the ways in which the 'just world' fallacy motivates victim-blaming, but there are other defences available to bystanders who seek to dispel troubling knowledge. Organised abuse highlights the severity of sexual violence in the lives of some children and the desire of some adults to inflict considerable, and sometimes irreversible, harm upon the powerless. Such knowledge is so toxic to common presumptions about the orderly nature of society, and the generally benevolent motivations of others, that it seems as though a defensive scaffold of disbelief, minimisation and scorn has been erected to inhibit a full understanding of organised abuse.

Despite these efforts, there has been a recent resurgence of interest in organised abuse and particularly ritualistic abuse (eg Sachs and Galton 2008, Epstein et al. 2011, Miller 2012). It is clear that cases of organised abuse continue to surface in a range of contexts, such as mental health services and child protection agencies. However, the representations put forth of organised abuse continue to be marked by the traces of disavowal, even amongst those who take allegations of organised abuse seriously. Herman (1992) has observed the 'dual imperative' that shapes the disclosures of sexual abuse survivors, whose desire to disclose and seek help can be thwarted by the impulse to remain silent and thus maintain the comforting fiction that their abuse did not take place. This dual imperative can result in a destabilised and fragmented narrative that is, through its incoherent or 'hysterical' presentation, effectively self-invalidating. A similar dynamic can be detected within some overwrought representations of organised abuse that effectively communicate the distress of victims and their supporters (and the management of vicarious trauma is a serious challenge for professionals in this area) but in a manner that infects their claims with an irrational edge that provokes scepticism and disbelief. Internal to such claims is the tension between the acceptance that organised abuse has occurred and the struggle to explain how or why.

This book aims to address these tensions by providing a critical overview of debates over organised abuse before going on to examine the lives of 21 adults who described organised abuse in childhood. It draws on a range of perspectives from sociology, criminology and psychoanalysis in order to situate organised abuse within the study of gendered violence more broadly, and to explore the ways in which organised abuse intensifies but also transgresses against normative modes of masculine power. The book will consider a range of theorists who have argued that the social construction of gender is replete with fantasies of masculine control and transcendence that can be embodied through eroticised violence. In such acts, the perpetrator claims his position as masculine 'subject' by forcing the victim to occupy the position of the subordinate 'other' or 'object', whether the victim is a woman, child or another man. The book's title 'Organised sexual abuse' refers to the sexual abuse of adults as well as children since, for some victims, organised abuse does not end in childhood and may persist into adulthood. The secretive nature of these practices is maintained not only by the collusion of perpetrators but also by the socially legitimised power that perpetrators of organised abuse enjoy over their victims as parents, teachers and other authority figures. Whilst organised abuse refers to a relatively uncommon and extreme form of child abuse, it nonetheless raises larger questions about gender, age and power.

The majority of the available literature on organised abuse is concerned with the psychotherapeutic treatment of survivors but the focus of this book is not on the survivor as client but rather on the survivor as witness. The book draws on the life histories and experiences of survivors to develop a criminological model of organised abuse. This model may enrich the understanding of the clinician or therapist and thus provide useful background information for treatment, and it may also serve as a validating resource for survivors who feel ready to examine their background from a sociological or criminological perspective. However, it should be recognised that this book does not provide guidelines for treatment or recovery from organised abuse. Furthermore, the material presented here is often disturbing and all readers should be mindful of the potential for vicarious traumatisation. Readers who have survived sexual abuse and organised abuse are respectfully requested to remain vigilant regarding their emotional wellbeing.

Some readers may find it a curious or even unscientific endeavour to craft a criminological model of organised abuse based on the testimony of survivors. One of the standard objections to qualitative research is that participants may lie or fantasise in interview. It has been suggested that adults who report severe child sexual abuse are particularly prone to such confabulation. Whilst all forms of research, whether qualitative or quantitative, may be impacted upon by memory error or false reporting, there is no evidence that qualitative research is particularly vulnerable to this, nor is there any evidence that a fantasy- or lie-prone individual would be particularly likely to volunteer for research into child sexual abuse. Research has consistently found that child abuse histories, including severe and sadistic abuse, are accurate and can be corroborated (Ross 2009, Otnow et al. 1997, Chu et al. 1999). Survivors of child abuse may struggle with amnesia and other forms of memory disturbance but the notion that they are particularly prone to suggestion and confabulation has yet to find a scientific basis. It is interesting to note that questions about the veracity of eyewitness evidence appear to be asked far more frequently in relation to sexual abuse and rape than in relation to other crimes. The research on which this book is based has been conducted with an ethical commitment to taking the lives and voices of survivors of organised abuse seriously.

The book begins with an examination of the challenges involved in developing a coherent explanatory framework for organised abuse. The chapter 'A subject of smoke and mirrors: Understanding organised abuse' takes its title from a description of ritualistic and sadistic abuse proffered by Professor Roland Summit (Summit 1994: 5), a pioneer in this field. 'Smoke and mirrors' is a useful metaphor for the ways in which organised abuse has eluded conceptualisation and understanding. The chapter provides an overview of the often incendiary debates over organised abuse before going on to suggest that critical theories of gender, crime and intersubjectivity may offer new insights into the phenomenon.

The second chapter draws together the available literature on organised abuse and develops a simple typology of cases based on the context in which they arise: network (or extra-familial), familial and institutional. Ritual abuse is discussed as an abusive behaviour that demarcates a particularly challenging form of organised abuse. By synthesising clinical and case review data with case studies and survivor accounts this chapter suggests that organised abuse can sensibly be understood in terms of the intersections of gender, age and power in a range of contexts.

The themes of gender, age and power is examined further in Chapter 3 from an historical perspective. This chapter argues that the construction of masculine sexuality by the 18th-century libertines as a 'natural' and predatory instinct has important parallels in modern society, including organised abuse. The work of the Marquis de Sade is used to illustrate the ways in which organised, sadistic and even ritualistic abuse can be understood as symbolic enactments of a pervasive ideology of masculine sexual aggression.

Chapter 4, 'Organised abuse and the pleasures of disbelief', uses Žižek's (1991) insights into the political role of enjoyment to analyse the hyperbole and scorn that has characterised the sceptical account of organised and ritualistic abuse. The central argument of this chapter is that organised abuse has come to public attention primarily as a subject of ridicule within the highly partisan writings of journalists, academics and activists aligned with advocacy groups for people accused of sexual abuse. Whilst highlighting the pervasive misrepresentations that characterise these accounts, the chapter also implicates media consumers in the production of ignorance and disdain in relation to organised abuse and women's and children's accounts of sexual abuse more generally.

The fifth chapter is autobiographical and describes the circumstances that led to the research upon which this book is based. It is called 'Down the rabbit hole: my story' because it describes my inadvertent 'tumble' into the world of organised abuse through my friendship with a young woman, 'Sarah'. This chapter provides an account of this friendship and how it endured through a period of intense stress, as the men who had subjected Sarah to organised abuse in childhood attempted to draw her back into the cycle of abuse and violence as an adult. This account is provided with the intention of highlighting the diversity of experiences with organised abuse and the ways in which men's experiences as witnesses to gendered violence can serve as the basis for resistance to it.

The following five chapters report on the results of life history research with adults with histories of organised abuse. Chapter 6 provides an overview of the common themes that characterised survivors' experiences of abuse, neglect and invalidation in childhood, and in particular how their accounts of life at home and school foreground the powerlessness of children. The seventh chapter is based on the accounts of participants whose organised abuse was arranged by their parents and other family members. It describes the 'two worlds' of severe sexual abuse at home and the charade of normalcy at school and in the community.

Chapter 8 focuses on the ways in which sexually abusive groups are characterised by processes of control, exchange and sadism. These themes are illustrated by the accounts of participants who were subject to network or institutional abuse; that is, organised abuse outside the family. The chapter combines sociological and psychoanalytic theory to describe the ways in which children are objectified, and their inner life denied, as they become entrapped within the dynamics of power and control that structure sexually abusive groups. This process is explored in more detail in Chapter 9, 'Ritual and torture in organised abuse', which argues that ritualistic abuse and torture are practices through which perpetrators of organised abuse attempt to intensify relations of domination and subordination.

The final chapter examines the controversial reports of murder and atrocity that have surfaced in accounts of organised abuse. Rather than dismiss them out of hand, this chapter suggests that these accounts can be considered credible in light of the sadistic, narcissistic fantasies that are manifest within sexually abusive groups. The book concludes by considering the challenges that organised abuse continues to pose to contemporary policy and practice in relation to sexual abuse and understandings of gendered violence.

Terminology

At present, there is no commonly accepted definition or description of complex cases of sexual abuse involving multiple abusers and multiple children. Generic terms such as 'sex ring', 'paedophile ring' or 'sexual exploitation' are unclear, since they tend to imply the abuse of children by predatory strangers when the relations between victims and abusers are often more complex than this. Cases are often categorised according to the forms of sexual abuse engaged in by perpetrators (eg a 'ritual abuse' case or a 'child pornography' case) but abusive groups tend to engage in multiple forms of abuse (eg both ritual abuse *and* the manufacture of child abuse images). Hence these distinctions are somewhat artificial and are often drawn according to the interests and priorities of the investigator/researcher rather than on the characteristics of the case. The simultaneous abuse of children and women, and the abuse of children into adulthood, adds an additional layer of complexity to the study of multi-perpetrator sexual offences by challenging taken-for-granted distinctions between rape and child sexual abuse.

This book employs the terms 'organised sexual abuse' and 'organised abuse' as relatively simple and inclusive descriptors for any occurrence of sexual abuse in which multiple victims have been exploited by multiple perpetrators acting in concert, in which some of the victims are children. This definition of organised abuse is drawn from La Fontaine (1993) and is consonant with the use of the term by other researchers (Bibby 1996a, Gallagher et al. 1996), however it acknowledges the co-abuse of children and women by some abusive groups. In this book, where a case of sexual abuse involves multiple victims (children or children and adults), multiple perpetrators, multiple incidents of abuse and evidence of premeditation and coordination between perpetrators, then it is categorised as a case of 'organised abuse'. The exclusion of any case of sexual abuse or exploitation from this definition of organised abuse is not a statement about the seriousness of the harm inflicted on the victim/s' or the gravity of the crimes committed by the abusers. This project is not based on a hierarchy of victimisation with 'organised abuse' at the top, but rather on a 'connective model' (Kelly 1998) that explores the commonalities that emerge from diverse experiences of organised abuse.

The book refers regularly to 'victims', 'survivors' and 'perpetrators'. These are contested terms in the literature and are often associated with simple dichotomies and absolutes, eg good victim/bad perpetrator, broken victim/recovered survivor. As the book will discuss, the lines of demarcation here are not fixed, since a 'survivor' may still be periodically 'victimised' by abusive groups despite their efforts to prevent such victimisation, 'victimisation' may include forced perpetration, and a 'perpetrator' may have an extensive history of 'victimisation'. Whilst acknowledging their ambiguities, the terms are used in this book as a kind of shorthand to situate social actors in terms of prior or ongoing victimisation and/or perpetration in organised abuse. 'Victim' refers to children or adults currently being victimised (which may include forced perpetration, which is understood as an important dimension of victimisation) and 'survivor' refers to children or adults who are no longer being victimised, or who are taking decisive steps to bring ongoing victimisation to an end. In general, the term 'perpetrator' is used to refer specifically to adults who are active in the planning and commission of sexual abuse and organised abuse. It should be acknowledged that, from the perspective of a survivor, an adult may be meaningfully and accurately described as a 'perpetrator' although an observer might be more circumspect in light of the 'perpetrator's' life history and circumstances. It is a testament to the empathy and compassion displayed by the survivors interviewed for this book that they often reflected on these ambiguities themselves, even when describing people in their past who had subjected them to extensive harm and violence.

Chapter 1

A subject of smoke and mirrors

Understanding organised abuse

The figure of the child at risk is a potent one in Western culture, and the sexual abuse and exploitation of children has long been a focal point of social anxiety. Child sexual exploitation is often invoked in public discourse to advance a range of agendas, only some of which are related to the wellbeing and security of victimised and vulnerable children. Reports of child prostitution and exploitation in the 'third world' have become an important part of the rationalisation of Western border control and national security policies (O'Connell Davidson 2005). In the United States, accusations of mass child molestation have been a feature of homophobic slander since the Cold War, in which nationalist propaganda conflated socialism, child sex crimes and homosexuality as a combined threat to social order (eg Fejes 2000). In Australia, allegations of 'paedophile rings' have been used to justify a range of punitive interventions into Indigenous families and communities (Brown and Brown 2007). In Britain, reports of Muslim 'sex rings' that prey on white teenage girls have stirred up a predictable response from racist and right-wing groups (Taylor 2012). What emerges clearly from these heated discussions is the way in which organised abuse can be invoked for maximum political gain and impact.

The rhetorical power of organised abuse comes from its unthinkable heinousness. When it is referred to in Western media and commentary, it is pervasively attributed to the 'Other' in the psychoanalytic sense: that which is considered radically different and outside the 'self'. Hence organised abuse is frequently associated by Westerners with ethnic communities and developing countries, with the implication that they are more dangerous and less civilised, or it is alleged to be committed by groups considered perverted and pathological, whether paedophiles, homosexuals or some conflation of the two. The invocation of organised abuse is a blunt but often effective way of polarising debate in order to raise suspicions about a particular social group or else to recast complex debates in black-and-white terms. State authorities and social movements have played a sometimes conflicting but combined role in shaping this debate. Sociologists and historians have made useful contributions by pointing to the political and cultural dynamics that shape overblown discourses about child endangerment and protection (Kincaid 1998, Jenkins 1998). However, they have sometimes reduced the subject of organised abuse to the moral panics that surround it, without considering the possibility that representations of organised abuse, however sensationalised, may have their origins in lived experience.

There are a range of useful and illuminating analyses of the media construction of organised abuse as it became front-page news in the 1980s and 1990s (Kitzinger 2004, Atmore 1997, Kelly 1998), but this book is focused on organised abuse as a criminal practice *as well as* a discursive object of study, debate and disagreement. These two dimensions of the topic are inextricably linked because precisely *where* and *how* organised abuse is reported to take place is an important determinant of how it is understood. Prior to the 1980s, the predominant view of the police, psychiatrists and other authoritative professionals was that organised abuse occurred primarily outside the family where it was committed by extra-familial 'paedophiles'. This conceptualisation of organised abuse has received enduring community support to the present day, where concerns over children's safety is often framed in terms of their vulnerability to manipulation by 'paedophiles' and 'sex rings'. This view dovetails more generally with the medico-legal and media construction of the 'paedophile' as an external threat to the sanctity of the family and community (Cowburn and Dominelli 2001) but it is confounded by evidence that organised abuse and other forms of serious sexual abuse often originates in the home or in institutions, such as schools and churches, where adults have socially legitimate authority over children.

As mandatory reporting laws and community awareness drove an increase in child protection investigations throughout the 1980s, some children began to disclose premeditated, sadistic and organised abuse by their parents, relatives and other caregivers such as priests and teachers (Hechler 1988). Adults in psychotherapy described similar experiences. The dichotomies that had previously associated organised abuse with the dangerous, external 'Other' had been breached, and the incendiary debate that followed is an illustration of the depth of the collective desire to see them restored. Campbell (1988) noted the paradox that, whilst journalists and politicians often demand that the authorities respond more decisively in response to a 'crisis' of sexual abuse, the action that is taken is then subsequently construed as a 'crisis'. This has been a particularly pronounced tendency of the public reception to allegations of organised abuse. The removal of children from their parents due to disclosures of organised abuse, the provision of mental health care to survivors of organised abuse, police investigations of allegations of organised abuse and the prosecution of alleged perpetrators of organised abuse have all generated their own controversies.

These were disagreements that were cloaked in the vocabulary of science and objectivity but nonetheless were played out in sensationalised fashion on primetime television, glossy news magazines and populist books, drawing on 'common sense' notions about what constitutes a credible allegation of sexual abuse and what does not. Whilst these controversies have mostly faded away, the uncertainties and anxieties that they raised about the existence of sexually abusive groups and the reliability of victim testimony remains. This has had serious consequences for the children and adults who are describing histories of organised abuse and require support from health and welfare services and access to the legal system. They constitute a group of sexual abuse victims and survivors whose experiences are, literally, unspeakable. Their histories, memories and testimony have been placed beyond belief and, for many, beyond hope. As Campbell (1988: 71) observed:

> Detection is always contingent. It depends on a co-operation and a consensus about what matters, what is wrong, what hurts, what is visible and what is knowable. Detection is above all about what is *evident* and what is *evidence*. But all this is dependent on political consciousness. Seeing is believing, we're told, and yet evidence, like beauty, is in the eye of the beholder. If you don't believe it is possible for children to be sexually abused *en masse* by the men in their lives, then you don't see the signs, even when they are staring you in the face.

Mollon (2008: 108) suggests that some forms of child sexual abuse are outside of the 'dominant symbolic structure' that determines 'what we normally believe to be true, possible and within the nature of reality'. Such abuse cannot by represented or acknowledged without threatening the integrity of prevailing systems of meaning, and the furore over organised abuse suggests that it represents just such a disruption. In allegations of organised abuse, customary images of parents, homes, schools and childhood are dissociated from their idyllic connotations and placed in relation to taboo acts and substances. Narratives of organised abuse are replete with the most perturbing of symbolic inversions and transgressions and as such have been treated as a contaminant or 'matter out of place', as Douglas (1966) defines impurity. The repeated attempt to discredit disclosures of organised abuse by claiming they are caused by watching horror films (La Fontaine 1998), or comparable in credibility to accounts of alien abduction (Bader 2003) and past life memories (Spanos et al. 1994), can be understood as a strategy of defence and trivialisation that wards off the threat that organised abuse poses to the symbolic order. Fairy tales, movies, books, talk shows and newspaper articles have all been blamed for inciting confabulated recollections amongst the suggestible.

The possibility that the representations that children and women have made of organised abuse may be grounded in lived experience has simply been unimaginable for some commentators. This has been compounded by the 'linguistic turn' in the humanities and cultural studies, where narratives of organised abuse have proved a popular subject for deconstruction and textual analysis. The role of therapy and social work in the construction of testimony of abuse and trauma, in particular, has come under sustained post-modern attack. Frosh (2002) has suggested that therapeutic spaces provide children and adults with the rare opportunity to articulate experiences that are otherwise excluded from the dominant symbolic order. However, since the 1990s, post-modern and post-structural theory has often been deployed in ways that attempt to 'manage' from afar the perturbing disclosures of abuse and trauma that arise in therapeutic spaces (Frosh 2002). Nowhere is this clearer than in relation to organised abuse, where the testimony of girls and women has been deconstructed as symptoms of cultural hysteria (Showalter 1997) and the colonisation of women's minds by therapeutic discourse (Hacking 1995). However, behind words and discourse, 'a real world and real lives do exist, howsoever we interpret, construct and recycle accounts of these by a variety of symbolic means' (Stanley 1993: 214).

Summit (1994: 5) once described organised abuse as a 'subject of smoke and mirrors', observing the ways in which it has persistently defied conceptualisation or explanation. The aim of this chapter is to review the ways in which organised abuse has been conceptualised by those researchers and clinicians concerned about it (the views of those authors who do not take organised abuse seriously will be considered in Chapter 4), and to introduce the sociologically-informed account of sexual abuse and organised abuse that is the foundation of this book. In doing so, a secondary aim of this chapter is to reveal the challenge that organised abuse poses to common understandings of child sexual abuse. Explanations for serious or sadistic child sex offending have typically rested on psychiatric concepts of 'paedophilia' or particular psychological categories that have limited utility for the study of the cultures of sexual abuse that emerge in the families or institutions in which organised abuse takes place. For those clinicians and researchers who take organised abuse seriously, their reliance upon individualistic rather than sociological explanations for child sexual abuse has left them unable to explain the emergence of coordinated, and often sadistic, multi-perpetrator sexual abuse in a range of contexts around the world. This chapter proposes an alternative approach that integrates sociological, criminological and psychoanalytic theory.

Conflicting approaches to organised abuse

Over the last 30 years, survivors of organised abuse and the range of professionals who support them have been working in coalition to bring to light the seriousness of organised forms of child sexual abuse. Emerging from this partnership has been a body of literature on organised abuse that includes autobiographies, case descriptions, clinic-based research studies and treatment recommendations. A significant proportion of this literature has been concerned with ritual abuse, a form of organised abuse in which perpetrators engage in sexual abuse in a ritualistic or ceremonial way (McFadyen et al. 1993). Sceptical claims that allegations of organised abuse are the product of therapeutic and social work malpractice is contested by the range of professionals reporting contact with victims and survivors, including domestic violence and rape crisis workers (Scott 1998, Cooper 2004), general practitioners (Jonker and Jonker-Bakker 1991), paediatricians (Buck 2008), police officers (Healey 2008) and school teachers (Hayden 1991). One of the key challenges that has faced workers is how to make sense out of lives in which multiple forms, contexts and perpetrators of abuse cluster and intersect in bewildering ways. Such extreme forms of child abuse have deleterious mental health consequences, and the coherence of eyewitness testimony of organised abuse appears to decline according to the seriousness of the violence disclosed by the victim. Politicising such narratives has necessarily required considerable intervention and interlocution by workers, in the form of high-lighting particular commonalities and advancing particular explanations (Clapton 1993).

Ritual abuse has proven particularly challenging for workers to under-stand and explain. The task of developing a reasonable explanatory framework for these disclosures has been complicated by the enthusiastic promulgation of conspiratorial and religious theories by evangelical churches and workers on one hand, and the bellicose scepticism of advocacy groups, journalists and academics on the other. The role of religious and occult ideologies in sexually abusive groups will be examined in more detail in Chapter 9, how-ever it is useful to note here the shortcomings of drawing a firm distinction between 'organised abuse' and 'ritual abuse'. Qualitative and quantitative research with adults and children reporting ritual abuse has found that it occurs alongside other forms of organised abuse, particularly the manufacture of child abuse images (Scott 2001, Snow and Sorenson 1990, Waterman et al. 1993), and hence subsuming such non-ritualistic experiences under the moniker 'ritual abuse' is misleading at best and incendiary at worst. Moreover, it is unclear why an abusive group that invokes a religious or metaphysical mandate to abuse children should be considered as largely distinct from an abusive group that invokes a non-religious rationale to do so. The presump-tion evident amongst some authors writing on ritual abuse that a professed spiritual motivation for abusing children necessarily reflects the offenders *actual* motivation seems naïve at best, and at worst it risks colluding with the ways in which abusive groups obfuscate responsibility for their actions.

Research on organised abuse emphasises the diversity of organised abuse cases, and the ways in which serious forms of child maltreatment cluster in the lives of children subject to organised victimisation (eg Bibby 1996b, Itzin 1997, Kelly and Regan 2000). Most attempts to examine organised abuse have been undertaken by therapists and social workers who have focused primarily on the role of psychological processes in the organised victimisation of children and adults. Dissociation, amnesia and attachment, in particular, have been identified as important factors that compel victims to obey their abusers whilst inhibiting them from disclosing their abuse or seeking help (see Epstein et al. 2011, Sachs and Galton 2008). Therapists and social workers have surmised that these psychological effects are purposively induced by perpetrators of organised abuse through the use of sadistic and ritualistic abuse. In this literature, perpetrators are characterised either as dissociated automatons mindlessly perpetuating the abuse that they, too, were subjected to as children, or else as cruel and manipulative criminals with expert foreknowledge of the psychological consequences of their abuses. The therapist is positioned in this discourse at the very heart of the solution to organised abuse, wielding their expertise in a struggle against the coercive strategies of the perpetrators.

Whilst it cannot be denied that abusive groups undertake calculated strategies designed to terrorise children into silence and obedience, the emphasis of this literature on psychological factors in explaining organised abuse has overlooked the social contexts of such abuse and the significance of abuse and violence as social practices. The fact that most perpetrators of organised abuse are men, and that their most intensive and sadistic abuses are visited upon girls and women, has gone largely unnoticed, as have the patterns of gendered inequity that characterise the families and institutional settings in which organised abuse takes place. Organised abuse survivors share a number of challenges in common with other survivors of abuse and trauma, including health and justice systems that have been slow to recognise and respond to violence against children and women. However, this connection is rarely made in the literature on organised abuse, with some authors hinting darkly at the nefarious influence of abusive groups. Fraser (1997: xiv) provides a note of caution here, explaining that whilst it is relatively easy to 'comment on the naïveté of those grappling with this issue ... it is very difficult to actually face a new and urgent phenomenon and deal with it, but not fully understand it, while managing distressed and confused patients and their families'. Nonetheless, it remains the case that the psychological literature on organised abuse has not provided a coherent explanation for the emergence of sexually abusive groups in a range of contexts, or for the difficulties that victims experience in disclosing their abuse and accessing care and support. The psychological model of organised abuse emphasises individual rather than social factors and so it tends to characterise organised abuse as a drama of psychological energies.

Similar deficiencies can be found in attempts to theorise organised abuse that draw from psychiatric understandings of 'paedophilia' (eg Wyre 1996). This is a perspective that has proved particularly influential in public inquiries into allegations of organised abuse (for examples from Australia, see NCA Joint Committee Report 1995, Wood Report 1997, for examples from Britain, see Corby et al. 2001). These public inquiries have integrated the psychiatric notion of 'paedophilia' with existing stereotypes of organised crime to generate a model of 'organised paedophilia' or the 'paedophile ring', in which otherwise solitary sexual offenders with deviant sexual interests conspire to sexually abuse children for pleasure and/or profit. This psychiatric model may accurately describe some abusive men and groups but it has proven problematic as a catch-all explanation for organised abuse. Attempts to establish the existence of 'paedophile rings' often founders on semantic debates over whether alleged perpetrators meet the diagnostic criteria of a 'paedophile', sometimes leading to the confused and misleading conclusion that no 'paedophile ring' existed even where there is strong evidence that multiple perpetrators have colluded in the sexual abuse of multiple children. Like the psychological model outlined above, the psychiatric understanding of 'organised paedophilia' is a framework that is focused primarily on individual psychological factors and overlooks the role of violence in criminal groups and the contexts in which such groups emerge.

The underlying assumption of literature on 'organised paedophilia' is that members of sexually abusive groups are motivated by a pathological sexual interest in children but this does not accord with evidence that suggests that abusive groups can simultaneously abuse children and women. It is increasingly recognised that sexual offenders may not specialise in one particular victim category, and a significant proportion of child sexual abusers have also offended against adults (Cann et al. 2007, Heil et al. 2003). Furthermore, many of the behaviours of abusive groups appear to be designed to elicit fear and pain from the victim rather than to generate sexual pleasure for the perpetrator per se. The two, of course, are not mutually exclusive, but there is a sadistic dimension to organised abuse that is not explicable as 'paedophilic'. A survivor of organised abuse from Belgium, Regina Louf, made this point clearly when she said:

> I find the expression 'paedophile network' misleading. For me paedophiles are those men who go to playgrounds or swimming pools, priests … I certainly don't want to exonerate them, but I would rather have paedophiles than the types we were involved with. There were men who never touched the children. Whether you were five, ten or fifteen didn't matter. What mattered to them was sex, power, experience. To do things they would never have tried with their own wives. Among them were some real sadists.
>
> (Louf quoted in Bulte and de Conick 1998)

A credible theoretical account of organised abuse must necessarily (a) account for the available empirical evidence of organised abuse, (b) address the complex patterns of abuse and violence evident in sexually abusive groups, and (c) explain the ways in which sexually abusive groups form in a range of contexts, including families and institutions. The data on organised abuse has been simplified or distorted in an attempt to force it to conform to mechanical psychological models of dissociative obedience or else to the psychiatric framework of 'paedophilia'. Psychopathology alone is an inadequate explanation for environments in which sexual abuse has a social and symbolic function for groups of adults. Abusive groups do not emerge in a vacuum but rather they are formed within pre-existing social arrangements such as families, churches and schools. The following section will introduce existing theories that link men's violent or criminal behaviours to structures of gender and power, and consider how these theories can provide a way of identifying the underlying factors and social processes that prompt the development of sexually abusive groups.

Criminality and violence as a gendered practice

A number of theorists have drawn attention to the pervasive ways in which the masculinity of sex offenders has been elided in medical and psychiatric literature. They have suggested that sex offending is, for some men and boys, a way of constituting and embodying a masculine sense of self (Glaser and Frosh 1993, Messerschmidt 1999, Cossins 2000). This work has been part of a broader shift in sociological and criminological thought away from essentialist explanations for crime towards a symbolic interactionist view of gender as a situated accomplishment (West and Zimmerman 1987) and performance (Butler 1990) achieved through social interaction. Gendered behaviour is not innate to men and women but rather '[w]hen persons "do gender", they engage in on-going interactional processes in which they invoke, construct and enact dichotomous images of two genders' (Gilgun and McLeod 1999: 170–1). An understanding of sexual violence as gendered performance is grounded in the work of feminist theorists from the 1960s and 1970s who argued that rape, incest and domestic violence are not symptoms of psychopathology but rather strategies used by some men to feel powerful and in control, and thus to feel 'like a man' (eg Summers 1975, Millett 1971, Brownmiller 1975). Feminist-informed research with rapists and wife batterers has documented the ways in which perpetrators' justifications for rape and violence overlapped with social idealisations of physical and sexual aggression as the natural and proper expression of authentic masculinity (Dobash and Dobash 1979, Scully 1988).

Disputing the medico-legal construction of sexual violence as a rare pathological aberration, feminist theorists have situated rape and abuse within the context of a society that has institutionalised male privilege and female subordination. Some radical feminists went further and characterised male violence as a purposive strategy undertaken by men in the perpetuation of this social order. Whilst the identification of the role of violence in the patterning of gender relations is an important insight, Connell (1987: 215) suggests that it is 'too easy' and too simplistic to explain a collective project of oppression as a conspiracy. In an earlier article, Carrigan, Connell and Lee (1985) argued that the link established by radical feminists between men's practices of violence and the social structures of masculine domination presumed an improbable degree of intentionality and awareness on the part of individual men, who were characterised as 'agents of patriarchy'. 'The overall relation between men and women', they stated, 'is not a confrontation between homogenous, undifferentiated blocs' (Carrigan, Connell and Lee 1985: 590). In this way, they contested the essentialism that has often undermined radical feminist theorising whilst keeping intact the focus of radical feminism upon practices of gendered subordination and control.

Carrigan, Connell and Lee (1985) proposed that male domination represents a historically contingent, but enduring, patterning of gender relations. Whilst this patterning is institutionalised through the collective practices of the state, the workplace, schools and the family, it is embodied by men in their everyday lives, and experienced as a constitutive force in their interpersonal and sexual relations. This model was subsequently expanded by Connell (1995) and others into a body of work called critical masculinity theory or 'critical studies of men' (Kimmel et al. 2005). This literature rejects the argument that there is one particular 'sex role' for men in society and instead examines the multiple constructions of masculinity that form within institutions, communities and cultures. Some forms of masculinity are considered more socially honourable than others, and Connell (1995) labelled the construction of masculinity that achieves cultural dominance as 'hegemonic masculinity'. This construction has the function of legitimising masculine domination by associating socially valued characteristics with men and boys, whilst less valued or despised characteristics are associated with femininity or with the masculinities of subordinate groups such as gay men or ethnic minorities. The ways in which the privileging of hegemonic masculinity is institutionalised and perpetuated at a social level is called the 'gender order', shaped by the divisions and distributions of labour, authority and sexual desire (Connell 1987).

In most Western societies, the hegemonic mode of masculinity emphasises aggression, dominance and sexual performance as key domains within which boys and men are expected to establish their masculine identities (Donaldson 1993). This mode delivers considerable benefits to men and boys by assigning them a superior cultural status in comparison to girls and women, which in turn is reflected by the superior financial and social capital accrued by men. Nonetheless, the price of male privilege is a considerable burden of anxiety and vulnerability since few, if any, boys or men meet the standards of hegemonic masculinity (Connell 1995). In response some may reject hegemonic masculinity outright and identify with alternative understandings of masculinity, whilst others seek to reinterpret hegemonic masculine ideals in a manner more suited to their circumstances. The ways in which working class or marginalised boys and men engage in hyper-masculine displays of transgression and thrill-seeking, for example, has been identified as a form of 'protest masculinity' that reworks hegemonic masculine principles in the context of socioeconomic disadvantage (Connell 1995). However there is considerable ambiguity in relations between 'hegemonic' and 'protest' masculinities, since the violence and criminality associated with the anti-hero is celebrated in 'hegemonic' as well as 'protest' masculinity as an authentic expression of masculinity (Tomsen 2008). Hence criminality occupies an ambivalent and contradictory position in contemporary constructions of masculinity, maintaining a surreptitious attraction and fascination for many men and boys.

Masculinity and sexual offending

Messerschmidt (1993) has called attention to the gendered nature of crime, and proposed that the disproportionate participation of men in a range of violent and criminal practices can be explained in terms of men's efforts to embody and reproduce hegemonic ideals of masculinity. He argues that criminal activity, as a form of 'doing gender', is a situated performance shaped by the access of men and boys to social and financial resources (Messerschmidt 1993: 93). Transgression and risk-taking maintains an appeal for a range of young men as a way of accruing masculine prestige amongst their peers, but Messerschmidt notes that white and middle-class teenagers, whilst engaging in 'pranks' and minor displays of rebellion, avoid committing offences that would disrupt their pathways towards a respectable professional position (Messerschmidt 1993). In contrast, working-class youth, for instance, and marginalised black youth, are more likely to resort to major acts of violence and theft as a way of asserting masculinity in contexts of structural powerlessness.

Whilst much of his work maintains a strong focus on the role of socioeconomic disadvantage and racial subordination in the genesis of male offending, Messerschmidt (1993) develops a more psychodynamic explanation for sexual offending. He suggests that sexual violence is a strategy through which men humiliate and devalue women, 'thereby strengthening the fiction of masculine power' (p 114), whilst also affirming the social construction of a man's 'essential nature' through the 'violent control of women' (p 152). In subsequent research with juvenile offenders, Messerschmidt (1999, 2000) emphasises boys' experiences of powerlessness and inadequacy within the gender patterning of hegemonic masculinities, and he analyses sexual assault as a resource that some boys draw on to overcome their subjective sense of disempowerment. In one case study, Messerschmidt (2000: 293) identifies how the boys' experience of risk, pleasure and dominance in the commission of sexually abusive acts formed the basis of what he describes as a compensatory 'supermasculine' identity. The participant Sam stated: 'Like, well, I'm a guy. I'm supposed to have sex. I'm supposed to be like every other guy. And so I'm like them, but I'm even better than them [the popular boys] because I can manipulate. They don't get the power and the excitement [that comes with sexual abuse]' (Messerschmidt 2000: 292).

This work provides intriguing insights into the role of anxiety, identification and self-construction in the practice of sexual abuse, although Messerschmidt does not elucidate further on the link between masculinity, abuse and subjectivity. Jefferson (2002) suggests that the theoretical apparatus of critical masculinity theory has generally underplayed the 'inner dimension' in men's maintenance and reproduction of power relations. However, this 'inner dimension' would appear to be a crucial factor in men's engagement in sexual abuse, which is inflected with fantasies of domination and control. Liddle (1993: 103) points to the perpetual instability of men's attempts to perform, obtain and incorporate the impossible ideals of masculinity. This results in numerous anxieties over dependency, adequacy, power, success and competency, all of which are culturally associated with sexual conquest and release. If a compulsory, aggressive heterosexuality is the 'first propensity' of male sexuality incited by the contemporary gender order, then Liddle (1993) suggests that child sexual abuse is the 'second propensity'. In his view, it is the 'disturbing rendezvous' of desire, vulnerability and powerlessness in child sexual abuse that marks it as the practice through which some men, in particular circumstances, attempt to resolve emotional conflicts over dependency through the satisfaction of desire.

Cossins (2000: 124) also emphasises the ways in which child sexual abuse accords with hegemonic ideals of masculinity, since 'the accomplishment of masculinity and experiences of potency are more likely to occur with those who are perceived to have less social power than the individual man in question'. Her 'power/powerlessness' theory contextualises sexual abuse in terms of the vulnerabilities and powerlessness that men can experience within a social order characterized by male competition and aggression. She suggests that 'different masculinities contain normative sexual elements that some men reproduce and affirm through child sex offending in cultural environments where the lives of men are characterised by varying degrees of power and powerlessness' (2000: 147). In formal and informal hierarchies in which males are subject to the control of those superior in status to them, and the 'jostling' and bullying of other males who seek to accrue status by subordinating others, sexual abuse is a practice through which men and boys can dominate another without risking retaliation or humiliation. The desire for control over a vulnerable 'other' may be explicitly recognised by offenders, however Keenan (2012: 238) notes that experiences of disempowerment may lead some men to sympathise with minors as 'friends' or 'equals', leading to a disingenuous 'blindness to power in the sexual and emotional sphere'. The degree to which sexual abusers acknowledge their power over children may vary but it seems that the attractions of child sexual abuse are linked to the sexual anxieties that some men experience in their efforts to defend and affix masculine selfhood. Cossins (2000) suggests that a minority of men eroticise the power imbalance inherent in adult-child relations, since these relations serve as a relatively unthreatening space for the accrual of experiences of (illicit, secretive) masculine pleasure, control and self-validation.

Abuse, domination and intersubjectivity

For Cossins (2000), the appeal of child sexual abuse for some men and boys emerges from the interaction between victim and perpetrator within a shifting field of interpersonal relations structured by gender and age. Whilst significant benefit accrues to men through these structures, men's experience of the relational field is beset with the anxiety that attends potential humiliation or shaming by peers or by girls and women. Hence sexual abuse is a practice through which boys and men can seek affirmation of their dominant status without the vulnerabilities that attend consensual, mutual sexual relations. This resonates in many regards with Benjamin's (1995, 1990) psychoanalytic theories of gender and subordination. Her work is based on the insights of Winnicott (1960: 586), whose suggestion that 'there is no such thing as an infant', only the infant-mother dyad, since 'without maternal care there would be no infant', recognised the importance of relationality in developmental processes. However, Benjamin (1990) enriched this perspective with the insights of Hegel and feminist philosophy to explain how processes of recognition and interaction give rise to inequality and coercion in gender relations. This section will examine the relevance of Benjamin's work, and the intersubjective psychoanalytic tradition more generally, to the study of sexual abuse.

Benjamin (1990) describes infancy as a state of profound dependence in which the child experiences fear and rage in its efforts to control its primary caretaker, usually the mother. Ideally, the child learns to regulate these destructive impulses over time by recognising that its mother is not simply an object that serves the impulses of the child. This recognition is crucial to healthy psychological development since the infantile desire for control and domination only leads to frustration. Every individual is psychologically, emotionally and materially dependent on others. Even 'independence' itself is a state that is only achieved when a person is recognised as independent. Hence 'independence' is paradoxically a state of dependency and the 'autonomous' subject must continually reconcile their desire for self-assertion and control with a recognition of the identity and needs of others. This is a tension that Benjamin (1990) suggests can be experienced as intolerable, fuelling the impulse for domination.

> When the conflict between dependence and independence becomes too intense, the psyche gives up the paradox in favour of an opposition. Polarity, the conflict of opposites, replaces the balance within the self.

> This polarity sets the stage for defining the self in terms of a movement
> away from dependence. It also sets the stage for domination.
>
> (Benjamin 1990: 50)

In a society structured by sexual difference, the collapse of mutuality into polarity, Benjamin (1990) argues, is a gendered process that differentially effects male socialisation and development. The male child establishes a sense of self through differentiating himself from his mother and, in a culture where men feature symbolically as subjects and women as objects (or as lesser or inessential subjects), this can involve a repudiation of 'Otherness' as a whole. 'An objectifying attitude comes to replace the earlier interactions of infancy in which mutual recognition and proud assertion could co-exist ... He is, of course, able cognitively to accept the principle that the other is separate, but without the experience of empathy and shared feeling that can unite separate subjectivities' (Benjamin 1990: 76). From the perspective of polarity rather than empathy, the 'other' is related to as an object rather than subject, and rationality and calculation rather than emotion and sympathy becomes the basis for interaction and engagement. Benjamin (1990) explains violation as a further elaboration of the process of psychic polarisation. Through an act of violence or domination, the 'master' gains by force the recognition of the other without entering into a relation of equals that would require him to recognise her subjectivity in turn. In this fashion he gains the recognition he needs to affirm his dominant status whilst maintaining his rigid internal boundaries and averting an inchoate fear of vulnerability and dissolution into the other.

Intersubjective theory provides a crucial link between the psychology of offender motivation and the socio-structural antecedents that shape and inform that motivation. The encoding of sexual difference itself in terms of a complimentary binary of masculinity/femininity represents, for Benjamin (1990), a defensive splitting of the subject in an effort to ward off the intolerable tensions that are produced in the intersubjective process. Research on empathy deficits amongst sex offenders is ambiguous, however it seems that violent or abusive men are not incapable of empathising with others but that, in particular situations and for particular reasons, they draw on their capacity to view, experience and treat others as objects rather than subjects (Walker and Brown 2011). This strategic 'objectification' of others enables men to resolve conflicts over dependency through acts of domination and violation. Where infantile fantasies of omnipotence and control become enmeshed within the maintenance of masculine selfhood, then the self is predicated on grounds that are continually falling away and the individual is confronted with masculine prerogatives that are unstable and anxiety-producing. Child sexual abuse becomes a way of assuaging or diminishing this anxiety for some men (Socarides 2004). As a 'container' for vulnerability, the powerlessness of a child demarcates them as particularly suitable objects of domination within this process.

Jefferson (2002) warns against reductive interpretations of gendered violence as performances or embodiments of masculinity, noting that such offences are socially despised precisely because they are considered un-masculine. However, it is at this point that a more subjective or phenomenological perspective is useful. The secrecy and illegality of child sexual abuse can maximise, rather than undermine, the offender's experience of excitement and control (Messerschmidt 2000). It is relevant here to note the work of Lyng (1990) on 'edgework' and the ways in which deliberate strategies of risk-taking and transgression can be used by boys and men to establish a sense of excitement, belonging and superiority. The more illicit and risky a criminal activity the greater the 'adrenalin rush', leading to intense embodied experiences that are integral to the attractions of some crimes (Ferrell 1997). This effect is particularly acute in group contexts, and the following section will consider this in more detail.

Organised abuse as a collective masculine performance

Group or 'gang' related crime has been researched extensively, and studies suggest that crime and violence is often used by groups of boys and men to delineate the boundaries and structure of their peer group, and to generate and perpetuate a sense of masculine solidarity (Messerschmidt 1993, Matza and Sykes 1961, Franklin 2004). In male peer group contexts, sexual violence can have a similar function. In his study of drug dealers in Harlem, Bourgois (1996) documented the initiatory dimensions of gang rape amongst youth gangs, and the ways in which sexual violence was used to create misogynist bonds between perpetrators. Philadelphoff-Puren (2004) has observed the ways in which relations between men have been enacted in the traditions of the 'gang bang' in Australian sporting teams and 'team bonding' rituals involving urinating and defecating on women. In her analysis of group sexual assault and homophobic violence in a high school setting, Franklin (2004) describes how gang rape can be understood as a 'participatory theatre' of masculinity, in which the victim is treated as an object upon whom perpetrating men and/or boys enact a performance of sexual aggression and domination. In doing so, she argued that they attest to and affirm the masculine performance of one another through sexually abusive acts, thus generating a sense of belonging through a shared understanding of the victim as degraded and subordinate and themselves, in contrast, as powerful and domineering.

Messerschmidt's (1993) analyses of gang rape in the 'Central Park Jogger Rape' case, which involved five black youths prosecuted (although later found innocent) of the rape and battery of a woman, suggests that groups of men may utilise collective sexual violence to 'strengthen the fiction of male power' in the context of disempowerment and subordination. This analysis of gang rape as a compensatory masculine practice is contested by evidence of the prevalence of gang rape amongst high-prestige and exclusive groups of boys and men. Drawing on her experience as a judge who has presided over numerous cases of multi-perpetrator rape, Judge Forer (in Sanday 2007: 23) describes as 'facile' the view of gang rape 'as a phenomenon of the under-class'. The only difference that she observed between the white, middle-class men and the impoverished black youth charged with multi-perpetrator rape that she encountered in the courtroom was that the former have far greater resources available to them to avoid prosecution. In her research on university gang rape cases, O'Sullivan (1998) has identified the prestige, secrecy and sense of unaccountability associated with fraternity membership as a crucial factor in the development of a culture of gang rape. Other con-tributing factors include a view of femininity as 'other' and a threat to mascu-linity identity and solidarity, resulting in the diminution in affective recognition and empathy described by Benjamin (1990) in her account of sexualised domination.

In literature on gang rape, sexual violence takes on initiatory, sadistic and ritualistic dimensions as it serves to construct and regulate relations between men that are premised on the subordination of feminised 'others'. In her study of multiple perpetrator rapes by university fraternities, Sanday (2007: 7–8) provides a detailed account of the homosociality of sexual violence:

> The woman involved is a tool, an object, the centrefold around which boys both test and demonstrate their power and heterosexual desire by performing for one another. They prove their manhood on a wounded girl who is unable to protest ... The event operates to glue the male group as a unified entity, and helps boys to make the transition to their vision of a powerful manhood – in unity against women, one against the world.

Like gang rape and other instances of collective sexual violence, organised abuse can be conceptualised as a collective masculine performance. Through the exchange and mutual abuse of victims, perpetrators of organised abuse generate a shared sense of power, control and masculinity. The experience of dominance that arises through the power differential that is inherent in child sexual abuse may be amplified by the involvement of other like-minded men, and indeed the role of the child may be little more than an object within the perpetrator's collective performance of masculinity. Kelly and colleagues (1995) observed that organised abuse is not limited to the exchange of children for sexual pleasure or profit, but may also generate power and status within groups of men who accrue subcultural capital in the process of providing children for abuse with other men. They identify that such systems of exchange are not unique to organised abuse, and that privileged access to the bodies of women and children is a common marker of masculine prestige in a number of different cultures and societies. In organised abuse, children may be reduced to objects of domination through whom perpetrators sustain and regulate their relations with one another, and develop a sense of masculine identity and belonging.

Conceptualising organised abuse as a collective strategy of masculinity provides new insights into the sadistic and ritualistic practices that have been observed in organised abuse cases. Collective sexual violence can produce a sense of transcendental control and mastery over the victim that perpetrators have described as 'godlike' (Kelly 2000, Caputi 1988) and can become enmeshed within pseudo-religious ideologies. This was in evidence in Sanday's (2007) study of gang rape by American fraternity members. The fraternity 'initiations' described to Sanday included animal sacrifice, being forced to drink animal blood, being smeared in vomit, being bound and gagged, being locked in coffins and other methods of torture. Once they were fraternity 'brothers', members frequently physically victimised one another, and collectively sexually abuse women, in a constant reaffirmation of the masculinist ideology of the fraternity. In one fraternity, this ideology was codified within an idiosyncratic religious framework that attributed the 'secrets of the brotherhood' to a Greek goddess. The physical and sexual violence of the fraternity was thus an expression of a gendered regime of power that had come to take on extraordinary metaphysical significance for the brothers, giving rise to seemingly bizarre rituals and occult beliefs. Given the widespread incredulity that has greeted accounts of ritualistic child sexual abuse, this account of the enmeshment of sadism and ritualism within an ethos of masculine *fraternite* is revealing and important.

Conclusion

Child sexual exploitation is a heavily politicised phenomenon that features in a range of competing debates and discourses. Empirical data on the contexts and harms of organised abuse has often been overshadowed by the claims of moral entrepreneurs and sceptics alike. Their disagreements have been fuelled by the challenges that organised abuse poses to prevailing understandings of child sexual abuse. In order to understand the crimes of groups of sexual offenders, a socially informed perspective is necessary, however practitioners and researchers have been constrained by their focus on individual victims and offenders. The prevailing view of sexual offenders as mentally ill has obscured the gendered dynamics of organised abuse, as has the focus of clinicians on explaining organised abuse in terms of psychological factors such as dissociation, trauma and attachment. Their efforts to articulate a comprehensive theory of organised abuse have also been challenged by the fact that the most serious of allegations of child abuse have been emerging from within contexts in which it is widely believed that children are loved and protected, such as families, churches and schools. This has given rise to a form of cognitive dissonance that has fed a groundswell of disbelief and outrage whenever authorities have sought to act upon allegations of organised abuse.

This chapter shows that organised abuse becomes less inscrutable through a multi-disciplinary theoretical lens. Critical theories of masculinity and psychoanalysis offer new tools to make explicable what has otherwise been considered unthinkable: the sexual abuse of children, and women, by groups of adults acting in concert. For some men, group contexts provide the opportunity for the formation of illicit sexualities and the expression of violent masculinities, giving rise, in turn, to florid subcultures of masculine supremacy. Organised abuse involves the collision of risk, transgression and sexuality in the company of like-minded others, constituting a collective 'edgework' experience that is linked to ideologies of masculine sexual domination and superiority. Connell and Messerschmidt (2005) have emphasised the importance of recognising the constitution of hegemonic masculinities in localised contexts, and the interaction of local gender configurations with regional or even global models of masculinity. In the case of organised abuse, particular cultural configurations of aggressive masculine sexuality are intensified and reworked within local abusive contexts to produce forms of masculine identification and relations that reproduce but also transgress against dominant norms of masculine power. However, through 'edgework' the subjective experience of transgression can be reconfigured into a gendered one that reconfirms, rather than contests, the masculine identification of the perpetrators. This theoretical approach foregrounds the ways in which groups of men can use violence and coercion in order to generate a shared sense of masculine identity and belonging through the subordination of children and women. As will be discussed in the following chapter, it is therefore necessary to consider the power differentials between men, women and children in the contexts in which sexually abusive groups emerge.

Chapter 2

Organised abuse cases

Network, institutional, familial and ritual

Context is crucial to understanding multi-perpetrator sexual offending. The bonds between the offenders, the relationship between offenders and victims and the place or institution in which the offence takes place are all factors that shape the severity of the crime and the motivations behind it. Whilst some sexual offenders are highly motivated to abuse children, men and sometimes women who might otherwise have found such behaviour abhorrent can be drawn into collusion or perpetration due to peer influence and other environmental factors (Harkins and Dixon 2010). This chapter will examine three contexts in which organised abuse has been repeatedly identified: (a) in extra-familial networks of offenders, (b) in children's institutions, and (c) in nuclear and extended families. It will also discuss ritual abuse, which is a common characteristic of familial cases of organised abuse although it has been documented in extra-familial contexts. These four categories – network, institutional, familial and ritual – emerge from two key studies undertaken in Britain by Creighton (1993) and Gallagher and colleagues (1996) and provide a logical basis to arrange and analyse the diverse literature on organised abuse. Any literature review of organised abuse is necessarily constrained by the inadequacies of the available data and the complexity and fluidity of cases of organised abuse. Indeed, some cases of organised abuse defy simple categorisation or explanation but, as this chapter shows, there is a clustering of common characteristics in particular contexts that can assist us in understanding how relations of gender, age and power enable sexually abusive groups to form in some circumstances.

The limitations of data on organised abuse

Whilst allegations of organised abuse have generated a wealth of controversy and commentary, empirical research and data on the subject are scarce. Epidemiological and clinical research studies suggest that a significant minority of sexually abused adults and children report multiple perpetrators and other indicators of organised abuse, however sexual abuse surveys rarely ask questions that would provide firm figures on the extent of organised abuse in the community (Salter and Richters forthcoming). Attempts to gather information on the extent of organised abuse in developed countries have been stymied by the failure of governments to collect data, and by their unwilling-ness to publish the data available to them (Renold and Creighton 2003, Kelly and Regan 2000). There is no standard, commonly accepted terminology to describe cases of sexual abuse involving multiple victims and multiple perpe-trators and so workers may categorise cases of organised abuse in different ways (Gallagher et al. 1996). Organised abuse may also be a difficult form of abuse for authorities to respond to and record appropriately. Clinicians and protective parents have documented the systemic obstacles they have faced when attempting to report a child's disclosure of organised abuse to the police or child protection authorities (Brooks 2001, Coleman 2008, Kinscherff and Barnum 1992).

There are numerous practical obstacles to identifying the numbers of children and young people abused by groups and networks. Organised abuse is a secretive enterprise that is rarely the subject of specialist or targeted policing and investigation practices (Kelly 1998). When organised abuse is detected by the authorities, most cases are detected accidentally (Gallagher 1998) or due to the perseverance of victims in spite of the inaction and inat-tention of authorities (e.g. Davies 1998, Fowley 2010, Owen 2010). However, the capacity of victims to report organised abuse is constrained. The factors that inhibit disclosure such as threats of death or harm during abuse and a relation of dependence with a perpetrator (Briere and Conte 1993, Loewenstein 1996, Schultz et al. 2003) are common features of organised abuse (Creighton 1993, Gallagher et al. 1996). Specific perpetrator strategies, such as drugging children (to reduce resistance and interfere with recall) or forcing children into sexual contact with other children (to engender a sense of guilt and com-plicity) also inhibit disclosure (Burgess and Lindeqvist Clark 1984, Gough 1996). For all these reasons, organised abuse may be a particularly difficult form of sexual abuse to detect (Gallagher 1998).

Research into organised abuse

In the early 1990s, two key studies of organised abuse by Creighton (1993) and Gallagher et al. (1996) in Britain gathered data sets of cases reported to the authorities and examined relationships between abuse types, perpetrators and victims. Previously, research on the subject had been 'siloed' according to abuse type and context, with relevant research taking place in relation to child pornography (Schoettle 1980, Pierce 1984, Tyler and Stone 1985) and/or child prostitution (Gitta 1984, Weisberg 1985, Janus and Heid Bracey 1986), 'sex rings' (Burgess and Lindeqvist Clark 1984, Wild and Wynne 1986, Wild 1989), multi-perpetrator sexual abuse in child care settings (Finkelhor and Williams 1988, Faller 1988, Kelley 1989) and ritual abuse (Cozolino 1989, Gould 1987, Kluft 1989). Whilst this research highlighted overlapping patterns of multi-perpetrator, multi-victim abuse, it was only with the coining of the term 'organised abuse' that an inclusive framework was provided through which these similarities could be examined in more depth (La Fontaine 1993).

Creighton (1993) surveyed 71 child protection teams of the National Society for the Prevention of Cruelty to Children in Britain regarding their experiences of child protection cases involving reports of organised abuse in the period December 1989 to April 1991. She found that 41 per cent of the agencies were aware of a case of organised abuse in their area in the period December 1989 to April 1991, and 20 per cent of teams reported working with children who were suspected of having being victimised in organised abuse during this period. These teams were then interviewed in order to gain more information about the cases, and they reported 19 cases of suspected organised abuse involving 61 children from 43 families. The child protection teams were asked to categorise these cases according to three non-defined categories of abuse: 'network', 'ritual' and 'child pornography'. The usefulness of her findings are limited by the small sample and a lack of standardised definitions but there was a striking consistency to the ways in which workers categorised the cases they had worked on.

Respondents reported 10 cases of 'network abuse', which they indicated referred primarily to extra-familial cases characterised by networks of men who abused post-pubescent children and who exhibited a clear gender preference. These abusive groups targeted either boys or girls but rarely both at once, and they were more likely to target boys. The majority of perpetrators were strangers to the children's families and the children in these cases often had fractured or difficult relationships with their parents. Some of the victims were in out-of-home care at the time of the abuse. Workers reported that the victims in network abuse cases were initially encouraged to contact perpetrators by other children, and they were provided various rewards to keep them quiet about the abuse. In this study, the three reported 'pornography' cases were similar to the 'network' cases although they involved a preponderance of female rather than male victims.

There was a significant difference between these 13 cases and the six reported 'ritual' cases. In the 'ritual' cases, victims were significantly younger and predominantly girls (83 per cent), with immediate and extended family members constituting 57 per cent of perpetrators and friends of the family another 31 per cent. Whilst mostly abusing girl children, these familial abusive groups were considerably less gender exclusive than in the 'network' cases, with some boys abused at the same time as girls. They abused fewer victims than the 'network' or 'pornography' groups but the abuse was of greater intensity, involving sadistic and ritualistic abuse.

These key distinctions between extra-familial 'network' abuse and familial 'ritual' abuse were also present in the more rigorous and comprehensive study undertaken by Gallagher and colleagues (1996), which involved a multi-method approach to develop a data set of child protection cases involving allegations of organised abuse. The researchers first sent a survey to all police, social and welfare agencies requesting data on cases of organised abuse for the period 1988 to 1991. Respondents identified 211 separate cases, and 'ritual abuse' was the predominant form of abuse reported (29 per cent), followed by 'paedophile ring' (20 per cent) and organised abuse at a 'non-residential institution' (14 per cent). The authors then undertook a comprehensive review of child protection cases within eight local authority areas, encompassing 20,000 files across 32 sites. In the sample of 78 child sex rings drawn from case review, 33 were constituted only of male perpetrators, and these groups primarily abused children of one gender or another (boys in 17 rings, girls in 13, both in 3). The victims of these groups were usually in their teens and they reported organised abuse such as the manufacture of child abuse images, but not ritualistic abuse. A higher number of rings (41) were comprised of both male and female perpetrators, and these groups predominantly abused only girls (19 rings) or both boys and girls (15 rings). The victims of these groups were younger and were more likely to report sadistic and ritualistic abuse.

The similarities between the findings of these two studies are clear. On the one hand, there are examples of extra-familial organised abuse in which groups of men act on a shared sexual preference for one gender, targeting vulnerable teenagers from unstable families or those in out-of-home care. On the other hand, the studies found patterns of family-based organised abuse with perpetrators of both genders, in which young children, predominantly but not exclusively girls, are subject to sadistic abuse, sometimes in ceremonial or ritualistic ways. Gallagher and colleagues (1996) also emphasised institutional settings of organised abuse, in which children were subject to organised abuse through a school or other institution. These three settings for organised abuse – extra-familial, familial and institutional – resonate in important ways with the literature on organised abuse that was published following these studies, whilst the role of ritualistic practices in organised abuse has been the subject of sustained debate and controversy. The following sections will examine these four categories in more detail.

Network abuse

Network abuse describes the kinds of abuses that has previously been documented in research on 'sex rings' or 'paedophile rings': networks of mostly extra-familial male abusers acting on a shared sexual interest in children (Burgess and Lindeqvist Clark 1984, Wild 1989, Hunt and Baird 1990). These groups commonly display a preference for one gender or another, rarely abusing boys and girls at once, and they usually target post-pubescent victims (Creighton 1993, Gallagher et al. 1996). Reports of network abuse are typified by high numbers of victims but short periods of abuse, with relatively limited progression of abuse, as multiple victims are inducted into and then quickly exit/escape from the abusive group. Since perpetrators of network abuse are mostly extra-familial they have limited influence over their victims in comparison to familial offenders, and they must employ a combination of inducements, threats and emotional manipulation to coerce the child into sexual activity. This may be effective for a period but since the initiation of network abuse typically begins in the early teens it seems that victims have greater psychological capacity to resist these strategies and exit from network abuse.

In their study of extra-familial 'sex rings', Burgess and colleagues (Burgess et al. 1984, Burgess and Lindeqvist Clark 1984) documented how perpetrators identify potential victims in a range of ways, including through work or leisure activities, and then engage in 'grooming' behaviour to entice the victim into sexual abuse. The victim may then be introduced to other perpetrators, at which point the victim may be subject to prostitution, the manufacture of child abuse images and other forms of exploitation. There is limited research into the experiences of children within network abuse, but the available literature emphasises how perpetrators encourage the development of a group subculture and peer dynamic between abused children which engenders a sense of guilt and complicity in the abuse (Svedin and Back 1996, Burgess and Lindeqvist Clark 1984).

Recent cases of network abuse have emphasised how the development of online technologies has facilitated the formation of sexually abusive groups. They have also provided examples of the ways in which women as well as men can become involved in network abuse. In a recent British case, a childcare worker, Vanessa George, took sexually abusive photographs of dozens of the children she worked with at the behest of Colin Blanchard, whom she had met online through a dating website. Blanchard had also recruited three other women online who were subsequently jailed for sexually abusing children at his request. In one email between George and Blanchard, George states 'I'll do what you want if you put a ring on my finger' (S. Morris 2009). During sentencing, the presiding judge described Blanchard's 'pernicious grooming' of the four women. The police spokesperson subsequently emphasised that, although the convicted women may never have abused children of their own initiative, nonetheless '[n]o one should be under the misapprehension that they were somehow forced into abusing children – they willingly took part' (Morris 2011).

The network abuse of older children in their early-to-mid teens may involve grooming by men posing as 'boyfriends' who then emotionally manipulate the child into participating in prostitution and other acts (Swann 1999). Children victimised in this way are often vulnerable or homeless teenagers with disrupted family backgrounds (Elaine and June 2005) but they may include middle-class teenagers (eg Reid 2010). Flattered by attention and impressed with displays of money and status, the victim's attachment to his/her 'boyfriend' may preclude acknowledgement or reporting of their exploitation and inhibit cooperation with the police. In many respects, this form of abuse corresponds with forms of 'pimping' experienced by vulnerable women as well as minors. Research with street-based sex workers in the 1980s found that the majority had been prostituted prior to the age of 16, often by 'boyfriends', and hence this form of network abuse is a well-established entre into adult sex work (Silbert and Pines 1985, Weisberg 1985, Gitta 1984). Such perpetrators may operate as part of an organised network of perpetrators who foster and exploit the emotional dependency of their victims, whom they offer to other men in order to accrue money, status and access to other sexually exploited children. In Britain, recent allegations of such abuse by men of 'Middle Eastern' background has been the subject of sustained controversy, however it has highlighted the vulnerability of some teenaged girls, particularly those in care, to the emotional and financial manipulation of network abusers (Norfolk 2012).

Institutional organised abuse

Institutional abuse refers to the sexual abuse of children by people who work with them in an institutional setting, in which one or more staff members engage in or arrange the sexual abuse of children in their care (Gallagher 2000a). Reports of institutional organised abuse are diverse, describing organised abuse in residential care, special schools, boarding schools, primary and high schools, day-care centres and preschools, and voluntary organisations. Some of the earliest reports of institutional organised abuse involved day-care centres and preschools. In their sample of 270 substantiated cases of sexual abuse in child care arrangements throughout America, Finkelhor and Williams (1988) found that 17 per cent involved allegations of multiple perpetrators. The authors observed that '[i]t is very clear that the multiperpetrator cases have dynamics which set them apart' (Finkelhor and Williams 1988: 38), with the largest average number of victims, the most extended and serious forms of abuse (including the production of child abuse images and ritualistic practices) and an over-representation of female perpetrators in comparison to other child care cases or in research on sexual abuse in general. They reported that 25 per cent of cases in their sample involved the perpetration of abuse by the owner or director of the child care business, raising the possibility that 'abuse was the reason for which the day-care operation was established' (Finkelhor and Williams 1988: 28).

The childcare abuse scandals of the 1980s and 1990s led to increased oversight of childcare arrangements and screening of childcare workers, and although sexual abuse and organised abuse cases continue to be uncovered in childcare and day-care centres, there appear to be considerably fewer cases than 20 years ago. Today the most common reports of institutional organised abuse involve historical complaints of abuse in religious institutions and residential children's institutions. In Australia, a recent public inquiry into the abuse of children in care in South Australia collected testimony from the former wards of a range of residential schools and homes that painted a disturbing picture of open cultures of institutionalised sexual abuse (Commission of Inquiry 2004). Former residents of one school described how staff colluded with other men, including police officers and social workers, in the sexual abuse of child wards, often incorporating former wards into the abusive activity. The abuse was allegedly kept secret by the collusion of the abusers, some of whom reportedly included bureaucrats in the child welfare system, and the general social disinterest in the welfare of state wards that was widespread at the time.

The paradigm of institutional care in Western countries has historically been marked by neglect and depersonalised and punitive responses by care-givers (Goffman 1961, Foucault 1967). A trend away from residential chil-dren's homes has occurred over the last 30 years as the poor life outcomes of children placed in residential care have become evident. Nonetheless, stud-ies of the prevalence of the sexual abuse of children in residential care suggest that rates of sexual victimisation are disproportionately high, although a significant proportion of perpetrators are other children rather than staff (Gallagher 1999, Hobbs et al. 1999). Research has identified a convergence of factors that have contributed to the high rates of abuse and violence at residential children's institutions, including the closed and self-regulatory nature of the facilities, the absence of substantive oversight, the powerlessness of children in care and their emotional vulnerability (Doran and Brannan 1996). However, the gendered nature of authority in institutional settings, and the gender dynamics of institutions more generally, has often gone unex-amined. Green (2001: 20) emphasises the ways in which masculine power structures in children's institutions have condoned or minimised the effects of 'aggressive and misogynistic male sexual behaviour'. In children's institu-tions, male authority can be expressed through institutionalised regimes of discipline, surveillance and control that facilitate and even condone sexual abuse (Parkin and Green 1997). In some instances, this has given rise to what Stein (2006) has called 'organised systematic abuse' in children's institutions, defined as 'the abuse over time of children and young people by different members of staff working within the same home, or other adults from outside the home' (p 16).

Where staff have been found to be sexually abusing children in care, the majority have acted alone (Gallagher 2000a). An overlap between institu-tional abuse and organised abuse has been widely reported although cases of organised abuse represent a small proportion of cases of institutional abuse referred to the police for investigation (Gallagher 2000a). Nonetheless, institutional organised abuse is likely be underreported since it involves the deliberate targeting of very vulnerable children who are unlikely to report abuse or be believed when they do (Hawkins and Briggs 1997). Sexually abu-sive men may seek to obtain influential positions in the child-care system with the intention of sexually abusing children and enabling other men to do so (Hawkins and Briggs 1997, Stein 2006). Abusers may then utilise the knowledge gained through their legitimate employment as the children's caretakers to identify vulnerable children and entrap them in abuse (Colton and Vanstone 1996, Gallagher 1999). Colton, Roberts and Vanstone's (2010) research on sexual abuse by men who work with children has emphasised the premeditated manner in which such men seek out employment that provides access to children, and the strategic manner in which they assess and minimise the risk of detection through grooming and other practices. These men may also be embedded within larger networks of abusers and this adds an additional layer of complexity to their abuse, since they may then provide the child for abuse to other men. Sexually abusive staff may also manipulate other staff into overlooking, colluding with or even participating in the sexual abuse of children (Jones 1995).

It has been common for institutional authorities to silence complaining children whilst protecting abusive staff, and some critics have described this pattern of institutional cover-ups as evidence of 'organised paedophilia' (eg Hawkins and Briggs 1997). The line between complicity and conspiracy in such instances is often uncertain, since there is considerable crossover between organised institutional abuse and what Kelly and Scott (1993) have called 'disorganised' sexual abuse, where a child is vulnerable to sexual abuse by multiple people due to a lack of organisation by child protection services. The severe sexual abuse of a child in care may not be evidence of collusion between abusers but rather it may indicate the absence of basic safeguards and protections. Nonetheless, the capacity of large church-run or state-run institutions to evade scrutiny and the zeal with which sexually abusive groups may attempt to hide their offences should not be underestimated. In 2002, it emerged that the state-run orphanage Pia Casa in Portugal had been targeted by a sexually abusive group that included diplomats, doctors, lawyers and journalists for over two decades (Tremlett 2010). Evidence of the abusive network was first provided to the police and politicians in the early 1980s, however key dossiers disappeared, other evidence was subsequently destroyed and witnesses reporting being threatened and intimidated (Taylor 2010).

Familial organised abuse

Familial organised abuse involves cultures of sexual abuse within families, in which multiple adults abuse children within the family (and often outside it) while enabling perpetrators from outside the home to sexually abuse their children.[1] Authorities have been slow to recognise familial organised abuse and, even where familial perpetrators are involved in organised

---

1 Where extra-familial perpetrators are absent, such abuse is better described as 'polyincest' (see Faller 1991), however it is common for polyincestuous families to be in contact with

abuse, investigators tend to focus on the extra-familial perpetrators (Gallagher et al. 1996). However, familial perpetrators have been documented since 'sex rings' and 'child pornography' first began to be investigated in the 1970s and 1980s (see Pierce 1984, Incardi 1984, Tate 1990). Research in the 1980s highlighted the participation of family members, particularly incestuous fathers, in facilitating the sexual exploitation of children (Wild 1989, Wild and Wynne 1986, Schoettle 1980). It is now well recognised that incest can include the facilitation of sexual abuse by perpetrators outside the victim's immediate or nuclear family (International Society for the Study of Trauma and Dissociation 2011).

Familial organised abuse is distinguished from network abuse cases, such as those examined by Burgess and colleagues (1984), by what could be called its polymorphous perversity. Whereas groups involved in network abuse tend to target specific gender and age categories, familial organised abuse commonly involves the abuse of female and male children, the abuse of children and women, and the abuse of familial and extra-familial victims (Cleaver and Freeman 1996, Gallagher et al. 1996, Creighton 1993). These studies find that, in familial cases of organised abuse, abuse tends to begin at a younger age, with a predominance of female victims, involving comparatively low numbers of victims compared to network abuse but a high intensity and prolonged duration of victimisation. Sexually abusive families may overlap with one another and provide one another with access to their children leading to a complex web of relations between victims and perpetrators that can be difficult to untangle. Victims may not know that other children from other families are also being abused, and if they do, they may not know enough information about other victims for them to be identified. Investigating such cases is, as Gallagher (1998) described, like 'grappling with smoke'.

Cleaver and Freeman (1996) provide a case study of familial organised abuse of rare detail. Through their research with parents suspected of child abuse, they developed close relationships with research participants that enabled them to identify an 'abuse network' across eight families. Through their analysis, they illustrated the 'cross-configuration' of patterns of organised abuse within families, in that the abuse 'extended vertically through the inter-generational family structure and laterally through the involvement of wider kin and family friends' (Cleaver and Freeman 1996: 232). In these families, sexual abuse was routine. Children were engaged in sexual activities from a young age with various members of the family, with the abuse quickly progressing to include penetrative assaults. The authors noted that sexual abuse was characterised by male perpetration, however women in the family had important roles within the culture of abuse. Women, usually

abusers who are not related by blood to victims or familial perpetrators (Crowley and Seery 2001).

mothers or grandmothers, were involved in abusive activities which 'ranged from recruitment or tacit acceptance to restraining children or concealing its effects to being perpetrators themselves' (Cleaver and Freeman 1996: 237). Relationships between men and women within this family network were based on a system of exchange 'in which the male perpetrator's offer of love and financial assistance was traded for sexual access to the woman's children' (Cleaver and Freedman 1996: 239). The families involved in the organised abuse all adopted and promoted an 'abuse culture' that fostered secrecy and interdependence.

Such an intergenerational familial abuse of sexual abuse was evident in the French sexual abuse prosecutions of 2005, in which 63 people across 21 families in the town of Angers were convicted of raping, abusing or prostituting 45 victims (Walt 2005). The victims included 19 boys and 26 girls aged between six months and 12 years at the time of abuse. The couples traded their children between them for petty amounts of cash or groceries. Intergenerational abuse was evident in some families. One victim, nine-year-old 'Marine V', who reported being raped by about 30 men, including uncles, her father and grandfather as well as neighbours. The men abused and prostituted their children and grandchildren, and whilst their spouses were less active in the abuse of the children they facilitated the abuse in other ways, such as acting as the 'treasurer' of the abusive group. In their defence, many of the women testified that they were also victims of incest and sexual abuse. Like other cases of familial organised abuse, the sexually abusive group only came to light when a victim approached the police to complain, despite the fact that the majority of the families involved were either known to social services or under their direct supervision.

Whilst the men and women prosecuted in this case were predominantly poor and welfare-dependent, the victimised children described a group of perpetrators who wore suits and ties and hid their faces behind masks when they abused them. A lawyer for one of those convicted in the case reported that these men were part of a sophisticated and wealthy network of sexual abusers who paid considerably more to abuse the children than other clients: up to €456 in one instance (Walt 2005). Such intimations of middle- or upper-class sexually abusive networks have been a feature of European investigations into organised abuse (Kelly 1998). However, Sinason (2002: 16) observes that '[i]t is far easier to pick up the signs of abuse in working class or 'underclass' children than in intact and outwardly functional middle-class families'. In her autobiography, Fowley (2010: 17–18), a survivor of familial organised abuse in England, reflected on the invisibility of her abuse in a well-to-do family that showed no outward signs of dysfunction:

> Apart from the abuse my life felt pretty normal. We were well looked after, well fed, clean, well dressed, and we got on OK. Mum and Billy [step-father] were not drinkers and they rarely went out, so there

was no shortage of money. No teacher would have singled me out as a child from a problem family, no social workers ever came knocking at our door, and we never had cause for a policeman to arrive on our doorstep.

Fowley's (2010) case attracted widespread attention in the United Kingdom due to the successful prosecution of some of her abusers, including her mother, and Fowley's resilience in waving her right to anonymity and speaking publicly about her abuse. Her story is similar in many respects to other less-publicised accounts of familial organised abuse that also describe sexual abuse by parents, grandparents, relatives and family 'friends'. However, these accounts have often included descriptions of sadistic abuses that have defied belief to the point of drastically polarising media coverage. This is particularly the case where ritualistic abuse is reported, as will be discussed in Chapter 4. Although ritual abuse has been reported in extra-familial and institutional contexts, this form of abuse is most commonly associated with familial organised abuse, and the controversy associated with it has had the effect of undermining the legitimacy of many reports of familial organised abuse. Ritual abuse is a complex issue that will be considered in more detail in the following section.

Ritualistic abuse

Ritualistic abuse refers to organised abuse that is structured in a ceremonial fashion, often incorporating religious or mythological iconography (McFadyen et al. 1993). The ritualistic activity is typically structured by 'deviant scriptualism', in which abusive groups parody traditional religious symbols and ritual practices (Kent 1993a, 1993b). The majority of cases of ritualistic abuse involve female victims and facilitation by parents (Creighton 1993, Gallagher et al. 1996), although early research on sexual abuse in child-care arrangements emphasised the presence of ritualistic abuse in some cases (Finkelhor and Williams 1988, Waterman et al. 1993). Studies of sexually abused children in day-care centres have provided compelling evidence that children reporting ritualistic abuse report more serious forms of sexual abuse than non-ritualistically abused children (including those subject to other forms of organised abuse), and they have more severe symptoms of post-traumatic stress disorder (Finkelhor and Williams 1988, Waterman et al. 1993).

Gallagher (2000b: 321) described allegations of ritualistic abuse as 'one of the most contentious issues in child protection' throughout the 1990s. Whilst ritualistic abuse is not a ubiquitous aspect of disclosures of organised abuse, it is associated with the extremes of child maltreatment, including murder, bestiality and the torture of children (Smith 1993, Hudson 1991, Driscoll and Wright 1991). Clinical psychologist Youngson (1994) argues that cases involving ritualistic abuse are qualitatively different from other forms of child abuse, however severe. Children and adults subject to ritualistic forms of abuse are profoundly traumatised, phobic of doctors and the police, and often convinced that the abusive group has supernatural powers (Mollon 1996). Cases involving ritualistic abuse are distinguished from other forms of organised abuse by the young age at which victimisation starts, the involvement of parents as primary abusers, the extremity and diversity of abusive practices, and the prolonged period of abuse (Creighton 1993, Gallagher et al. 1996).

Studies of children's and adult's disclosures of ritual abuse have identified a common catalogue of abuses: forced ingestion of human waste, Satanic iconography and occult paraphernalia, animal mutilation or killing, and the use of drugs (Smith 1993, Driscoll and Wright 1991, Young et al. 1991). Victims and survivors have described ritually abusive groups engaging in elaborately structured phases of torture designed to induce dissociative and traumatic psychopathology, with the apparent intention of maintaining abso-lute control over the victim and reducing the likelihood of detection (Sachs and Galton 2008, Epstein et al. 2011). As will be discussed in Chapter 4, a substantial group of commentators have argued that such descriptions align so closely with the content of myth, novels and films that they are most likely confabulations drawn from the same. However, this view is challenged by the recent substantiation of organised, sadistic and ritualistic abuse during the prosecution of child sex cases in Europe and North America.

In 2005, seven members of a fundamentalist Christian church in the American town of Ponchatoula, Louisiana were indicted on charges of sexu-ally abusing three children, all of whom were related to some of the accused. The eyewitness statements of the children described child abuse in 'satanic' rituals, animal sacrifices and group sexual abuse, and this was corroborated by the diary entries of some of the accused. An FBI agent testified that physi-cal evidence of such ritualistic activities had been uncovered during the police investigation (Ellzey 2007). The former pastor of the church was sentenced to four concurrent life terms, another church member was sentenced to three life sentences and a third pleaded guilty and received a 10-year sentence (Hastings 2009). Child sex charges against one of the accused who had ini-tially notified the authorities of the abuse, and subsequently agreed to testify against other church members, were dropped.

The Ponchatoula case is illuminating for a range of reasons. It highlights the ways in which familial organised abuse and institutional organised abuse often overlap where ritualistic abuse is alleged. In this instance, it seems that sexually abusive men developed connections with one another through their participation in a church, and then, in their practice of organised abuse, they adopted and inverted the ritualistic tradition of the church. This accords with the descriptions of ritualistic abuse that will be analysed in Chapter 9. Other survivors have reported that priests, pastors and church members were actively involved in their organised abuse, and they have described ways in which Christian iconography and ritual traditions have been parodied by sexually abusive groups. Commentators have often been at a loss as to what to make of such reports, but as Goodwin (1994a) points out they are not without historical precedent. The organisation of illicit sexual activities in ways that mock religious sensibilities has been a long-standing feature of libertine philosophy, and in the fiction of the Marquis de Sade, priests and other men ecstatically engaged in the 'satanic' rape of children. This historical connection between child sexual abuse and irreligiousity will be considered in more detail in the following chapter.

Perpetrators of ritualistic abuse draw on a range of religious traditions to legitimise their abuse of children, and this includes occult and pagan mythology. In 2011 in Swansea, Wales, Colin Batley was found guilty of 35 charges relating to his role as the leader of a 'satanic cult' that sexually abused children and women, manufactured child abuse images and forced children and women into prostitution (de Bruxelles 2011). His partner and two other women were also convicted on related charges, with one man convicted of paying to abuse a victim of the group. The groups' ritualistic activities were based on the doctrine of Aleister Crowley, an occult figure whose writing includes references to ritual sex with children. Crowley's literature has been widely linked to the practice of ritualistic abuse by survivors and their advocates, who in turn have been accused by occult groups of religious persecution. During Batley's trial, the prosecution claimed that Crowley's writings formed the basis of Batley's organisation and he read from a copy of it during sexually abusive incidents. It seems that alternative as well as mainstream religious traditions can be misused by sexually abusive groups.

The literature on ritualistic abuse suggests that ritualistic sexual practices with young children are a characteristic of particularly abusive groups, and that such practices typically occur alongside a diverse range of other abusive practices, such as child prostitution and the manufacture of child abuse images. One of the shortcomings of the available literature, however, is the general presumption (implicit or explicit) that abusive groups are motivated by a religious or spiritual conviction. In clinical and research literature, abusive groups are generally referred to as 'cults', and 'cult abuse' is a term that has been used interchangeably with 'ritual abuse'. It is questionable whether 'cult' is an accurate or useful descriptor for these abusive groups, who are usually constituted of multiple abusive families and family 'friends' and contacts who are collectively engaged in multiple forms of sexual violence. In her critique of ritual abuse literature, Goodwin (1994b: 486) argues that the focus on 'ritual' and 'religion' is fundamentally misplaced:

In many ways it is unfortunate that this element [ritualistic abuse] became so prominent in many of the early investigations that the phenomenon was named 'ritual abuse' rather than severe or sadistic abuse. This has led to the misconception that this was some sort of new phenomenon, that religious rather than sexual, monetary or power motivations were central to it, that its roots could be found in the history of religion rather than the history of crime, and that to perceive or study the phenomenon constituted some sort of fundamentalist witchhunting.

Goodwin suggests that ritualistic abuse is one expression of an historical continuum of sadistic sexual practices that she traces back to the Marquis de Sade and his libertine contemporaries in the 18th century. She highlights the historical continuity between de Sade's libertinism and ritualistic abuse, but she does not elucidate upon its implications for the study of organised abuse beyond advocating for a shift in focus towards the issues of sexual violence and power. The next chapter explores this potential link between libertinism and ritualistic abuse in more detail. However, the position that ritualistic abuse is best understood in terms of sexuality and power was examined by Scott (2001), whose qualitative research with adult survivors of ritualistic abuse synthesises research on ritualistic abuse and organised abuse with social theory on violence against women and children. Using a grounded theory approach, Scott (2001) explored how her participants' accounts of ritualistic abuse were enmeshed within histories of family violence, abuse and neglect, as well as networks of perpetrators engaged in sadistic practices with children, child prostitution and the manufacture of child abuse images. Her findings challenge many of the assumptions of the ritual abuse literature, as well as those of its detractors. She suggests that the harmful and traumatic experiences of ritually abused children are driven by routine power-and-control relationships, such as those between a parent and a child, and that their ritualistic abuse experiences should be seen in relation to a wider picture of severe family dysfunction, psychopathology and isolation.

Gender, age and power in organised abuse

With few exceptions (see Kelly 1998; Scott 2001), gender is a neglected factor in the literature on organised abuse. This is surprising, since research has highlighted specific dynamics of gender and age in sexually abusive groups. Speaking generally, the limited prevalence data available suggests that girls are the primary targets of abusive groups (Wild and Wynne 1986, Wild 1989). In their study Gallagher and colleagues (1996) found that 45 per cent of cases involved only the abuse of girls, and 24 per cent of cases involved the abuse of boys and girls. Less than a third of cases involved the groups that only targeted boys. In mental health settings, the overwhelming majority of clients reporting histories of organised and ritualistic abuse are women and girls (Coleman 1994, Scott 1993, Driscoll and Wright 1991, Shaffer and Cozolino 1992, Creighton 1993). Some surveys of adults and children reporting ritualistic abuse, or samples of cases of ritualistic abuse, do not report on the gender of victims (Cook 1991, Snow and Sorenson 1990, Hudson

1990) which highlights the lack of priority afforded to gender in early inquiries into ritual abuse.

Simple prevalence measures hint at, but do not provide, the full picture of gender dynamics within organised abuse. Whilst higher numbers of victims are often reported in cases of organised abuse in which boys are targeted, the frequency, severity and period of abuse of each male victim is limited in comparison to circumstances in which girls are targeted, or where boys and girls are targeted (Creighton 1993, Gallagher et al. 1996). In contrast, whilst fewer victims are reported in cases of organised abuse involving the abuse of girls, or girls and boys, the abuse is often more severe and prolonged (often involving ritualistic abuse) (Gallagher et al. 1996, Creighton 1993). This pattern accords with the different contexts in which boys and girls are vulnerable to organised abuse, with boys primarily abused in extra-familial contexts and girls in intra-familial contexts. Research on sexual abuse finds that familial abusers target fewer victims, but subject them to more intensive and prolonged abuse, whilst extra-familial abusers may abuse each victim only briefly but abuse higher numbers of victims (Abel et al. 1987). It seems that this gendered pattern is also present in relation to organised abuse.

Gallagher and colleagues' (1996) research highlighted significant patterns of bias in the identification and reporting of organised abuse cases that has important gendered implications. When they compared survey responses on organised abuse cases from police and social services to their case review findings, they found that police and social workers under-reported familial perpetrators and familial cases of organised abuse and over-reported cases of organised abuse involving male victims. This accords with sexual abuse research which finds that cases of incest and familial abuse (which predominantly involve girl victims) are under-represented in the criminal justice system, which indicates that they are less likely to be detected and prosecuted (Bagley and Pritchard 2000). Kelly (1996) suggests that extra-familial cases of organised abuse are better recognised than familial organised abuse since they conform to pre-existing assumptions about 'paedophiles' and 'sex rings'. It seems that the particular contexts in which girls are likely to be subject to organised abuse, such as families, are under-recognised by the authorities and less likely to be recorded appropriately even when investigated.

The duration of victimisation is an important distinguishing factor between male and female victims of organised abuse. Whilst the organised abuse of boys tends to cease in their early-to-mid teens, the organised abuse of girls may be very prolonged and persist into adulthood. This is particularly the case where ritual abuse is reported. Scott (1993) reported that, amongst the 191 who contacted a ritual abuse hotline in a 24-hour period,[2] 20 said that

---

2 Scott (1993) states that the helpline, available for 24 hours after a BBC programme on ritual abuse was screened in Britain in 1992, was unable to cope with demand, registering 4,500 attempted calls in the first hour of operation.

they were subject to ongoing abuse. Only three of these 20 callers were male, and female callers reporting a history of ritualistic abuse outnumbered men by a ratio of 2:1. The number of victims in cases of organised abuse is therefore only one measure of the severity of the abusive activity and may provide a misleading picture of the gendered dynamics of organised abuse. Other relevant indices include the age of abuse initiation, the diversity, severity and frequency of the abusive acts, and the period of time that a victim was subject to organised abuse. The evidence suggests that, whilst abusive groups that preferentially target male victims may abuse higher numbers of children, those groups that victimise girls or boys and girls subject children to more intensive, frequent and prolonged victimisation, including the victimisation of some girl children into adulthood.

There is one gendered issue that has been widely remarked upon in relation to organised abuse, and that is the disproportionate participation of women as perpetrators in organised contexts. This phenomenon was first noted in day-care cases of organised abuse in the United States (Finkelhor and Williams 1988, Waterman et al. 1993) and it has also been reported in surveys of adult survivors (Smith 1993, Driscoll and Wright 1991) and in reports from clinicians working with adults and children with histories of organised abuse (Robinson et al. 1994, Motz 2008). Cases of organised abuse constitute, in fact, a significant proportion of all detected cases of female sexual offending against children. In Vandiver's (2006) review of all female offenders identified in the national FBI sexual abuse incident database in 2001, 46 per cent had at least one co-offender. Of these women, 48 per cent had more than one co-offender, and 7 per cent had ten or more co-offenders.

Faller (1987, 1995) documented the high level of mental illness, substance abuse and cognitive deficits amongst female sexual offenders, and suggested that many of the women in her studies had been coerced into sexually abusive behaviour by co-offending men. Her position that women's sexually abusive behaviour in organised contexts was frequently a product of 'male dominance' (Faller 1987, 1995) is an atypically political account of women's involvement in organised abuse. Simplistic readings of reports of women as perpetrators of organised abuse has prompted the claim that gender is irrelevant to the perpetration of organised abuse (eg Tomison 1995), and some survivors have insisted that women were 'as bad' or worse than male perpetrators (Scott 2001). This insistence may come, in part, from the ways in women's complicity or active participation in sexual abuse is understood to breach hegemonic norms of femininity and motherhood (Peter 2006). The literature on ritual abuse, in particular, suggests that both men and women who abuse in such contexts have also been abused in childhood, just as they offend in adulthood – the archetype of the 'predisposed' or 'intergenerational perpetrator' described by Peter (2006).

The unspoken assumption in much of the relevant literature is that women's participation is organised abuse is produced under the same circumstances as men's. At the very least, it seems that many therapists feel that the difference between men's and women's involvement in organised abuse is unimportant when conceptualising organised abuse as a whole. Scott's (2001) research challenges these assumptions. She noted that, whilst abusive incidents may be orchestrated in a manner that 'rendered women and men equal in the pursuit of power and pleasure' (Scott 2001: 130), the lives of women in abusive groups described by her participants were characterised by submission to the demands of husbands, fathers and other men. This submission was frequently achieved through violence and abuse. It seems that, whilst abusive groups can involve both men and women, their roles and experiences are not equivalent. The evidence suggests that organised abuse is a form of abuse in which women's reasons for abusing children may be very different from those of their male co-offenders.

Conclusion

The emergence of cases of organised abuse in the 1980s posed several challenges to the accepted wisdom of psychiatrists, police officers and other authoritative voices on sexual abuse. The diverse configurations of victims, perpetrators, contexts and abuses in organised abuse cases defied easy categorisation and explanation. Some child and adult survivors described experiences of florid and excessive violence, such as ritual abuse, that appeared inexplicable and unimaginable. The most rigorous efforts to explain organised abuse to date have involved comparison between statistical or descriptive 'snapshots' of cases in a search for discrete patterns, which has yielded provocative similarities between the contexts in which cases of organised abuse emerge and the patterns of abuses reported by survivors. This chapter has grouped the available data on organised abuse under four key categories – network, institutional, familial and ritual – that have emerged from these statistical studies in order to clarify the available evidence base and highlight important similarities between cases.

These categories highlight the diversity of contexts in which organised abuse emerges and the ways that common arrangements within families, institutions and communities can be co-opted for sexual abuse. They provide a useful way of conceptualising and grouping cases of organised abuse although it is important to note that experiences of victimisation or perpetration can elude categorisation according to particular kinds or settings of abuse.

A victim may be exposed to multiple sexually abusive groups who are interconnected through a web of relations between perpetrators, who may be relatives, friends, associates, procurers and clients, between whom children are circulated as a form of capital in the generation of profit, pleasure or status depending on the context (Itzin 2001). Relations between perpetrators may form due to a shared interest in sexually abusing children, as appears to be the case in 'network' abuse, but in familial and institutional settings the organised abuse of children can develop as part of a culture of power, violence and fear.

There is considerable variation between cases of organised abuse, however underlying their differences are a set of linkages between gender, power and abuse that have often been neglected in the literature. The following chapter aims to examine the cultural and historical context to these linkages by highlighting how violence and transgression have come to play an important role in modern understandings of male sexuality. The association of masculinity with sexual aggression is often taken for granted in discussions of sexual offences but it will be argued that this association is an historically contingent one with important consequences for our understanding of organised abuse.

Chapter 3

The historical context
Liberalism, libertinism and ideologies of masculine sexuality

In his experience as a sex researcher, Plummer (2010: 167) wonders at the 'strange subterranean worlds' and sexual subcultures that are nestled within 'everyday community life'. He suggests that sexual subcultures often provide novel alternative readings of the dominant culture, parodying social roles and symbols and imbuing the hypocrisies or excesses of the social order with an erotic charge. Similarly, this chapter takes an historical and cultural view on organised abuse and examines the ways in which organised abuse elaborates upon normative power differentials between men, women and children. In particular, the chapter is concerned with the sexual underpinnings of liberal democracies and the ways in which traditional liberal theory relegated women and children to the status of lesser subjects or even objects that fall under the 'natural' dominion on men. Liberal theory has furnished modern democracies and the civil rights movement with the crucial theoretical frameworks of rights, consent and equality but it is marked by a set of contradictions in relation to the subordinate status of children and women. These contradictions have served as the focal point around which fantasies of domination, control and even destruction have converged, and these fantasies over time have come to inform the widespread conceptualisation of masculine sexuality as a predatory and sadistic instinct.

By examining the continuity of ideologies of masculine sexual sadism from the 18th century to the present day, this chapter seeks to identify the social conditions for the emergence of organised abuse and to consider the cultural resources that perpetrators draw on to construct a sense of self through their conduct. That liberalism emerged from within, and was reflective of, a misogynist cultural tradition is well-recognised by feminist historians and political philosophers (Pateman 1988, Thornton 1990), however the manner in which the gendered underpinnings of liberalism were reworked within libertinism is less acknowledged. This chapter will focus on the work of the Marquis de Sade because it is in his literature the eroticisation of modern masculine privilege is formally enshrined within a philosophy of sexual cruelty. His work describes the practices of sadistic and ritualistic abuse, the simultaneous abuse of women as well as children and sometimes men, the wearing of uniforms during abuse and other features commonly reported by survivors of organised abuse (Goodwin 1994b). Clear linkages are evident in the work of Sade between liberal notions of freedom, individuality and choice and the sexual exploitation of children and women. Through an analysis of his work, this chapter aims to illuminate the role of sadistic sexualised violence in the context of historical and contemporary masculinities. Whilst much has changed since the time of Sade, many of the same social and economic structures that perpetuate gender inequality persist, and hence the libertine eroticisation of such inequities continue to resonate for some men in contemporary society.

Ideologies of masculine sadism

A recent Australian online newspaper article (Sheehan 2011) questioning the routine quality of men's sexually coercive behaviour prompted an online comment that illustrates the investment that many men have in claiming a prerogative for physical and sexual predation:

> Men are hunters. We are predators. We are excited by the thrill of conquest and victory. It's how we are wired. Sexual conquest means a greater chance of passing on your genes.
>
> There's nothing wrong with this unless it's criminal. The only people that have a problem with it are those who don't have game (and are intimidated) and those that would seek to repress men.

In this comment, the reader suggests that sexual activity represents men's 'conquest' of women and a 'victory' in a battle between the sexes. The possessive plural 'we' positions the author and other men as sexual 'hunters' fuelled by a genetic compulsion. By implication, women are either passive objects to be acted upon by men or else they are 'prey' whose sexual engagement with men is limited to flight or submission. The author suggests that the only people who would disagree with the logic of his sexual Darwinism are lesser-status men 'who don't have game' and are intimidated by him, or 'those that would seek to repress men', ie feminists or women out of step with the natural order he describes.

This enmeshment of masculine self-aggrandisement with fantasies of sexual domination reflects the underlying sentiments of numerous television shows, films and other cultural productions. The modern media consumer is continually exposed to atavistic representations of male heterosexuality in which violence or criminality are framed as primordially masculine accomplishments (Salter and Tomsen 2012). In both the academic and 'pop' variants of psychology and criminology, violent men have been understood to suffer from an 'overflow' or surplus of masculinity or testosterone, a substance that has come to take on mythical gendered properties in the social imagination.

Hence violent men are reviled as uncontrolled deviants in some circumstances (particularly, as the comment above suggests, when their violence breaks the law) and admired as paragons of masculine irrepressibility in others such as during war and sport, when violence is legally sanctioned, or in other circumstances where coercion is considered socially legitimate and indeed inevitable, eg the sexual 'hunt' of women.

This link between masculinity and sadism is so ubiquitous in Western cultures that it often goes unnoticed, insinuating itself into common reasoning by virtue of its taken-for-granted status. Various provocation defences in the criminal justice system accept the logic that men are burdened with an instinct for physical and sexual aggression and their capacity for restraint rests on a hair trigger that is activated by, for example, a short skirt in the case of rape, a sexual insult in the case of domestic violence and homicide, or a come-on in the case of anti-homosexual assault and murder. However, the ideology of masculine sadism does not describe a 'natural' fact but rather a historically contingent construction of masculine sexuality intimately bound up with the social and economic order ushered in by urbanisation, industrialisation and modernisation. Sadism, as Foucault (1964: 210) observed, 'is not a name finally given to a practice as old as Eros; it is a massive cultural fact which appeared at the end of the eighteenth century'. As the following sections will show, it is in this historical shift that the roots of contemporary organised abuse can be found, alongside other forms of gendered violence that are enabled and even encouraged by the social conditions of modernity.

Liberalism, gender and sexual violence

Organised abuse, like all forms of child sexual abuse, occurs most often in the spaces of childhood that are designated in liberal democracies as 'private' spaces such as the home, or in sites such as schools and residential institutions that are neither wholly 'private' nor fully 'public'. The 'private' sphere has been idealised in liberal thought as a space apart from the regimes of law that regulate life in the *polis* and the world of business and politics. In this space, men have been empowered in liberal democracies to pursue personal fulfilment, whether spiritual, emotional or sexual, with limited state interference (although with notable exceptions, eg homosexuality). Founding liberal philosophers such as Rousseau assumed that men enjoyed a natural dominion over women, who were considered constitutionally unsuited to the rigors of 'public' life whilst perfectly formed for domestic labour and childrearing (Pateman 1988). The maximisation of the happiness of men, according to liberal theory, has involved providing men with the greatest freedom to arrange their familial and intimate relations in whatever manner they wish, and the wellbeing of children and women within such arrangements have been a secondary consideration.

Feminist critics have argued that, since liberal thought was formulated in the 18th century, the figure of the liberal 'citizen' has been gender-neutral in principle but masculine in practice, and many of the 'rights' and protections accorded to him have not been extended to children and women (MacKinnon 1989, Pateman 1988, Smart 1991). Pateman (1988) has argued that liberalism legitimised a social and legal regime whereby men were compensated for their subjection to the demands of state authority in 'public' life with the crafting of a zone of impunity around homes populated by women and children over whom they exercised virtually untrammelled control. It is nonetheless true that liberalism has provided a vocabulary of equality and rights that would prove integral to subsequent women's movements and other civil rights movements. The liberal notion of an individual moral and agentic subject (even an implicitly masculine one) created the foundation upon which notions of sexual consent and other critical feminist concepts could be advanced. However, the high rhetoric and abstractions of liberal theory have legitimised the subordination of women to men through the operations of institutions, such as the criminal justice system, whose legitimacy is founded on liberal notions of justice and equality (MacKinnon 1989). Men's crimes against women and children have been persistently veiled as a mostly 'private' matter that is not a legitimate focus of the attention of 'public' agencies such as the police or justice system.

Liberal thought was being formulated in the 18th century in the advent of unprecedented urbanisation and industrialisation in Europe and North America. This was an era of social and economic change that would profoundly impact on gender relations. As relations of production were restructured to form the nascent capitalist economy, established forms of aristocratic masculinity based on lineage and honour gave way to constructions of masculinity that reflected the new distribution of money and power: in particular, 'bourgeoise' masculinities with a focus on professional expertise, and working-class masculinities that emphasised masculine solidarity and homosociality (Cohen 1999, Liddle 1996). During this period, the gendering of work became less flexible and more culturally prescribed, and women and children were increasingly excluded from economic participation. Female idleness became a bourgeois ideal and the capacity to maintain a wife and children in the home the mark of a successful and wealthy man. The notion that the lives of women and children should be restricted to the 'private' sphere was simply untenable for many of the poor and working class who were dependent on the income of all family members, but it was an ideal that symbolised the increasingly gendered nature of labour and income. Literature throughout the 18th and the 19th centuries extolled the 'natural' complementarity of men's and women's roles within the spheres of public and private life, although such claims prompted fierce contestation from women's advocates (Rendall 1999).

The gender-polarised social order legitimised by liberalism was inextricably bound up with a reconfiguration of sexuality in ways that expressed and reinforced women's devaluation within the social order. As a family income increasingly became understood as a male income, the work available for girls and women was seasonal and piecemeal at best, or else involved domestic service where physical abuse and sexual exploitation were commonplace (Simpson 1987). Throughout the 18th century, there was a noticeable trend towards marriage, and early marriage, since women had few prospects other than unemployment and poverty without the economic support of a husband (McKeon 1995). Wives and children had few protections against men who chose to exercise their patriarchal prerogative through physical or sexual abuse, or who squandered the family income on gambling and alcohol. Far from signifying a 'separate but equal' division of social power, the 'public-private' divide instead represents the mutually enforcing economic and emotional complexities of masculine domination in the new capitalist order. Within the prevailing liberal ethos, the economic marginalisation of women was justified by an ideology of feminine gentility and incompetence and the rise of a 'cult of womanhood' that valorised the obedient wife who was virtuous by dint of her subordinate disposition (LeGates 1976).

The ethos of feminine domesticity in the 18th century, Cohen (1999) suggests, coexisted alongside an emphasis on rough homosociality as a way of establishing masculinity. The 'obedient' wife was just one manifestation of masculine privilege. So too were the increasing numbers of prostitutes and the pornography and erotica that circulated throughout the coffee houses and men's clubs of the era. The male sociability of the new 'public' sphere incorporated carnivalesque displays of heterosexual aggression in a period in which understandings of consensual and coercive sex were virtually indistinguishable from one another. In contrast to the more diffuse modes of sexuality that preceded it, the sexual culture of the 18th century celebrated penetrative heterosex as the sexual act *par excellence* and the most basic expression of masculine attainment (Hitchcock 1996). In the North American context, Sanday (1996) has documented increased reports of urban gang rape during this period. Pornographic literature featured women as passive objects who, through penetration, could be 'taken' or 'possessed' by men (Harvey 2004). Detectable in the pornography of the 18th century was a theme of sadism and cruelty that had been largely absent from the erotica of the preceding century (Simpson 1987). In the 18th century, the power differentials between men and women that had become embedded within the division of labour within the capitalist economy, and the structures of power within the liberal state, were also intrinsic to the prevailing structure of sexualisation in which masculine power and female powerlessness was eroticised.

Children were not exempt from the processes of objectification that had become a normative element of masculine sexuality. The rape of a young child was abhorred by the 18th-century public but there was considerable ambiguity over the line of delineation between child and adult, and an entrenched suspicion that behind the resistance of a girl or woman to sexual coercion was concealed consent. Voltaire could decry the 'deflowering of a girl of 8' in 1764 whilst maintaining that older girls and women were culpable for their rape even when they violently fought with an attacker (Vigarello 2001: 65). The value of 'childhood' in the 18th century was dependent on its conformity to bourgeois ideals of 'innocence'; that is to say, a lack of worldly experience. Involvement in delinquency or work disqualified many of the children of the poor and the working class from this definition of 'childhood' and hence they could be considered fair game in the sexual economy. In 18th-century France, sexually abused children as young as six or seven were accused by judges of solicitation and active involvement in their own abuse (Vigarello 2001: 85). The available historical literature suggests that the prostitution of 12 or 13-year-old girls was common in 18th-century England (Brewer and Bullough 2005) and specialised brothels were established for clients with an interest in children below the age of 10 (Simpson 1987). A significant proportion of reports of rape involved victims younger that 12 (Simpson 1987). The rape of a child was rationalised by perpetrators as well as by the media and the courts according to a prevailing myth that sex with a virgin could cure venereal disease, but Wolff (2005) argues that the prevailing image of the 'innocent', vulnerable child may have encouraged child sexual abuse in a culture that eroticised 'deflowering' the young and vulnerable.

In the gender order of the 18th century, masculinity was associated with a position of privilege in a sexual economy characterised by the objectification and exchange of women's bodies. With their entry into the labour market vitiated by deep inequalities, women's social and economic status was determined primarily by the mode of exchange of her sexual labour: through marriage for 'respectable' women, and through prostitution for the impoverished or the unlucky. Whilst virtuous femininity was defined by the restriction and exclusivity of sexual relations, the performance of authentic masculinity could straddle both sides of the sexual economy: 'respectable' dominion over house and home alongside transgressive forays into prostitution, pornography and other sexual manifestations of women's and children's powerlessness. Sexual appetite and aggression had become integral to the maintenance of masculine identity and status, whilst the vulnerabilities of children and women marked them as suitably disempowered objects for the performance of masculinity. As the next section will discuss, these performances took on structured and symbolic forms through the masculine fraternities and clubs that proliferated during the 18th and 19th centuries. In these clubs the philosophy of libertinism was born, in which the high-minded ideals of rationality and liberty were bound to a predatory masculine sexuality. It was in the context of libertinism that the symbolism of ritualistic and sadistic sexual abuse was first theorised as the righteous celebration of masculine entitlement.

From liberalism to libertinism

The European and North American societies of the 18th century were not sexually permissive by any means, however the diversity of human sexuality was a topic of enduring interest and a key point of resistance to the authority of church and state. Intellectual circles pointed to the sexual practices of ancient paganism and 'exotic' foreign cultures to construct a new history of sexuality. They argued that European sexual prohibitions were the arbitrary impositions of a corrupt priesthood and that sexual expression, rather than sinful or amoral, was conducive to wellbeing and social harmony. This linkage between irreligion, sensual pleasure and self-realisation formed the basis of the writing and philosophy of the libertines, whose advocacy of hedonism was designed to both shock and liberate (Turner 1987). Libertinism drew on the hedonist tendencies of Enlightenment philosophy which proposed that pleasure and happiness were the ultimate grounds of morality and the ends that human beings naturally pursue. However, as Rousseau and Porter (1987: 3) observed, 'the more sexual desire was installed as the hub and premium mobile of the "moral order", the more that order became amoral and immoral'. By the 18th century, the broad church of libertinism came to harbour extremes of sexual nihilism in which masculine erotic sadism was writ large as a universal, metaphysical principle. The prerogative of masculine dominion over women and children, as imagined in liberal philosophy, was mythologised by the libertines as a right of sexual access to women and children, upon whose bodies could be written the fiction of transcendental selfhood (Cameron and Frazer 1987).

Developing a historical genealogy of libertine discourse and behaviour is complicated by a number of factors, including (a) the secrecy of libertine groups and fraternities and hence the scarcity of reliable historical records of libertine activities, (b) the intertwining of fact, fiction and exaggeration in moralistic attacks on libertinism, and (c) the ways in which libertine principles and convictions are presented through parodies and satires of prevailing hypocrisies over sex and gender. Turner (1987) points to the varieties of uses of the term 'libertinism' since the 18th century and emphasises that libertinism does not describe a coherent ideological programme or canon. However, common to the various postures and attitudes associated with libertinism is the simultaneous glorification of sexuality and the mocking of established conventions, including religion, in the pursuit of masculine self-realisation. Whilst trading in abstractions such as fraternity, liberty and happiness, libertine philosophy was realised and embodied in the sexual objectification and dehumanisation of women and girls, through whom sensual pleasure was generated and religious morality was flouted. Whilst their anti-clericism and republican spirit were genuine, it also served to rationalise acts of sexual domination and to mythologise the masculine solidarity that was generated through the subordination of women and girls, intertwining misogyny and sexual coercion with lofty ideals of rationality and liberty.

This was an ethos embedded within many of the private men's clubs and orders that proliferated throughout 18th-century Europe and North America (Lord 2008). They have been celebrated by Habermas (1989) for their pursuit of reason and free thinking, but some of these clubs were fervently libertine in flavour, engaging prostitutes, other women and one another in sexual rituals. Koselleck's (1988) view of these clubs and orders is that they were the hypocritical construct of an emerging social class of bourgeoisie that obscured their shared class interests by laying claim simultaneously to Enlightenment 'reason' and occult 'mystery'. Such an argument can be extended to the gender politics of these fraternities, in which sexual performance and the objectification of women served as a practice of solidarity between 'brothers'. Deneys (1991) suggests that the sexual economy of libertinism had many parallels with the emerging capitalist economy in which women featured as a form of capital to be exchanged between men, producing value in the process through sexual 'conquest' and other badges of masculine honour. The fraternal orders and clubs provided important forums in which free discussion of atheism and resistance to Church control and state hypocrisy could take place but this privileged anti-authoritarianism harboured an ethos in which masculine self-identity could be found through coercive sex and transgression.

The Marquis de Sade and libertine excess

The nihilistic overtones of libertine sexuality would find their greatest advocate and systematiser in the Marquis de Sade, the French nobleman and philosopher whose surname was adopted by Krafft-Ebing a century after his death to label the eroticisation of violence as 'sadism'. Since Kraft-Ebbing, psychiatrists and sexologists have argued that sadistic behaviour is evidence of a sexual pathology. However, Sade's philosophy of sexual cruelty describes the social and cultural rather than biological origins of transgressive and violent masculine sexuality. In novels such as *Justine, or the Misfortunes of Virtue, Juliette* and *The 120 Days of Sodom*, Sade described a 'private' sphere replete with the coercion and violence otherwise understood as characteristics of 'public' conflict. His work is a searing expose of a gendered hierarchy characterised by masculinist aristocratic and ecclesiastic privilege on one hand and the inequities of the developing capitalist order on the other (Carter 1979). According to Sade, women and girls in such conditions are faced with two main choices: resist their subordinate position in the natural order and endure the abuse and violence which is their lot, or ally themselves with their abusers in an effort to gain some status and ameliorate the harm inflicted upon them.

Whilst his libertine contemporaries opposed conventional religious morality, Sade wrote fiction and philosophy that flouted and inverted religious doctrine in accordance with a nihilistic teleology in which violence and murder are intrinsic to the 'natural' cycle of creation and destruction (Airaksinen 1995). He proposed that there should be no inhibitions to sensual pleasure nor should there be any discrimination between sexual impulses. Sexual violence was celebrated by Sade as a human manifestation of natural forces, and hence it is the prerogative of the Sadeian hero to cultivate a principled indifference to the suffering of the victims of his pursuit of sensual pleasure. It is in the pornographic philosophical treatises of Sade that the defining elements of organised child sexual abuse first appear in the historical record. His works frequently describe groups of men who enslave children and women and subject them to organised, sadistic and ritualistic abuse with disturbing parallels to contemporary reports. For Goodwin (1994a: 483–4), Sade describes ordeals that are not just similar to those described by children and adults with histories of ritualistic abuse, but rather they are virtually identical in structure and detail:

> To mention a few: locking in cages, threatening with death, burying in coffins, holding under water, threatening with weapons, drugging and bleeding, tipping upside down and burning, wearing of robes and costumes, staging of mock marriages, defecating and urinating on victims, killing of animals, having victims witness torture, having them witness homicides, pouring or drinking of blood, and taking victims to churches and cemeteries.

The only contemporary element missing in Sade's account of organised and ritualistic abuse, Goodwin (1994a: 484) notes, is the manufacture of child pornography, however, 'its place is taken by use of peepholes and uses of stages at the orgies, where each libertine could be seen to perform with his entourage of victims'. She suggests that contemporary reports of ritualistic abuse are neither unprecedented nor inexplainable, as sceptics suggest, nor are they evidence of underground 'cults' or a trans-historical 'Satanic' tradition. Instead, it seems that cases of ritualistic abuse may be evidence of the persistence of the libertine notion of the male sexual prerogative which is derived from the historical patterning of gender relations and the associated practices of group sexual violence and ritualistic abuse.

Goodwin (1994b) is not the only contemporary commentator to highlight the similarities between the philosophy of sexual cruelty espoused by Sade's heroes and modern reports of sexual violence. Cameron and Frazer (1987) argue that the Sadean construction of masculine sexuality in terms of violent transcendence over others has come to permeate the cultural order, informing the conduct of serial killers who have found power and pleasure in the murder of the weak and the vulnerable. In serial killer Ian Brady's (2001) published account of his crimes and motivations, he articulates a philosophy of sexual murder that draws explicitly on the work of Sade. Caputi (1988) gathered reports from soldiers and murderers recounting the 'godlike' experience of power and control they experienced in the conduct of sexual atrocities that have many similarities to the pretensions of Sade's characters. In Sanday's (2007) study of gang rapes by university fraternities, she documented how the bond shared by initiated 'brothers', and perpetuated by the tradition of the 'train' or gang rape of vulnerable women, was encoded through secretive ritual practices and esoteric religious mysteries. In a riposte that could have been torn directly from the pages of Sade, one fraternity 'brother' reflected how, through initiation into the fraternity, members came to feel they were the 'masters of life' because they knew its 'tiny, black, hollow core' (Sanday 2007: 163).

The contemporary 'management' of sexual offences is beset with distinctions between sex offences on the basis of age, gender and particular forms of sexual behaviour. Sade presents an entirely different configuration of sexual crime and one that more closely mirrors cases of organised abuse. Sade did not distinguish between the abuse of a girl or the abuse of a woman, nor did he delineate between ritual, sadistic and sexual forms of abuse. Instead, these practices interconnect with one another according to context and the particular interests of the abuser; what they have in common is their utility in the production of power and pleasure. The role of women in the perpetration of organised abuse has often been observed and, similarly, in Sade's books the positions of abused and abuser are not fixed by gender. Nonetheless, the context of abuse remains ruled by the association of masculinity with power and violence. Even where a woman can affect some respite from abuse through establishing an alliance with her abusers, she only does so on the terms set out by her abusers and her subordinate position within the gendered hierarchy remains unchanged.

In contrast to the individualising and clinical accounts of sex offences that dominate the modern scientific literature on sexual offences, Sade offers a thoroughly sociological perspective. He contextualised the acts of organised abuse that he described within a 'black market' of exploitation, abuse and pain that is produced by, and inextricably bound up within, the gendered structures of the free market, in which the economic and social privileging of men finds expression through the debasement and enslavement of women and children. The excesses of free market forces may be kept in check in the 'public' sphere by the force of law and custom, but Sade reveals that, behind the veil of 'privacy' lies a sexual marketplace red in tooth and claw. He suggests that beneath the formal symbolic order of liberal theory and its high-minded ideals are the profoundly unequal relations of power they legitimate, and the sadistic drives and urges they produce. These tendencies are evident not only in organised abuse but in a range of sexual atrocities committed mostly by men against women and children in a hapless search for the transcendental masculine identity celebrated by liberalism.

Sadean abuses in contemporary society

Ideologies can produce their own excesses as their explicit and implicit logics are reworked, reinterpreted and deployed for reasons that appear, at first glance, far removed from the rationalising tropes through which ideologies legitimise themselves. This was well recognised by Marx and Engels, for whom the contradictions of capitalism gave rise to unintended emotional and psychological responses in the working classes that could be incorporated into alternative visions of social and political life. Similarly, the patterns of affect and sexuality that formed within early liberal democracies found articulation within ideologies of libertinism and masculine sadism. Whilst libertine excess appears, within a liberal framework of rights and justice, as a crime or aberration, it can be also understood as the eroticisation of the liberal presentation of the 'public-private' divide and the gendered inequities therein.

Masculine privilege has come to be symbolised or signalled by a range of libertine practices that, in contemporary society, continue to be deployed in degrading ceremonies that reinforce gendered relations of domination and subordination. The role of sacrilege and ritualistic abuse in the work of Sade is comparable to its contemporary application in Abu Ghraib, where Muslim captives in Iraq were terrorised by American soldiers who desecrated Islamic scripture, forced them into proximity with taboo substances, raped and forced them to engage in sexual acts with one another. In this process, the frameworks of meaning and interpretation supported by religious ideology were systematically destroyed and replaced by the basic principle of the supremacy of power and the domination of the weak by the strong. This is the ideological truth asserted by Sade, who describes sex on coffins in crypts, the penetration of orifices with crucifixes and a range of other blasphemies also reported in cases of organised abuse. In these acts, the worldview of the victim is deconstructed and remade according to the view of the torturer, who integrates culturally potent symbols into the production of pain and horror to inscribe a visceral sense of degradation and shame upon the victim.

In Sade's world, this shame is emancipatory in that it reveals the 'natural' state of human affairs and thus enables the victim to eschew the false constructs of virtue that had previously consigned them to subordination. In many regards, Sade's depiction accords with the fantasies of perpetrators of torture and abuse who, by coercing their victims into compliance and even perpetration, come to believe that their victims 'want', 'deserve' or 'need' their abuse and are all the stronger for it. In organised abuse, just as in Abu Ghraib, this process is associated with masculinist hierarchies in which women may be co-opted into performances of degradation and humiliation, but nonetheless their ritualistic and sadistic practices signify the designation of the 'weak' and feminine from the masculine and masterful.

The similarities between military torture and organised abuse have been noted elsewhere (Golston 1993a, Golston 1993b, Kelly 2000), however the notion that the 'private' sphere might harbour torture of a degree comparable to those inflicted in the context of 'public' war and conflict is frequently dismissed out of hand. Abu Ghraib has gone down in infamy despite the best efforts of the American military and government to keep it secret because the 'public' contexts of such abuses are amenable to documentation and investigation in ways that the 'private' spaces of organised abuse are not. Importantly, Abu Ghraib occurred in the 'East' rather than the 'West', the global 'South' rather than the 'North'; in short, in an area of the world designated as a 'zone of fear' by Western governments and media agencies. Colonialist ideologies of racial barbarism and primitivism facilitate (and even encourage) the identification of violence and sadism in developing countries, which are constructed by Western media and authorities as lawless and risky in contrast to the 'zones of safety' within the 'civilised' West (Ignatieff 1998). Žižek (1994) describes how, during the Balkan conflict, Western journalists competed with one another to provide images of 'lacerated child bodies, raped women' as 'fodder for hungry Western eyes'. Implicitly, these images delineated the savage Balkan 'other' from the normal Western citizen. The unbearable fact, he suggests, is that *there is no difference*', and that the efforts of citizens of Sarajevo to 'maintain the appearance of normal life' in the midst of war have many parallels with our own efforts to 'live in the fiction of peace' (p 2).

Within the 'discourse of disbelief' (Scott 2001) that has developed around organised abuse and ritualistic abuse, there is an assumption that such excessive abuses are alien to the 'civilised' Western world. In many regards this mirrors the hegemonic view of 'global difference', defined by Connell (2007) as the 'difference between the civilisation of the metropole and other cultures whose main feature was their primitiveness'. However, the rape, torture and evisceration of women and children are not 'primitive' practices foreign to 'first world' nations. Child abuse images categorised on the COPINE scale[1] as 'category 10', meaning that they depict the sexual torture of children (eg the child is subject to sadistic abuse or forced into sexual contact with an animal) circulate on the internet (Taylor et al. 2001). There is a group of child sex offenders who fantasise about torturing and murdering children, with one pornographic magazine intercepted in the 1980s stating that 'All the great extremes – genital torture, forced unlubricated rape, butchering – reach their pinnacle when the victim is a small child' (quoted in Tate 1990). The author of this magazine, Peter Sotos, was convicted of child pornography

---

1 The COPINE scale is a rating system, developed by staff at the Combating Paedophile Information Networks in Europe (COPINE) project, that categorises the severity of child abuse images. The COPINE scale rates child abuse images from 1–10, which 10 being the most extreme category. A simplified scale from 1–5, based on the COPINE scale, was developed by the UK Sentencing Panel and is widely used in the Australian criminal justice system (see Griffith and Simon 2008).

offences but his subsequent writings on child torture and murder have attracted a cult following led by novelist Dennis Cooper who has bemoaned the failure to recognise Sotos' work as 'significant contemporary literature'.[2]

Throughout the 20th century, the depiction of illicit sadistic sexuality in 'high' as well as 'low' culture has been viewed as a courageous 'unveiling' of a fundamental truth about human life (Kramer 1997). Caputi (1988: 30) notes that sexual violence is frequently mythologised as 'some mysterious force of nature, the expression of deeply repressed "human" urges, a fact of life, a supernatural evil, a monstrous aberration – anything but the logical and eminently functional product of the system of male domination'. However, in the reification of male sexual violence into a universal, ahistorical 'truth' the line between representation and enactment is unclear. In an interview in which Sotos described his interest in 'extreme sexual violence and sadism', he assured the interviewer he had found ways to 'enjoy their pleasures without getting my hands ostentatiously dirty' (Tate 1990: 170). In the recent British investigation into child sexual abuser Roger Took, the police uncov-ered internet chat logs in which Took described his participation in the gang rape and murder of a child in Cambodia with such frequency and consistency that the authorities treated the incident as a potential fact (Metcalf 2008). However, police were unable to ascertain whether the murder described by Took had taken place and instead he was prosecuted for child pornography offences and sexual offences against his stepdaughters.

The similarities between high-minded representations of sexual violence and the actual practices of some perpetrators suggests that brutality and sadism, far from being an exotic characteristic of developing countries, are instead symptomatic of entrenched associations between power, masculin-ity and violence in Western culture (Kramer 1997). However, when such violence is reported to have occurred in developed countries this linkage is denied and instead the crime is framed as an aberration and explained according to the particular psychological or developmental characteristics of the offender. Kelly (2000) contests the de-politicisation of serious physical and sexual violence against women and children in Western countries. Drawing on a gendered lens, she has highlighted the political significance of the commonalities between reports of sadistic sexual violence in armed conflict and those alleged to occur in organised abuse:

> What is being enacted in most of these settings are reinforcements of the primacy of relationships between men, and the accompanying subordination of women which underpins male supremacy. Men affirm one another as men through the exclusion, humiliation and objectifica-tion of women. What we need to explore in more depth is whether any

2 see http://denniscooper.blogspot.com/2006/07/peter-sotos-day.html.

hierarchical grouping of men, organised as men, creates conditions in which coercive heterosexuality is promoted and enacted. These groupings would include sports teams, private clubs, gangs, secret societies as well as the military.

(Kelly 2000: 57)

The fact that women and children frequently present in mental health settings in developed countries with trauma-related psychological problems of a dimension comparable to survivors of ethnic cleansing or prisoners-of-war challenges the taken-for-granted assumption that atrocity and torture are activities restricted to 'public' political conflict overseas (Herman 1992). It would seem that the politics of gender produces its own atrocities and torturers. However, hegemonic liberal idealisations of the 'private' sphere as an idyll free from the troubles of 'public' life, and 'West' as free from the barbarism of developing countries, obscures the politics of gender, and the intensification of the powerlessness of women and children by acts of abject and terrifying violence.

Abusive groups are not foolish. They do not operate in 'public' spaces where they will be subject to the panopticon of legal surveillance and regulation. Instead, they have colonised the 'private' spaces in which men have long enjoyed legal impunity for the physical and sexual abuse of children and women. Cooper et al. (2006) argue that the 'private' spaces of the home and family serve in effect as a 'parallel state' operating within the nation state in which sexually abusive men can construct their own regimes of abuse, control and terror with little risk of detection. Despite the reforms of recent decades, signs of the persistence of children's and women's powerlessness can be read in the continuing prevalence of sexual abuse, sexual assault and domestic violence, and the obstacles that children and women experience in trying to make these 'private' crimes 'public'. The eroticisation of this powerlessness is what creates the impetus for organised abuse and, indeed, the other manifestations of the libertine 'tradition' in which sexual coercion and aggression serves as the foundation of claims to masculine status. Behind the latticework of analytic binaries that demarcate 'public' from 'private', 'civilised' from 'barbaric' and so forth is a cultural continuum of eroticised sadism. This continuum persists, in no small way, due to a collective investment in prereflexive norms and values that simultaneously denies the seriousness of gendered violence in developed countries whilst crafting 'private' spaces in which women and children can by battered, raped and even murdered by men upholding the masculine entitlement they have come to understand as their right.

Conclusion

By identifying its historical antecedents, this chapter argues that organised abuse is a product of a pervasive ideology of masculine sadism through which men find solidarity with one another through acts of collective sexual violence. In the examination of libertinism, it is clear that historical continuity is important in understanding coercive as well as consensual sexualities and sexual cultures. The forms of domination, control and violence on display in organised abuse are a particular arrangement of cultural material and symbols with an established historical association with violent endorsements of masculine privilege. This is not to say that the configuration of these associations has not changed in 300 years, or that they are employed in the same way today by all the men who seek to embody them. Acknowledging the impact of feminism on gender relations, Frosh (2002) provocatively asks whether gendered violence in contemporary society should be understood as both an expression of male power and as a 'retreat' by men faced by the decentring of once taken-for-granted privilege. The practices of organised abuse today may therefore have a range of different connotations today than they had in the past. Nonetheless, the emergence of new cases of organised abuse, and their similarities to abuses described 300 years ago suggest that the practice of sadism still retains its potent associations with masculine power and privilege, even as the political economy of masculine power shifts and changes.

If the liberalism and libertinism of the 18th century serves as a useful blueprint for contemporary misogyny and its excessive violence against children and women, then it may also offer tools for challenging and undermining this violence. Sociological research has revealed the interactions of multiple competing masculinities including anti-hegemonic masculinities that explicitly reject dominant narratives of male sexual aggression (see Connell 1995). Power and resistance are intimately linked according to Foucault (1979), and efforts to 'naturalise' male sexual aggression have prompted their own counter-formations and alternatives. Furthermore, it is clear from the practices of consensual sadomasochists that the eroticisation of power differentials can be 'read' against the grain of the gendered *status quo* in ways that are experienced as subversive, emancipatory and liberating, playing with rather than reinforcing gender roles and tropes. So just as liberalism has institutionalised gendered inequities whilst providing succor and inspiration to women's movements, libertinism can both intensify and subvert relations of domination and subordination. The question of how we can re-imagine these potentials is beyond the scope of this book, but it is an important one. By locating the historical origins of organised abuse, we can move beyond the limitations of contemporary understandings of sexual abuse to identify the broader cultural linkages between organised child abuse, violence against women and structures of gender and power. However, as the following chapter will show, these linkages give rise to processes of invalidation, denial and disbelief that camouflage the very abuses that they enable.

Chapter 4

Organised abuse and the pleasures of disbelief

In the 1980s and 1990s, the most prolific and widely read literature on organised abuse was written by sceptical journalists and academics who referred to the phenomenon, almost uniformly, as 'satanic ritual abuse'. Clinical and therapeutic literature preferred terms such as 'organised abuse', 'sadistic abuse' and 'ritual abuse' but sceptics insisted that these terms were just euphemisms for 'satanic ritual abuse' and outrageous allegations of satanic rituals, cannibalism and human sacrifice. This argument has been repeated with such enthusiasm in the press that it is no exaggeration to suggest that scepticism is the dominant mode through which allegations of organised abuse came to public attention. The public has been repeatedly warned that 'satanic ritual abuse' has been the obsession of 'witch hunters' since the Middle Ages, and that this melodrama is being repeated today by a coalition of social actors driven by a puritanical desire to impose their conservative, authoritarian agenda upon society. This chapter seeks not only to question the accuracy of this representation but also to highlight its ideological formation within social movements for people accused of sexual abuse.

The previous chapter explored an undercurrent in the social construction of masculine sexuality, in which the free expression of sexuality was understood as a social good linked to notions of freedom, liberty and the natural order. However, in the 1980s revelations about the frequency of child sexual abuse have brought to light previously unacknowledged dimensions of masculine sexual coerciveness, which in turn destabilised common presumptions about the benevolence of masculine sexuality and power. This chapter will focus on the efforts of social movements to close over this breach by construing women and children disclosing sexual abuse, and the professionals who supported them, as a threat to the social order. Allegations of 'satanic ritual abuse' were presented as evidence that feminist and/or Christian 'zealots' had infiltrated the child protection sector and mental health services and, motivated by a hysterical antipathy to 'male sexuality', were coercing children and women concocting outrageous allegations against innocent men. This was presented as an unprecedented crisis in which all men were vulnerable to vilification or prosecution on the basis of a false accusation of sexual abuse.

This chapter will draw on Žižek's (1991) insights into enjoyment as a political factor to untangle the enmeshment of ideology and emotion within the sceptical account of 'satanic ritual abuse'. Blaming therapy, social work and other caring professions for the confabulation of testimony of 'satanic ritual abuse' legitimated a programme of political and social action designed to contest the gains made by the women's movement and the child protection movement. In efforts to characterise social workers and therapists as hysterical zealots, 'satanic ritual abuse' was, quite literally, 'made fun of': it became the subject of scorn and ridicule as interest groups sought to discredit testimony of sexual abuse as a whole. The groundswell of support that such efforts gained amongst journalists, academics and the public suggests that the pleasures of disbelief found resonance far beyond the confines of social movements for people accused of sexual abuse. These pleasures were legitimised by a pseudo-scientific vocabulary of 'false memories' and 'moral panic' but as Daly (1999: 219–20) points out 'the ultimate goal of ideology is to present itself in neutral, value-free terms as the very horizon of objectivity and to dismiss challenges to its order as the "merely ideological"'.

The media spotlight has moved on and social movements for people accused of sexual abuse have lost considerable momentum. However, their rhetoric continues to reverberate throughout the echo chamber of online and 'old' media. Intimations of collusion between feminists and Christians in the concoction of 'satanic ritual abuse' continue to mobilise 'progressive' as well as 'conservative' sympathies for men accused of serious sexual offences and against the needs of victimised women and children. This chapter argues that, underlying the invocation of often contradictory rationalising tropes (ranging from calls for more scientific 'objectivity' in sexual abuse investigations to emotional descriptions of 'happy families' rent asunder by false allegations) is a collective and largely unarticulated pleasure: the cathartic release of sentiments and views about children and women that had otherwise become shameful in the aftermath of second wave feminism. It seems that, behind the veneer of public concern about child sexual abuse, traditional views about the incredibility of women's and children's testimony persist. 'Satanic ritual abuse' has served as a lens through which these views have been rearticulated and reasserted at the very time that evidence of widespread and serious child sexual abuse has been consolidating.

The rise of the 'false memory' movement

Since the 1960s, health and welfare workers and feminists have successfully challenged the view of medical and legal authorities that sexual abuse was a rare and not necessarily harmful act in which children share responsibility with adults. The implications of this new paradigm were considerable, involving a shift away from the discursive power of the traditionally masculine disciplines of medicine and law and towards the standpoint of the primary objects of sexual victimisation; that is to say, women and children. Disclosures of sexual abuse began to be considered authentic representations of lived experience in therapeutic contexts, the media and the criminal justice system. Prior to this period, the communicative contexts in which women and children could disclose sexual abuse were few and heavily constrained. In interpersonal as well as institutional settings (eg court rooms or psychiatric clinics), the denials of the accused were afforded considerably more weight than the allegations of victimised children or women, which reflected the broader social context in which the legal and political rights of women and children were limited, and poorly protected, in comparison to men. Even where the victim was believed, community disgust at sex offences often stigmatised the victim as well as the offender. However, the opening up of new and more sympathetic therapeutic spaces, and increasing media coverage of sexual abuse, created alternative testimonial opportunities for victimised children and women away from the medico-legal traditions that had trivialised their accounts. This was a challenge not only to established expertise but to the project of governmentality itself and the gender order that it legitimises. Foucault (1964) had much to say about the ways in which psychiatric categories have served the interests of governmental authorities but little to say about the profoundly unequal distribution of power to men within such arrangements. The privileging of women's voices and expertise in public debate on child sexual abuse was a direct challenge to this distribution of power, and it was met by an extraordinary backlash that focused, to a significant degree, on allegations of organised abuse.

In the early 1990s, a group of people accused of sexual abuse formed the 'False Memory Syndrome Foundation' (FMSF). The FMSF's primary goal was to advocate on behalf of parents accused of child sexual abuse by their adult children, but the Foundation also became an important resource centre for people accused of sexual abuse by minors. Importantly, the Foundation attracted academics from a range of disciplines whose expertise had been contested or challenged by the legitimisation of children's and women's testimony of sexual abuse. A number of psychiatrists, psychologists and other researchers aligned themselves with the Foundation, claiming that only the careful 'scientific' scrutiny afforded by their respective professions could delineate 'true' from 'false' memories of sexual abuse. This was an argument that many took to the courtrooms as paid defence experts for people accused of sexual abuse and other offences against children and women (Whitfield 2001), giving rise to an unusual body of academic literature that presented the arguments of sexual abuse defence teams as scientific fact (Salter 2008).

With the support of these academics and clinicians, the Foundation claimed to have discovered a new psychiatric condition called 'False Memory Syndrome' at 'epidemic proportions' (Pope 1996: 957). This 'syndrome' purported to describe an illness created by false memory induction either through active therapeutic malpractice or due to a widespread 'moral panic' or 'sexual hysteria' about child abuse. This heady mix of psychological and sociological theory gave significant credibility to the 'false memory' societies that other advocacy groups for people accused of sexual abuse had lacked. By the mid-1990s, 'false memory' societies had been established throughout North America, Europe, Australia and other Western countries. As a social movement, the 'false memory' societies formed an aggressive and effective advocacy coalition that provided the media with compelling narratives of families devastated by accusations of child sexual abuse (Kitzinger 1998). These narratives proved influential in academic and media debates over allegations of child sexual abuse. Journalists and researchers sympathetic to the 'false memory' position warned that any man could be subject to a false allegation, risking prosecution and imprisonment in a criminal justice system that was characterised as riddled with injustices. During this period, the sympathy that had been evident in media coverage of sexual abuse victims since the late 1970s began to evaporate (Beckett 1996).

The construction of 'satanic ritual abuse'

The 'false memory' movement lacked the empirical evidence to prove that, as they claimed, many allegations of sexual abuse were the product of cognitive errors and widespread psychotherapeutic malpractice. Instead, they fed media controversies over allegations of ritualistic abuse in an attempt to suggest the existence of an 'epidemic' of suggestibility and unprofessional conduct in the mental health and child protection sectors. Kluft (1997: 33) provides a summary of this strategy:

> Groups purporting to speak for those who claim to have been falsely accused of child abuse have found it useful to exploit the skepticism surrounding alleged ritualized abuse as a starting point for their efforts to demolish the credibility of those making more mundane accusations. Their strategy has seemed geared to finding a straw-man target and then initiating a domino effect that serves their agenda.

In the 1980s, some (although not all) early attempts to prosecute allegations of ritualistic abuse had foundered on investigative failures, and the plight of child witnesses forced to testify under the same conditions to adults (Hechler 1988). This was a period in which there were no protocols or training on complexities of investigating multi-perpetrator, multi-victim sexual abuse cases, which could snowball from an initial report or suspicion of abuse into an unanticipated explosion in referrals, complaints and media attention (Gaspar 1996). The struggles of police and child protection services to manage these cases were recast by the 'false memory' movement as evidence of the unprofessionalism of any investigator who could take an allegation of organised abuse seriously.[1] The efforts of clinicians and therapists to develop effective treatment for clients with histories of ritualistic abuse, who presented with acute and complex problems previously unrecognised in mental health training or literature, were attacked as the iatrogenic cause of the very disclosures they were a response to. As media interest began to coalesce around the claims of the 'false memory' movement, substantiated cases of organised and ritualistic abuse were ignored or sidelined and important evidence was overlooked (Kitzinger 2004).

Academics associated with the 'false memory' cause developed a range of sceptical explanations for allegations of ritual abuse. The corollaries drawn in this literature between therapy/social work and fraud, deceit and quackery are not established through research but rather assumed from the very outset. This work shared a common intellectual strategy, in which academics transposed their preferred theoretical frameworks to allegations of ritual abuse rather than developing their explanations according to the available evidence. For example, Ofshe's research had previously focused on the dangers of cults. To support his claim that ritual abuse disclosures were iatrogenic he drew a parallel between cults and therapy, which he and journalist Watters characterised as 'high pressure' environments pervaded by cult-like New Age techniques (Ofshe and Watters 1996). Other sociologists more sympathetic to 'New Religious Movements' argued that allegations of ritual abuse were an attack on alternative spiritualities rather than an outgrowth of them (Richardson et al. 1991). Folklorists argued that 'satanic ritual abuse' was an urban legend (Victor 1993), 'false memory' researchers argued that it was a product of 'false memories' (Loftus and Ketcham 1994), religious historians drew parallels with historical examples of scapegoating and witch hunting (Frankfurter 2001), and so on.

Within the broad umbrella of the 'false memory' movement, competing and often contradictory explanations of ritualistic abuse proliferated. These explanations had in common the conviction that allegations of ritualistic abuse had no basis in fact despite little agreement amongst sceptics regarding the actual origins of such allegations. This literature advanced a simplistic portrayal of social work and therapy as fields characterised by fad, gossip and coercive influence that resonated strongly with the 'false memory' societies that authors had aligned themselves with. Despite their claims to be writing in the name of 'objectivity', 'reason' and 'justice', 'false memory' academics

---

1 In fact, these cases included strong medical evidence of sexual assault. The allegations of organised abuse that arose in Jordan, Minnesota in 1983 are frequently referred to in sceptical literature as an example of 'false allegations', however of the 29 children reporting sexual abuse in the case, ten showed medical signs of sexual assault, with one nine-year-old girl incontinent of urine and faeces (Tamarkin 1994b). The McMartin preschool case is perhaps the most infamous failure to prosecute organised abuse in the United States in the 1980s, but the strength of the medical evidence of sexual assault in the case is rarely acknowledged (Rust 1985–1986).

promulgated pejorative and unfounded characterisations of professional practice by constructing caricatures of ritual abuse allegations which, they claimed, established the frequently of malpractice amongst social workers and therapists. In this literature, ritual abuse is almost invariably referred to as 'satanic ritual abuse' and attended by a list of atrocities (eg murder, cannibalism, human sacrifice), followed by warnings that 'if therapists believe these type of claims, it seems likely that they would be even more likely to believe the less aggravated claims involving ordinary child sexual abuse' (Loftus 1993: 524).

The rhetorical importance of 'satanic ritual abuse' for the 'false memory' movement is illustrated by the fact that, of the 144 newsletters released by the FMSF between 1992 and 2011, 140 of them used the term. Scott (2001) argues that the deployment of the term 'satanic ritual abuse' was a deliberate strategy undertaken by 'false memory' activists and journalists sympathetic to the 'false memory' movement in an attempt to portray cases of ritualistic abuse in a salacious light. In doing so, they were able to shift the debate about sexual abuse allegations from the terrain of child welfare, reframing the issue in terms of the susceptibility of women and children to coercive influence. The emphasis on *satanic* ritual abuse was a particularly important part of this strategy, characterising child protection workers and therapists as 'anti-satanists' on a 'witch hunt'. This was a rhetorical strategy that substantively broadened the field of people evincing scepticism over women and children's testimony of organised abuse from the core of the 'false memory' movement to include a range of progressive and relatively liberal commentators.

Academics in literature (Showalter 1997), folklore (Victor 1993), religious history (Frankfurter 1994), philosophy (Hacking 1995) and anthropology (La Fontaine 1998) weighed in to condemn those social workers and therapists who 'believed' disclosures of ritualistic abuse without 'real' cause. Frankfurter's (2001: 354) characterisation of the 'abuse expert' who incredulously accepts the accounts of their client is typical of this literature:

> For abuse experts untrained in the dynamics of memory and unread in any but the most credulous accounts of historical 'devil-worship,' there was no reason to be critical of patients' testimony and every reason, they believed, to reverse 'centuries of silence' and put full trust in their patients' accounts

In this passage, as in other sceptical accounts of 'satanic ritual abuse', it is invariably the perspectives of other more 'scientific' and 'objective' disciplines that are privileged over the supposedly partial and subjective professions of social work and therapy. The term 'expert' is used ironically here; the 'abuse expert' is not credited with basic training, competence or critical faculties. This perhaps reflects the ways in which the 'caring' professions are often devalued in comparison to other professions. However, as a characterisation of workers with clients disclosing ritual abuse, it is contested by even the briefest purview of the literature written by practitioners who took disclosures of ritualistic abuse seriously. Encounters with organised abuse cases in the 1980s had prompted considerable shock and alarm in therapeutic circles but by the 1990s therapists and social workers were cautioning against unfounded speculation on the subject. They were often agnostic about disclosures of ritual abuse, and repeatedly emphasised the importance of prudence and care when working with these clients.

> The reports of my patients appear genuine and I am treating them very seriously. I do not, however, have any direct evidence that the stories are true. I am a therapist and my job is to treat whether or not the memories are in fact as recalled.
>
> (Fraser 1990: 57)

> To understand this area we must maintain scientific skepticism and clini-cal empathy. We need to avoid the hysteria of overreaction and the denial mechanisms triggered when one is confronted with horrible material.
>
> (Sakheim and Devine 1992: xii)

> I feel that the psychotherapist has to maintain an open mind about what is real and what is phantasy – holding reconstructive pictures in mind only as tentative hypothesis, ever ready to be revised as further material emerges. In this respect, my attitude to accounts of ritual abuse is no dif-ferent to that towards any other childhood experience.
>
> (Mollon 1994: 146)

The reasonable tone of such literature did not accord with widespread efforts to characterise these workers as 'conspiracy theorists' and neurotic zealots. Hence it was simply ignored by the 'false memory' movement and those sympathetic to them, or else the public was warned that the 'abuse experts' were attempting to conceal their true agenda behind a thin patina of respectability. The presentation of workers in the field of sexual abuse as devious and untrustworthy served as an ideological foil against which 'false memory' authors and those sympathetic to them established their own claims to objectivity and expertise. The fact that many of these authors had little or no understanding of the fields of child protection or therapy that they were criticising did not appear to blunt the vigour with which they pursued their critique. Their 'expertise' was derived from their distance from the prac-ticalities of investigating or treating sexual abuse; a field of work that, after all, was portrayed as a hotbed of hysteria and neurosis.

The case made by the 'false memory' societies that allegations of organised and ritualistic abuse are wholly fabricated is based, to a significant extent, on a report prepared by FBI agent Kenneth Lanning (1992). Lanning's report details his concerns about the potential impact of hyperbole and sensational-ism on investigations into ritual abuse. However, the report does not contain any empirical review or analysis of cases of ritual abuse, with Lanning acknowledging that he had never investigated a case of ritual abuse or interviewed a child or adult alleging ritual abuse (Bennetts 1993). Nonetheless, Lanning's report is pervasively mis-cited throughout 'false memory' literature as a 'case review' that conclusively discredits all reports of ritual abuse to American authorities. References to this report often involve fictitious details designed to lend it an air of definitive authority. For example, Ofshe and Watters (1993) claim that Lanning's report was based on a review of 'three hundred cases' of ritualistic abuse. Lief and Fetkewicz (1997: 303) announce 'When SRA is involved, we know ipso facto that the accusations are untrue' due to 'a decade of study by the FBI'. Wright (2006: 121) calls the report 'a comprehensive, eight-year study by the FBI on occult crime'. Lanning's report has taken on an almost scriptural or mythical significance amongst sceptics who continue to assert that the FBI has disavowed ritual abuse investigations, despite the fact that FBI agents have been involved in the investigation and prosecution of ritual child sex abuse cases (eg Ellzey 2007).

Other examples of 'false memory' research show serious methodological and ethical flaws. In Australia, a police investigator undertook qualitative research with women reporting ritualistic abuse, only to diagnose them with 'false memory syndrome' when most refused to consent to an unrequested physical examination for evidence of physical and sexual assault (Ogden 1993). He describes 'extensively investigating' the body of one woman after she disclosed internal scarring from sexual torture (Ogden 1993: 32). His research methods were not only egregiously unethical, but his conclusions that his participants were suffering from a factitious disorder because they would not provide him with medical evidence of sexual assault was spurious. It is common for sexual abuse and sexual assault victims to express reluctance to undergo a physical exam, and even where they do consent physical signs of sexual assault may be ambiguous or nonexistent. Despite these serious shortcomings, Ogden's work was reported in the Australian press as evidence of an epidemic of 'false memories' (Guilliat 1995), and he was appointed to the board of the Australian False Memory Association.

In her book claiming that allegations of ritualistic abuse are mostly confabulations, La Fontaine's (1998) comparison of social workers to 'nazis' shows the depth of feeling evident amongst many sceptics. However, this raises an important question: Why did academics and journalists feel so strongly about allegations of ritualistic abuse, to the point of pervasively misrepresenting the available evidence and treating women disclosing ritualistic abuse, and those workers who support them, with barely concealed contempt? It is of course true that there are fringe practitioners in the field of organised abuse, just as there are fringe practitioners in many other health-related fields. However, the contrast between the measured tone of the majority of therapists and social workers writing on ritualistic abuse, and the over-blown sensationalism of their critics, could not be starker. Indeed, Scott (2001) notes with irony that the writings of those who claimed that 'satanic ritual abuse' is a 'moral panic' had many of the features of a moral panic: scapegoating therapists, social workers and sexual abuse victims whilst warning of an impending social catastrophe brought on by an epidemic of false allegations of sexual abuse. It is perhaps unsurprising that social movements for people accused of sexual abuse would engage in such hyperbole, but why did this rhetoric find so many champions in academia and the media? The following section will examine in more detail the linkages between emotion and ideology in debates over 'satanic ritual abuse'.

The pleasures of disbelief

One of the enduring characteristics of the sceptical literature on 'satanic ritual abuse' is the tone of scorn and contempt. Social workers and therapists whose clients disclose ritual abuse have been described as vectors of memory contagion motivated by ideology, hysteria and professional self-interest. Women and children disclosing ritualistic abuse were characterised as 'blank canvasses' vulnerable to coercive influence, or confabulators who fantasise about rape and torture and project these fantasies onto innocent men. The gender dynamics of these characterisations were unmistakable. Not only were workers and survivors associated with the pejorative 'feminine' attributes of hysteria and neurosis, but advocates of the 'false memory' position were clear that they considered 'feminism' to be responsible for the social ills of which they claimed 'satanic ritual abuse' as a symptom. As much was acknowledged by a member of the advisory board for the British False Memory Society who expressed his concern about the 'feminist agenda' to Kitzinger (1998: 192):

> I think we are very sensitive, males ... not just me, all of us, I think we're all very sensitive now ... about the feminist agenda. I can't believe that this assembly of figures [the BFMS advisory board] of figures of approximately twenty men and one woman isn't something to do with men if you like rushing in to protect their image ... I think it's a defensive operation.

It was explicit in 'false memory' literature that masculinity and masculine sexuality was under attack by social forces driven by feminine neurosis and hysteria. Wakefield and Underwager (1994: 43) argued that the 'Furies' of 'radical feminism' were inciting a panic about ritual abuse for political reasons, entrapping 'many, many citizens' within experiences of 'conspiracy theory, victimization, and a "paranoid style of thinking"'. In his book on Australian allegations of ritual abuse, Guilliat (1996: 263) claimed that ritualistic abuse allegations are the product of a widespread hysteria about child sexual abuse driven by feminism and a deep-seated 'fear of male sexuality'. Victor (1998) characterised feminists as 'demonologists' susceptible to wild rumours and panics made by Christian fundamentalists and social conservatives. La Fontaine (1998) also characterised 'feminists' as the unwitting dupes of Christian conspiracy theories.

Warnings about clandestine conspiracies between Christians and feminists are a mainstay of sceptical literature on ritualistic abuse. Stranger bedfellows could not be imagined but such unfounded imputations of conspiracies and hidden agendas are a mainstay of ideological antagonism (Žižek 1996). Žižek (1993: 202–3) shows that what is at stake in such antagonism is a 'theft of enjoyment': 'we always impute to the "other" an excessive enjoyment: he wants to steal our enjoyment (by ruining our way of life) and/or he has access to some secret perverse enjoyment'. Emanating from the 'false memory' movement was the notion that therapists and social workers were taking a perverse pleasure in their work as they probed into 'private' places – bodies, minds, homes, families. As a result, it was claimed that men could no longer teach, touch, hug, bathe or play with children for fear of a false allegation of sexual abuse. Articles on false memories described how the sanctity of family life was at risk from baseless 'recovered memories' of sexual abuse. The inference was that feminism had destabilised, if it had not actually destroyed, the simple day-to-day pleasures that men found in their contact with children as fathers, teachers and community members. These were pleasures that feminism had supposedly 'stolen' from men that must be stolen back, and in this process the pleasurable excesses of revenge and retaliation were considered justifiable

This retaliation was not limited to hyperbole and invective. False memory societies supported malpractice lawsuits against therapists well-known for specialising in the intervention and treatment of organised and ritual abuse. Therapists who wrote and spoke publicly about organised and ritual abuse reported being stalked, picketed and threatened by 'false memory' activists (Calof 1998, Salter 1998). Where organised abuse had been investigated and prosecuted, the 'false memory' movement mobilised *pro bono* legal support for those convicted. With their support, some convictions were overturned but where appeals failed the case was canonised as an 'injustice' enacted by a legal system that, advocates claimed, was conspiring against men charged with sexual abuse (Olio and Cornell 1998). A range of high-profile, highly partisan books and documentaries on organised abuse cases emerged in which critical evidence was minimised, distorted or simply ignored, resulting in groundswells of public support for men convicted of organised and ritualistic sexual offences. These efforts were front-and-centre within a broader campaign designed to delimit the capacity of child protection services to intervene in child abuse, to undermine the credibility of testimony of sexual abuse, and to narrow the access of victimised women and children to mental health care and the legal system.

Underlying these efforts was an enduring nostalgia for an earlier social order of male right and sexual expression undisturbed by the supposed (over)empowerment of children and women. The 'false memory' movement described not only how allegations of sexual abuse had disrupted family life and severed family relations but a more general sense of social disintegration and *anomie* precipitated by the cultural prominence given to children's and women's testimony of sexual abuse. One letter to the FMSF compared disclosures of sexual abuse to 'lynching':

> Let it be known especially to mental health professionals that the character assassinations of a father and mother constitute moral patricide and matricide and are hate crimes not any less horrendous than lynchings. The advantage of lynchings was and is their relatively short duration, culminating in the termination of all pain.
>
> (FMSF newsletter 1999, vol 8 no 4)

In response to these concerns, the 'false memory' movement imputed a terrifying new force that was 'pulling the strings' behind the scenes and creating this misfortune: a secretive alliance between Christians and feminists, united in their shared antipathy to the 'natural' expression of male sexuality. However what 'we conceal by imputing to the Other the theft of enjoyment is the traumatic fact that we never possessed what was allegedly stolen from us' (Žižek 1993: 203). The therapist/social worker 'Other' attacked by the 'false memory' movement did not designate an actual threat but rather functioned as the foil for an ideological conception of masculine sexuality as basically harmless and benevolent. It was claimed that the presence of this 'Other' had disrupted the cordiality of family life and prevented men from being 'really themselves' around children. However, it was precisely the construction of the therapist/social worker 'Other' that enabled the reassertion of an idyllic view of masculine sexuality as harmless and safe, even as evidence of widespread male sexual maltreatment of children was coming to the fore.

The cultural idyll of childhood as a protected and peaceful phase of development not only disavows the ambiguities and vulnerabilities of children's lives in the 'gerontocracy' (James et al. 1998) but it precludes recognition of the severity of sexual violence in the lives of some children. Disclosures of such violence are a potential rupture in the legitimacy of hegemonic ideals. They reveal the discrepancies between cultural ideals and social realities and, in doing so, threaten to disrupt and subvert broader systems of representation and meaning. Descriptions of organised, sadistic and ritualistic abuse brought to the fore the implicit threat that all disclosures of sexual abuse pose to prevailing systems of representation, by emphasising the vulnerability of children to sexual violence in the very spaces, such as the home and families, that are legitimised as benevolent and protective. By challenging these legitimations, the women's movement and the child protection movement was challenging the gender order upon which they are based, in which male control of families and other important social institutions was presented as appropriate, natural and beneficial. The caricature of 'satanic ritual abuse' provided a point of mobilisation around which a diverse coalition of interest groups and individuals could contest the gains made by abused women and children by attacking those agents, such as therapists and social workers, who were working on their behalf. The zest with which their agenda was adopted and enacted within the community, and by a range of state authorities, suggests that they had tapped into a hidden reservoir of anti-feminist and misogynist sentiment that would have a serious impact on the wellbeing of victimised children and women.

The consequences of the pleasures of disbelief

In the sceptical literature on 'satanic ritual abuse', references to the severe and chronic mental and physical health problems of adults and children with histories of organised abuse are notable only for their absence. Whilst sceptics scornfully characterised allegations of organised abuse in terms of murder, cannibalism and ritual sacrifices, they ignored the mundane evidence of physical and sexual abuse that had led to the very child protection interventions and criminal prosecutions they claimed had no basis in fact. The majority of sceptics had little direct experience of adults or children with histories of organised or ritualistic abuse, and nor did they employ research methodologies that would familiarise them with the perspectives and needs of this population. On the contrary, through the 'false memory' movement, many sceptical academics and journalists developed close personal and professional relationships with adults accused of organised and ritualistic abuse. Throughout the 1990s, this sceptical coalition brought tremendous political and media pressure to bear on particular investigations into organised abuse on behalf of those accused. Their social and political agenda was sympathetically received by state authorities, influencing child protection decisions (Nelson 2008), custody cases (Brooks 2001) and public inquiries (Rogers 1999) in relation to organised and ritual abuse. As cases of organised abuse gained increasingly high-profile (and often global) media coverage, the claims of those accused were accepted at face value whilst social workers and therapists involved in the cases were restricted from challenging these claims by professional codes of confidentiality (Kitzinger 2004, Goddard 1994, Summit 1994).

The ensuing backlash resulted in multiple failures to protect children and vulnerable adults. In the United Kingdom, children who had disclosed organised and ritualistic abuse were returned to their parents despite continuing to disclose sexual abuse and engaging in disturbed and traumatised behaviour (Nelson 2008). In a Scottish case, eight children were returned home to their parents despite their testimony of organised abuse and medical evidence of child torture (Rafferty 1997). In Australia, a pregnant woman approached child protection services disclosing a history of ritual abuse but her concerns about her capacity to protect her child from sexual abuse were dismissed, since the department did not accept that ritual abuse occurs (South Australian Ombudsman 2004). In 2005, a report by Scotland's social work inspection agency found that, throughout the 1990s, social workers failed to remove three children from their parents despite clear evidence of physical, sexual and emotional abuse. The children had been in contact with over 100 health professionals throughout the 1990s, and they frequently disclosed organised abuse by their parents. Despite clear evidence of abuse, it seems that these disclosures of organised abuse were the primary reason why child protection authorities failed to intervene. Commenting on the case, the local social work director stated that case workers were operating in the wake of controversies over ritualistic abuse and they were therefore 'reluctant to make similar mistakes' (Seenan 2005).

The wholesale whitewashing of evidence of harm in cases of organised abuse not only compromised child protection efforts, but resulted in the denial of health care to survivors. Ofshe and Watters (1996) and a range of 'false memory' activists have lobbied against the provision of mental health treatment to people with histories of organised abuse and associated diagnoses, such as dissociative identity disorder (DID).[2] There is ample evidence that people with histories of organised abuse and/or a diagnosis of DID constitute a population of mental health patients with acute and complex needs (Ross 1995, Noblitt and Perskin 2000, Sachs and Galton 2008). Adults with undiagnosed or untreated DID have extremely high suicide rates several thousand times the American national average (Kluft 1995). However, Ross (1997) observes that, in his clinical experience, the suicide risk for this population reduces dramatically once they have established a working rapport with a mental health professional. Moreover, people with DID are at heightened risk of physical and sexual victimisation, and may require mental health care in order to bring ongoing abuse to an end (Middleton 2005). The 'false memory' campaign to restrict mental health care to this population not only contributed to their risk of suicide and self-harm, but complicated their efforts to protect themselves from ongoing abuse and violence.

2 Dissociative Identity Disorder (DID) (formerly known as multiple personality disorder) is a complex, chronic mental illness characterised by the presence of multiple, alternating self-states, personalities or identities (known as 'alters' in much of the psychological literature) as well as recurrent amnesia for current and/or past events (International Society for the Study of Trauma and Dissociation 2011). DID develops as a response to chronic and overwhelming trauma exposure in childhood, including organised abuse (Middleton and Butler 1998).

Conclusion

The final newsletter of the FMSF was released in 2011, and in the closing paragraph of her editorial, the FMSF founder Pamela Freyd stated 'But we must also thank, in a bizarre way, all those whose practices have given us laughs'. She goes on to refer to a woman who was diagnosed with DID by Dr Valerie Sinason, a well-known British specialist in the treatment of organised and ritualistic abuse. It is perhaps fitting that Freyd's final editorial closes with a reference to the pleasure that the FMSF has found in parodying the treatment of severe sexual abuse. The history of the 'false memory' movement has been characterised by a pervasive attitude of scorn and contempt towards those disclosing particularly traumatic sexual abuse and the workers who have offered them care and support. This was a tone that was uncritically adopted by many across the academic and popular media and seemed to resonate strongly within the general community.

This chapter has argued that factor of enjoyment is crucial in explaining the success of the FMSF in advancing their agenda, and the degree of contempt that continues to characterise references to cases of organised abuse. In online as well as 'old' media, 'satanic ritual abuse' is invoked whenever a journalist or commentator seeks to rationalise their derision for the testimony of sexually victimised women and children or those professionals and agencies who would accept their testimony as true. Behind these assertions is a view that masculine sexuality is essentially harmless whilst it is claimed that the minds of women, children, feminists and 'Others' harbour socially destructive forces that can easily turn against men. It is by *disbelieving* the testimony of women and children that such forces are kept at bay and men are protected. The construct of 'satanic ritual abuse' is now an endlessly elastic one that can rationalise virtually any claim of male victimisation by 'false allegations' of sexual abuse. When Jerry Sandusky, former Pennsylvania State University assistant coach, was charged with 40 counts of child sexual abuse against eight complainants, his lawyer compared the allegations against him to the 'moral panic' over 'satanic ritual abuse' (Sax 2011). The suggestion is that credible allegations of sexual abuse involve one victim and minor forms of abuse. An allegation more complex and serious than this, it is suggested, is likely to be the product of confabulation and hysteria.

Whilst many of the arguments of the 'false memory' advocates were based on widely circulated misunderstandings, we might follow Žižek (1991: 2) in suggesting that 'ignorance is *not* a sufficient reason for forgiveness since it conveys a hidden dimension of enjoyment'. Sedgwick (1994) also argued against reifying ignorance as an impersonal force that bestows 'passive innocence' upon those that experience it. Instead she emphasises the political qualities of ignorance and the ways in which a 'plethora of ignorances' circulate as part of 'particular regimes of truth'. From this perspective the ways in which particular understandings of organised abuse were promoted and others foreclosed or erased in public life can be understood as a collision of personal and collective interests in maintaining public non-awareness of a particularly disturbing form of gendered violence. As allegations of organised abuse grew, the threat that the increasing recognition of child sexual abuse posed to the gender order reached intolerable proportions. Social movements sought to resolve this threat by imputing it to an 'Other' (usually identified as the feminist/Christian zealot masquerading as a therapist or social worker) and creating an ideological antagonism in which the social order could be saved if this 'Other' was attacked and silenced. Sceptical literature on 'satanic ritual abuse' played out this simplistic fantasy, 'revealing' the feminist/Christian zealot as the 'real' threat who is then defeated through the superior intellect of the author. Calling the motives of these workers into question by characterising them as feminists, Christians and ideologues was a particularly effective strategy, since it crafted a target that groups from both the left and the right of the political spectrum felt justified in attacking. However, regardless of their purported political orientation these attacks shared a common and highly gendered vocabulary of 'hysteria' and contamination as misogynist views of women and children, suppressed in the aftermath of second-wave feminism, found cathartic and pleasurable release.

This chapter has argued that the credulity with which such blatant hyperbole was greeted in many quarters can only be understood in terms of the pleasures of disbelief, and the manner in which it served to occlude recognition of the growing evidence of the pervasiveness of sexual violence against children. Concerted attacks on the testimony of victims and those professionals, such as therapists and social workers, who had created new opportunities for them to disclose their abuse had a stultifying effect on the nascent response to organised abuse. The next chapter will provide a personal perspective on the consequences of this by describing the author's experience as a carer for a survivor of organised abuse, and highlighting the ways in which the prevailing climate of disbelief can entrap victims within a cycle of ongoing abuse and violence.

Chapter 5

Down the rabbit hole

My story

All researchers carry with them the accumulation of their background and personal history, and this shapes their work in important ways. This chapter provides an account of my history as the friend and carer of a survivor of organised abuse called 'Sarah' (a pseudonym). In a field as controversial as this one, allegations of personal bias and prejudice are widespread and questions about how and why I came to study organised abuse are inevitable. This chapter presents an answer to those questions, but hopefully it provides much more than that. The majority of the relevant literature on organised abuse has been written by survivors and the health professionals who have treated them. I occupy neither category although my experience encompasses aspects of both, having been prompted to research organised abuse as an academic after having witnessed directly its ongoing harms on someone I care about. My awareness of organised abuse developed in the context of my friendship with Sarah, which began in my late teens. It culminated in the year I spent in my mid-20s as Sarah's carer in order to prevent the abusive group from drawing her further into a life of violence and sexual exploitation. By documenting my experiences I hope to add a new perspective and voice to the burgeoning testimonial evidence of organised abuse.

This chapter reveals a set of intensely emotional experiences: the feelings of fear and powerlessness that came from witnessing Sarah's abuse, but also the depth of the friendship that enabled us both to survive it. In academic as well as professional circles, respectability is coded according to a personal bifurcation into discrete 'public' and 'private' personas. Feminists have been the most vocal critics of this distinction because much of their work concerns the political dimension of 'private' relations and behaviours. Challenging those forms of domination and exploitation enabled by the public/private division, according to hooks (1989), involves an analysis of the points where the public and the private intersect. My time as Sarah's carer is one of these points. The act of caring has been coded 'private' in every respect. It is emotional, undervalued, unpaid domestic labour concerned with the everyday routine of ensuring that a sick person is made better. As her carer, I spent a lot of my time trying to help Sarah to eat, to sleep, to maintain her employment and to access the health services that she needed, and to liaise with the police in an attempt to protect her from ongoing threats and assaults. As a gay man this experience was not complicated by romantic or sexual interest and this facilitated the establishment of an elevated sense of trust between Sarah and I. However, I soon learnt that my role in Sarah's life was viewed with some suspicion by law enforcement and health workers, who found it unbelievable that a young man might support a woman he was not sleeping with or related to. And yet it was precisely my position in Sarah's private world as her friend and carer that exposed me to the complexities of her enmeshment in the world of organised abuse. The captivity of victims of organised abuse is not signified by locks and bars but instead by complex psychological processes that require patience and empathy to decode.

It has primarily been those individuals engaged in the 'emotion work' (Hochschild 1979) of listening to victimised children and adults, and providing them with care and support, who have raised the alarm about organised abuse. The notion that social work, therapy, nursing, parenting or caring is a credible basis for making such claims have been disparaged by sceptical commentators who have invoked science, rationality and objectivity to craft a more authoritative position for themselves. There are authors and activists who have been nothing short of savage in their efforts to disparage victims of organised abuse and those who support them, and so I have not relished the possibility that, in writing down my experiences, they might set upon my story with similar ferocity. However, to omit my story from this book would only affirm the false distinctions between emotionality and rationality, the personal and the scientific, and the public and private that have derailed reasoned discussion of organised abuse. It also risks collaborating in the pervasive devaluation of the vitally important work of supporting victimised children and adults. This is what brought me to the field of organised abuse and it is something that I share with most of the people who have chosen to speak out on this topic.

This chapter proceeds in three parts that describes the three phases of my personal engagement with the issue of organised abuse: first as a friend, then as a carer, and finally as an advocate and academic. The history that follows is as accurate as it can be given that some details must be left deliberately vague in order to protect Sarah's anonymity. The narrative presented here has been reconstructed not only from memory but also from email records, my own diaries and a qualitative interview that I undertook with Sarah a few years after the events described here. As such, the chapter presents something of a dialogue between myself and Sarah – and between our past as well as present selves. In doing so, I describe my own tumble 'down the rabbit hole' and re-emergence into a world that was I no longer familiar with: one in which a young woman could be stalked, assaulted and terrorised over a period of years by a group of men without drawing the attention or interest of the authorities. The stark reality is that neither the police nor any other agency intervened to protect Sarah despite repeatedly being notified of her plight. The disinterest and inaction of the authorities in the face of evidence of organised abuse is irreconcilable with common stereotypes of police 'always investigating cases' and investigators 'always getting their man' (Tamarkin 1994a). This irreconcilability lies at the very heart of the debate over organised abuse, and this chapter details my own struggle to recreate a coherent worldview in the aftermath of a prolonged confrontation with extraordinary abuse.

Being a friend

Throughout the 1990s, as a teenager, I had read newspaper reports about adult women who, after attending counselling or therapy, were making outrageous allegations of sexual abuse by 'paedophile rings' and 'cults'. Like many others, I accepted the proposition that such allegations were evidence that the movement against child abuse had 'gone too far'. I had no reason to rethink my position until my late teens when I became friends with Sarah. I had known Sarah only a short time before I came to realise that there was a hidden dimension to her life. Sarah's nightmares and cries in the early hours of the morning were known to many of her friends but she was reluctant to acknowledge them. There were days when her face was pale, her eyes were dark and she spoke in short, clipped sentences. During these times she seemed to be labouring under an immense burden, and she had an air of fragility about her that was in stark contrast to the strong and gregarious woman that I was otherwise accustomed to. I was already familiar with the signs of sexual abuse, having grown up with relatives and friends who had been victimised. Much of Sarah's behaviour was similar to the other survivors that I had known but Sarah bore a degree of pain that I had not encountered before. It was the secrecy behind which she struggled to contain this pain that I found particularly disturbing, and I decided to break through it.

Sarah went on long walks at night, sometimes only returning in the early hours of the morning. One day, as she set off at dusk for her walk, I insisted on coming along with her. We had barely turned the first corner before I confronted her with my belief that something traumatic had happened to her. In my characteristically blunt fashion, I told her that I thought she had been sexually abused, and I asked her 'Who was it?' Sarah fixed me with a stare that I remember to this day. It was beyond shock, a kind of gaunt, pale horror. I began to list likely suspects. 'Was it a family member? Priest? Teacher?' I was met with a stunned silence that I tried to fill with reassurances that it was okay to acknowledge abuse, that I would believe her and that I knew other people that had been abused. Her response, when it came, was entirely unexpected. 'They were … there was a few of them' was all that she said. 'They' – plural – I was not prepared for. The rest of our conversation was short but before it came to an end I made her a promise that would prove fateful: that whatever she was going through, she didn't have to go through it alone.

The incident I have described may appear as a reckless intrusion into Sarah's privacy but I was 19 at the time and not conversant with the sensitivities around disclosure. Nonetheless, when we were discussing this incident in interview several years later Sarah cautioned me not to understate her agency in disclosing her abuse to me.

> It wasn't really – it actually wasn't that you – it wasn't involuntary. I had more control over it than you probably knew. In that, it was very bit-by-bit, and that is how I do it. You know what I mean? I gauge the trust, and then tell a little bit, and then gauge the trust.

And this is precisely how our friendship developed, 'bit-by-bit', as Sarah cautiously let me into her world. I witnessed how she sustained her hopes for her future in spite of the nightmares, terror and pain that frequently incapacitated her. At times she maintained a frenetic pace of work and study, only to be reduced by flashbacks and anxiety to a lump under bedsheets for hours or days. During these times she trusted me to come and visit her, and we'd watch videos and share a companionable silence until she felt better. We became close friends. With all the confidence of inexperience, I assumed that she and I could meet any challenge posed by her history. I knew nothing about organised abuse and, after our initial conversation, we did not discuss her experiences of it. She was unable to speak about it without great distress and I had presumed that I knew what I needed to.

This was a presumption that would be tested by my dawning realisation that her abuse was not in her past, but rather it was continuing in the present. I learnt much later that some of Sarah's 'walks' at night involved meeting the abusers from her childhood, who would contact her to arrange a time and place where they could collect her and take her to be abused. In hindsight, there had been signs. She sometimes had strange injuries that she couldn't explain, but she dismissed them and I didn't give them much thought. In interview, Sarah commented on the 'two sides' to her life during this period:

> I really did separate out my life. No one in my day-to-day life knew about that side of it. It was really weird, like that – at night what was happening, compared to the day.

This was a facade of normalcy that began to deteriorate. In her early 20s, Sarah was no longer willing to obey the demands of the abusive group, and she stopped acquiescing to their instructions to meet them for abuse. They responded with a barrage of emails and phone calls threatening to harm her and the people she cared about if she did not comply. Sarah tried to manage these threats by herself but the abusive group began to intrude further and further into the boundaries that Sarah had established around her 'day-to-day life'.

One day, Sarah's flatmates reported that two men had come to the door, ascertained that Sarah lived there, and promptly left without explanation. This episode left Sarah terrified although I reassured her that there was probably a mundane explanation for this visit. A few weeks later, stricken with grief and shock, she told me that two men had been waiting for her outside her house at night when she came home from work. She described this incident in an email to me at the time:

> There were two of them, and they were just hanging around in the vacant block across the road from my house. I didn't even notice them at first. I got out of my car to go inside, and they walked over as if they were just walking past. I didn't really think twice about them. Until things were already happening. I didn't recognise them at any point. Well, I didn't really get to see their faces, because it all happened too suddenly. It was what they said, oh and what they did, which was absolutely congruent with both the emails and past experience. They mentioned that they were never going to be out of my life, and that things would be much worse if I told anyone what had happened when I was younger.

This was the first of a number of incidents of violence and terrorisation. Sarah moved houses a number of times to maintain her safety, however flatmates at each house began to complain of men stalking through the back-yard at night or knocking on the door. Sarah frequently received emails and phone calls telling her to 'be ready' to leave when a man came for her. I slept on the floor of her room on a night after she received a text message saying that someone was coming to 'collect' her. We woke up in the early hours of the morning to the sound of multiple people knocking on the front door and the windows of the house, calling her name. The situation began to take on the unreal qualities of a horror movie but try as I might I couldn't convince Sarah to report her abuse to the police. At the time, I didn't recognise the degree of terror that the abusive group evoked in Sarah.

A game of cat-and-mouse ensued as Sarah began moving houses in an effort to stay ahead of the abusive group. Eventually she took to living in her car and sleeping in parkland in order to stay safe. She reasoned that it would be harder for the abusive group to track her if she maintained an irregular schedule and ensured that her living arrangements were unpredictable. However, I became worried that she was only a few steps away from homelessness and I arranged for her to stay with my family for a period of time. I didn't fully understand what Sarah was going through but, as the abusive group persisted with their campaign of stalking and terrorisation, I was faced with a simple choice: increase the level of support that Sarah was receiving or watch the situation deteriorate further. In an email to me at the time, Sarah identified how these repeated attacks were forcing her to acknowledge the severity of her abuse as a child, which was producing new opportunities for resistance:

> There has been a clicking over in my mind – a resolve to change things; a realisation that I can't just go on and take everything and kid myself that I can take it unceasingly and infinitely without scarring or caring ... It also involves a different angle of thinking about myself. A want to protect me, rather than the previous sense of surrender and inevitability. Maybe not yet tangible and effective, but these subtle changes in thinking patterns, I think are the beginning of making all the difference.

Sarah and I became resolved to move away from the city in which she was being terrorised, and find a new home town in which we could find her a life free from ongoing violence. I was also determined to connect Sarah with mental health services, with whom she had only intermittent contact, as well as with the police. I found Sarah's refusal to disclose her circumstances to a third party immensely frustrating. If we lived together, I felt I would be in a better position to bring in the help that I felt Sarah needed. We found a house, I packed my bags, and so began the year I spent as Sarah's carer.

Being a carer

With the benefit of hindsight, it now seems to me that Sarah's experiences of stalking and violence were very similar to those reported by women escaping domestic violence. She was being terrorised by threats she received over the phone and via email, and periodically men could be found waiting for her at home or work. To keep her safe we made sure that she was dropped off and picked up from work, either by me or by friends. Our new rental property was as secure as we could make it with our limited funds. We began formulating strategies to ensure that she was eating and sleeping well and accessing health services when she needed them. With encouragement, Sarah was skilled at finding the supports that she needed, and my role was to provide an anchoring and stable presence in the house so that she was not alone when she felt overwhelmed by depression or memories of abuse. Much of my 'caring' time was spent in her room at night as she struggled through another flashback, holding her hand and trying to coax her back to reality. The ways in which her memories could manifest in somatic ways was nothing short of startling. During one incident, her body temperature dropped dramatically and her lips turned blue. She was freezing cold to the touch and began speaking about a childhood memory of being submerged and nearly drowned in a tub of icy water. It was only when she began responding to some hot water bottles and several blankets that I decided not to call an ambulance.

I must confess that, until Sarah and I came to share a house, I had harboured some lingering doubts about Sarah's reports of organised abuse. The degree and authenticity of Sarah's distress was not in question but I wasn't entirely certain of its source. Nonetheless, it was not long before I was confronted with irrefutable evidence that Sarah's history of organised abuse was continuing in the present.

A month or so after Sarah and I moved in together, she didn't return home from work. Later that night I received a text message from her, and I eventually found her, semi-conscious, on the side of a city road. She was wet, as though she had been recently washed, and she had deep marks on her wrist and ankles where she had clearly been bound with a cord or rope. I immediately called an ambulance and rode with her, but once in the hospital, I quickly discovered how fluid and relative 'evidence' can be. In the eyes of the doctors and police, the marks on Sarah's wrists and feet were less significant than her refusal to permit them to examine her for a sexual assault. In the hospital, she became terrified at the prospect of an internal exam and her non-compliance was interpreted by both the police and the doctors that she could not be believed. In interview, Sarah recalled:

> One of the big things with me at hospital was that I didn't want the doctors taking photos of me, or touching me. And if I'd said, 'Yes, you can examine me' – I think they would have believed us more. But it was the fact that I wouldn't let them … and any other proof [such as the rope burn] that didn't fit into the specific things that you look for in a sexual assault was not seen as real.
>
> I remember them looking for – because you are meant to look under the finger nails, you are meant to look for defensive wounds – and of course I've got no blood under my finger nails, because in that situation [organised abuse] I don't defend myself. And things like that. I remember them getting my hand, and going 'Nah, there's nothing under her nails' as though the only alternative is that I'm lying.

This was a pattern of disbelief that would reassert itself with each subsequent hospital admission. Despite our best efforts, Sarah 'disappeared' once a month or so, only to appear semi-conscious in various parts of the city or outside the city limits in the bush. For the first three or four times that this occurred, I called an ambulance to take her to hospital. She often had welts and bruising, and I had no way of knowing the extent of her injuries without a qualified medical assessment. Importantly, I wanted a record of the attacks on her and some official acknowledgement of her plight. I held onto my faith that, as the evidence of Sarah's abuse accumulated, the doctors and police would intervene to improve a situation I was beginning to find intolerable and out of control.

However, the attending physicians and police had a standardised approach for assessing the credibility of complaints of rape. Since Sarah did not conform to this model, she was considered to be a malingerer who was not a legitimate focus of attention or concern despite her injuries. They made it clear that there were questions about the nature and legitimacy of my relationship with Sarah, questions that, particularly for the hospital, came to eclipse what was happening to Sarah. Since I was present at each of Sarah's admissions, the hospital staff accused us of engaging in some kind of *folie a deux* or, worse, they suggested that I was responsible for the injuries that the abusive group inflicted on Sarah. Sarah described the efforts of hospital staff to substantiate their suspicions about me:

> It was such a mind-fuck at the hospital. They got this psychiatrist to talk to me. And first off she's saying, 'So, do you think that Michael believes you?' And I'd say, 'Yes.' And she said, 'Do you think he believes you too much?' And I didn't know how to answer that question.
>
> And then there'd be 'And do you think Michael cares about you?' And I said, 'Yes.' And she said, 'Do you think he cares about you too much?' And I said, 'Maybe.' Because I was feeling guilty. They seriously asked me these questions.
>
> And then she asked, 'Well, why do you think he cares about you too much?' And I said something like, 'I made a mistake, I shouldn't have done it' – because I was feeling guilty, I was ashamed that I'd slipped up and the group had – gotten to me, and it was four in the morning and you were awake and scared and worried for me.
>
> But the hospital had gotten the answer from me they wanted, and I didn't realise what they were doing. And the next time I ended up in hospital, the same psychiatrist came to me and said, 'Well, you said some really interesting things about Michael last time. Do you remember?' And she had all these notes, saying 'Michael cares about me too much.' There was another note, something like 'I've made a big mistake.'
>
> And I was just going 'No, no, you don't understand.' And at the same time, I was thinking – god, this is like a TV show. This is like an interrogation sort of thing. They totally cornered me when I was completely vulnerable. But they wanted to believe so much that we were completely delusional.

During this hospital admission, we had been separated for several hours whilst staff attempted to encourage Sarah to implicate me in her abuse. Reassured by the amount of time they were spending with her, I had fallen asleep in the waiting room under the false assumption that, finally, she was receiving the care she needed. It was a great shock when I was finally permitted to see her and I found her limping to the toilet, hunched over in pain and shame. She had wrapped the hospital blanket around her as tightly as she could, like a cocoon, with only her eyes showing. Her eyelids were fluttering from trauma and dissociation as she inched down the corridor, desperately trying to cover the scant hospital gown with the blanket. Two police officers were leaning against the wall, watching her without offering assistance. The looks on their faces as they joked about her made it clear that we should never come back.

This final hospital admission was, as I wrote in my diary at the time, an event that fundamentally changed my perception of the 'way things are'. The fantasy that some outside force or agency would intervene to protect Sarah was gone. We soon discovered that we had no recourse to the police. Having been designated *persona non grata* during those hospital admissions, there was no amount of evidence that could convince them of the merit of our reports. This included an incident when I came home from work to find the house that I shared with Sarah had been broken into and our walls daubed with red paint and animal blood. Strange red symbols had been painted on our walls and bedclothes, and I found an animal organ lying in my bed. A baby's 'tippee' cup, full of animal blood and offal, was left on Sarah's desk, with a bright, childish sticker on it reading 'Drink me!' I called the police who took photos of the vandalism and did some fingerprinting. The advice from the forensics team was that we should change our names and leave the state. Once they left, we never heard from them again.

We lived in the vacuum created by the neglect of the police and medical services and in such a space the only action left to me was to care for Sarah as best I could. I tried to help her to eat, sleep and build her strength, all the while knowing that the next attack could be only a few days or weeks away. We made contact with local sexual assault services, psychologists and therapists, and found a number of workers who were familiar with organised abuse and sympathetic to Sarah's situation. However, they were poorly situated to respond to Sarah's primary need, which was not for therapy but rather safety from the ongoing abuse. It seemed that we were trapped in a vicious circle: struggling to stabilise Sarah's mental health because of ongoing abuse, but unable to stop the ongoing abuse due to Sarah's fragile mental health. In order to wear away at Sarah's resolve to protect herself, the perpetrators would engage in days or weeks of sustained threats via telephone, text message or email. For a few weeks, we heard from a woman who regularly telephoned the house, claiming that her children were being sexually abused in Sarah's absence because Sarah was not allowing herself to be abused as instructed. Occasionally the phone would be snatched away from her by a man who, in one memorable instance, threatened to kill me. I took to sleeping with a knife under my bed. When Sarah was feeling strong she was able to resist the entreaties, threats and attempts at blackmail, but if she was feeling vulnerable or frightened then she could leave the house and 'disappear' for hours.

After Sarah's 'disappearances' it could take days or weeks for the bruises and burns to heal. These were not simply the marks of violence but of torture. After one particularly awful episode, she reappeared at the front door at dawn having gone missing the night before. She was having difficulty walking and she winced when I tried to support her to walk to her bedroom. The skin on her stomach and back was red and inflamed, but I didn't ask why and she didn't tell me. It was a few days later, when the inflammation had gone down, that I saw the lines on her skin where someone had traced symbols on her body using a red-hot implement. My reaction was a horror compounded by despair. Here was further physical evidence of her ongoing abuse, but where could we go with it? What could we do with it? A previous email to the local detectives had 'bounced'. They had given me the wrong email address. They didn't return phone calls or messages. We were cut off from external assistance, and the hospital had made it clear that they suspected I might be responsible for the injuries Sarah incurred during abuse. We had to do our best between the two of us.

My initial optimism that I could affect a decisive break in Sarah's contact with the abusive group, and my faith in the authorities, now seemed to me to be hopelessly naïve. In this diary excerpt, I reflect on this dawning realisation:

> I thought I could make more of a difference than I can, in the immediate present anyway. She must be free to negotiate the terms of her contract with the torturers. It is a private world that I have no entry into.

I was becoming aware of the complexity of our struggle to keep Sarah safe, which in effect was a war fought on two fronts. The first was the world external to Sarah, a place where men could wait patiently for her outside our house or her work with the intention of pulling her into a waiting car. This was a world that might be frightening but at least it was a place where I could make some difference by, for example, arranging to meet her at her workplace to make sure she was safe as we made our way home. However, the second front was Sarah's mental environment which, I was slowly coming to realise, harboured forces that wished her harm just as forcefully as those anonymous men did. Sarah's attachment to the abusive group was anchored by the sedimentation of terror, shame and loyalty that had accumulated over many years. These were emotions of such intensity that they were often beyond articulation, compelling Sarah to place herself at risk despite her own deeply held desire to find a life free of pain and abuse.

Reading over my diaries from this time, it is undeniable that my time spent as Sarah's carer was often grim and frightening work. However, my feelings of exhaustion, despair and anger served as an important counterweight to Sarah's habitual response to her abuse, which was to numb and dissociate herself from the emotional after-effects. Even when Sarah felt vulnerable to the manipulations and threats of the abusive group, she knew that she could not obey their instructions to meet them for abuse without causing me great distress and anxiety. This sense of responsibility to me served as an anchoring point that Sarah could use to combat the compulsion to put herself at risk. Furthermore, my sense of horror at the predations of the abusive group enabled the expression of Sarah's own long-suppressed emotional responses. The very fact that I found her abuse unbearable validated her own intrinsic experience of victimisation as excruciating rather than something she deserved and must learn to bear. This served as a bridge from the secretive world constructed by the abusive group, with its predetermined logic of torture and exploitation, to a freer state in which she could determine the direction of her own life.

These were circumstances that should have eroded our friendship, and they were probably intended to. The abusers had crafted an unbearable situation in which we felt isolated and alone. They tried to turn us against one another, telling Sarah that I was one of them, and telling me on the phone that she was a 'slut' who 'wanted' what they did to her. However, our resolve held and strengthened and over time it became clear that we were incrementally but irrevocably altering the cycle of abuse and shame that had bound Sarah to the abusive group. In the context of our friendship, Sarah was shifting between the identities that had been constructed through dehumanising abuse and an emergent set of possibilities based upon a view of her as valuable and deserving of love: a view that she could trust me to hold even when she could not. As a friend and carer, I related to her as someone of intrinsic worth and so I served as the stable reference point for a different sense of self than one grounded in the humiliation and deprivation of abuse. Over time, the threatening emails and phone calls that Sarah received no longer seemed so compelling to her. The logic that the group used to manipulate her still resonated but she did not instinctively assent to it any more. She could distance herself from the threats and entreaties and consider the most constructive way to respond.

Sarah began to make important gains in many areas of her life. She found new friends. She began dating. She enrolled herself in an intensive programme for trauma survivors and made considerable improvements in her mental health. She began eating and sleeping more regularly. Her day-to-day conversations were increasingly concerned with mid- to long-term plans about her education and career. Over time it became clear that Sarah no longer needed the kind of intensive support that I was providing. She has always been fiercely independent by nature and she was determined to move forward with her life. In the meantime, I needed time and space to recover from a period of anxiety and exhaustion, and to consider the implications of what I had witnessed. Our lives had shared a common trajectory for a period of years and now we needed to follow different directions, although we parted with the mutual understanding that, together, we had achieved something very important.

Being an advocate and academic

The process of caring for Sarah had involved investigating the limited range of services available to her, and the dawning realisation that adults with histories of sexual abuse are offered very little assistance indeed. I joined the advocacy group Adults Surviving Child Abuse (ASCA) and eventually came to serve as a director for three years. I was also active in various online mailing lists and discussion boards pertinent to organised abuse and ritual abuse. Writing and talking about organised abuse was a way of resisting the sense of stigmatisation left by the disbelief of the doctors and the police. It also served as an outlet for the frustrations and helplessness I had felt as Sarah's carer. If I couldn't protect her then, at least, I did not have to bear the stifling silence that hung over our ordeal. Through my work with ASCA, and my contact with an expanding network of survivors and the workers who supported them, I began to develop a social and political context for our experience.

There was a systemic quality to the neglect and invalidation Alex experienced at the hands of the authorities, and this resonated with the methods of control drawn on by her perpetrators, who often told her that nobody would believe her. They were in fact quite correct. It was my own belief that the authorities would assist us that proved naïve and unfounded. I began to read the organised abuse literature but I couldn't find answers to my most pressing questions: How could Sarah's plight have been ignored by so many for so long? Why couldn't we find mental health services or crisis services to assist us? Why were the police and other agencies so unmoved by her distress and her physical injuries? The material I could find online was focused on ritual abuse and had a strongly conspiratorial slant, claiming that ritualistic abuse is evidence of secretive global networks of abusers. However, I felt that this presentation, in many ways, colluded with the abusers' delusions of grandeur. Despite their claims that they were, as they dubbed themselves, 'kings', 'masters' and 'gods', the abusers that had spat expletives at me down the phone had sounded much like bitter old men and I was not going to grant them the status of global puppet masters. What I wanted to know was how a network of thugs and rapists could terrorise Sarah under the very noses of the authorities without being stopped.

If I was nonplussed by the state of current explanations for organised abuse, then the sceptical literature appeared to be coming from another planet. Their insistence that allegations of organised abuse are nothing more than the product of 'recovered memories' disclosed in therapy years or decades after the events were supposed to have taken place had no relevance in Sarah's case. Sarah was not only describing events in the past but also in the present, and her disclosures were not made in a therapist's office, nor were they facilitated by me in any way except through the offer of a sympathetic ear. Moreover, sceptics simply assumed that mental health care was accessible and affordable and that women and children who disclosed sexual abuse in therapy and counselling were not only believed but they were encouraged to elaborate. The truth was that many (and probably most) women with trauma-related mental health problems cannot afford the mental health care they need, and they often find themselves in the public health system where disclosures of sexual abuse are viewed as a distraction if not an irrelevance. Behind the din of the 'false memory' movement was a silent mass of abused women unable to find adequate support who were frequently being subject to inappropriate and sometimes retraumatising treatment in a health system that was not attuned to their particular needs and vulnerabilities. Meanwhile, activists, academics and journalists claimed that the very therapy they could not find or afford was responsible for mental health problems that were going untreated.

While I was grappling with these questions, Sarah was making a new life in a new city, which was not without its own challenges. Her decision to move away was hard for both of us, but she wanted a fresh start away from the accumulation of bad memories. Despite the move, she still had to be vigilant, since it was clear that the abusive group was tracking her movements. On a few occasions, funeral wreaths were mysteriously left on the doorstep of her new house on dates that were significant for Sarah in relation to her abuse. She made sure that friends were available to escort her from work after being confronted with a strange man who demanded that she get into his car. Despite these ongoing efforts to revictimise her, she struck up a strong connection with the man who is now her husband, and who has known about Sarah's history since the early days of their relationship. Like me, Sarah's partner has been faced with the frank reality of Sarah's situation, having been the recipient of strange threatening text messages and, on one occasion, discovering that his car had been smashed in by unknown vandals. However, such incidents became less and less frequent over time and eventually ceased altogether. The fact that Sarah is now safe and well, with a family and flourishing professional career, is due to their joint resilience and perseverance.

It was Sarah who, observing my efforts to make meaning out of what we had been through, suggested that I apply to study organised abuse as a doctoral candidate. It was a timely suggestion. It seemed impossible for me to 'get on with my life' if this meant trying to 'un-know' that other people were enduring what Sarah had endured. It was in this spirit that I enrolled in postgraduate study and began the research that forms the basis of this book. I had expected to encounter some degree of scepticism and resistance in relation to research into organised abuse, and hence the support I have received as both a postgraduate student and now as an academic has been both a relief and a pleasure. It is only recently that I have had the chance to thank Sarah for nudging me onto the path to a career that I certainly had not imagined when I took that fateful walk with her over a decade ago, and asked her what was wrong.

Conclusion

Writing this chapter has not always been easy, and the notion of publishing it is not a comfortable one. It is not my professional life that is being exposed to scrutiny here but rather my personal life, since my awareness of organised abuse developed in the context of a friendship that began when I was still a teenager. I do not provide a biographical account here as an attempt to underwrite the claims I present in this book as an unproblematised 'truth' authenticated by my own experiences. Instead, I have included my story in order to make explicit the ways in which the theoretical and empirical material presented in this book is founded on personal experience. Calls to acknowledge the value of personal experience and knowledge in the social sciences have generally come from feminists and almost uniformly from women. However, in this chapter I highlight how men's personal experiences of violence against women can serve as the basis not only for personal transformation but also academic inquiry. This has required me to describe how I came to witness the predations of an organised group of sexual abusers, as well as the dynamics of the alliance that Sarah and I created in order to help her survive her ordeal.

Whilst women have been most active in emphasising the 'public' value of their 'private' experiences, this chapter illustrates that men also have an investment in the 'public' recognition of our 'private' experiences. In many regards, I am testifying here to the enduring power of the alliances that men can forge with women in a shared resistance to gendered violence and the mutuality that can flourish between men and women more generally. Some years have now elapsed since my time as Sarah's carer, and what has lasted for me is not the fear and fatigue but instead the admiration and even pride that came from watching Sarah fight with such determination to create for herself the conditions that others take for granted every day – the right to live a life that is secure, safe and free from violence. I am proud to say that today it is Sarah who determines the direction of her life. This is an accomplishment that speaks to the restorative powers of emotional support as well as to Sarah's own particular strengths and bravery. The path that leads away from the trauma and captivity of organised abuse is not a linear one and it is a form of abuse that leaves everyone who encounters it irrevocably changed. However, as Sarah's story shows, a life worth living is a realistic goal for survivors but it is dependent on a context of care that has, sadly, often been lacking in the experience of survivors. The next chapter will discuss in more detail the contexts in which organised abuse flourishes, and in particular the ways in which neglect and invalidation can entrap children and adults in profoundly abusive arrangements.

Chapter 6

The experiences of survivors
Extraordinary crimes in everyday life

Violence against women and children can be the primary organising principle of collective criminal action but it often falls outside the definition of 'real' crime unless it overlaps with some other policing or policy priority. Behind the rhetoric of concern over 'sex trafficking', for example, are a range of government priorities in relation to border control and national security that frequently eclipse the needs and opinions of women deemed to have been trafficked (Segrave et al. 2009). Organised criminal violence against children and women is often not, in and of itself, an imperative for action. In Australia, Cooper and colleagues' (Cooper 2004, Cooper et al. 2006, Cooper et al. 2008) research with women involved in bikie gangs, drug trafficking networks or ritually abusive 'cults' has documented patterns of multi-perpetrator stalking, battery and torture against children and women. They found that this violence is often ignored by police agencies whose focus is on the illicit profit-making activities (such as drug manufacture or money laundering) of these groups, not on their crimes against their partners or children (Cooper et al. 2008). Where physical and sexual violence has been arranged through 'informal' networks of friends or relatives then authorities do not consider it to be 'organised crime' in any meaningful sense (Cooper et al. 2008). European policy-makers have shown a similar reluctance to consider that the organised abuse of children and women for reasons other than profit should be categorised as 'organised crime' (Kelly et al. 1995).

This reflects a more general minimisation of the seriousness of gendered violence. The accounts of survivors of domestic violence of being tortured with cattle prods (eg Bibby 2011) and other experiences of extreme violence may be briefly sensationalised by media coverage but otherwise the full spectrum of gendered violence rarely receives public recognition. Most victimised women's experiences do not include these extremes but the silence surrounding such crimes has the effect of camouflaging the ways in which 'private' violence can escalate to include organised abuse, torture and even death. Furthermore, this silence renders the lives of children and women who have survived extreme abuse very difficult. They face systemic barriers to seeking help, finding support and being believed in medical, legal or social contexts when they tell the truth about their lives. Chapter 3 examined the ways in which notions of 'public' and 'private' life in liberal democracies have camouflaged the vulnerability of children and women to gendered violence. The politics of 'privacy' operates to filter social reality in ways that occlude the severity of 'private' crimes from 'public' recognition, rendering invisible those victims whose histories of violence are dissonant with the idealisation of 'everyday' spaces such as homes, schools and churches as safe environments.

This contradiction between 'extraordinary' abuses and 'everyday' life has been important in debates over organised abuse. It is a distinction that is also used throughout this chapter to introduce the findings of a qualitative study of adults with histories of organised abuse. In interview, participants described how organised abuse took form within the everyday power inequities and injustices of the 'private' spaces of childhood, such as homes, schools and churches (see Appendix I for more information on the research project and methodology). A great degree of powerlessness and vulnerability is an objective condition of childhood in Western societies, although children's experiences of these conditions vary greatly depending on their life circumstances (Jenks 1996). Many children only ever experience their subordinate position indirectly, through the seemingly arbitrary and erratic displays of adult authority that occur frequently in childhood. However, in this study, participants described how abuse and neglect in a range of sites made that powerlessness known to them in the visceral terms of helplessness, betrayal and exploitation. Their attempts at disclosure were usually ineffective and where their distress was detected by other adults it did not result in efficacious intervention or care and support, but instead they were labelled as 'difficult' or 'slow'. In their accounts of childhood, participants described how they learnt to adapt to the abuse they could not avoid whilst seeking to exercise those opportunities for agency and resistance that they could find. However, these experiences of powerlessness often persisted into adulthood, with many participants describing recent experiences of violence, abuse and invalidation. The aim of this chapter is to highlight the ways in which organised abuse can be understood as an 'extraordinary' configuration of the coercion that characterises the 'ordinary' intersections of age, gender and power. As participants make clear, these intersections are so ordinary that the violence that can result from them is easily overlooked, even when that violence takes on extraordinary proportions.

Renee's story

Sceptics have frequently compared allegations of organised abuse to stories of alien abduction and past life memories, suggesting that accounts of organised abuse contain similarly fanciful or impossible elements. However, where narratives of organised abuse are subject to study and analysis they have been found to be far more mundane (Scott 2001, Itzin 2001). In this study, as in others, survivors described sexually abusive groups in the context of common social arrangements such as homes, schools and churches. Their abusers were their parents, teachers and other adults with socially legitimised authority over them. In effect, they were held captive within profoundly abusive relations by mechanisms of power that were invisible because they are widespread and socially accepted. In this regard, organised abuse is similar to other forms of interpersonal violence against children and women and indeed organised abuse often occurs contemporaneously with emotional, physical and sexual abuse and domestic violence. The story of one research participant, Renee, illustrates the ways in which organised abuse is embedded within the spectrum of woman and child abuse.

In Renee's experience, sexual abuse was 'everywhere' when she was a child. It was present at home and at school. She even recalls walking to high school one day 'and there's this guy pulled over on the side of the road, car door open, guy in his fifties, bald, having a wank'. She recounted how she was sexually victimised by her stepfather and stepbrother at home, as well as by teachers at school.

> The school I went to, one of the PE [physical education] teachers went to jail [for sexual abuse]. There were other male teachers. We talked about it! 'Oh, Mr Smith's wife has gone away, he asked me if I wanted to come around to his place for a kiss.' It's almost like it was everywhere.
>
> ... My deputy head principal at high school, I have never actually said the words, [cries] but he was into abusing girls. Y'know, we all wore uniforms up to here [indicates shortness of school skirt]. I've got memories of him, because I was always getting sent to him – saying 'Step back a bit, step back a bit', so that he could see. And I remember him telling me to pull my dress higher, and going around the side of his desk and he is having a wank.

When Renee was eight, her stepfather arranged for her to pose at a local photography studio for child abuse images, and he provided her for abuse to a local group of men. Whilst this involved, at times, quite sadistic abuse it was not discontinuous with her experience of a social world dominated by the sexualised power of men over children. As she said, 'I just thought it [sexual abuse] was, this was just life, you know'.

Renee's experience of sexual abuse as 'just life' can be understood as a psychological adaptation to her persistent victimisation. It was a way of conceptualising and accommodating the frequency of sexual abuse in her life (see Summit 1983). However, this adaptation had important political dimensions. At both home and school, it was through the privileges enjoyed by men that Renee was sexually victimised. These two institutions were the primary sites of her sexual victimisation, with each site compounding and reinforcing the harms of the abuse she was experiencing in the other site. At home, her stepfather Mark had untrammelled access to Renee's body, having ensured her mother's compliance through a combination of violence, alcohol and drugs.

> There was a lot of drinking. Every Thursday, Friday, Saturday and Sunday were just – they would both go out with their own friends and get absolutely rotten. During the week there were always two or three drinks straight after work. Then the violence started. My stepfather started hitting mum and hitting us and that went on for a while.

The pervasiveness of sexual abuse imparted to Renee the message that she was devalued and disreputable and that sexual abuse was a natural part of her social landscape. She described herself as one of the 'dead shits' at school; misbehaving, drinking, unlikely to be believed if she reported abuse and therefore vulnerable to a few predatory teachers who targeted school children for abuse. Whilst Mark's authority was unquestioned at home, at school, the deputy principal and other male teachers used their positions of authority to sexually abuse Renee and her friends. The abusive deputy principal and her stepfather occupied comparable positions of authority over Renee in their respective spheres and they abused this authority in similar ways. In order to explain why Renee considered sexual abuse as 'just life' and 'everywhere', it is important to understand not only her victimisation in organised abuse, but how this experience resonated with other abusive experiences in her life, and the ways that these experiences were organised by common structures of gender, age and power.

Participant's descriptions of organised abuse had much in common with their other accounts of abuse and violence but it also had particular characteristics that set it apart. Not only was organised abuse associated with particularly severe forms of physical and sexual violence, but perpetrators engaged in creative strategies with the intention of enhancing the fear, pain and confusion of victims. As will be discussed in more detail in Chapter 8, Renee described incidents of abuse by men who dressed up as children's cartoon characters and police officers to intimidate and disorientate her. They staged mock forensic interviews and physical 'examinations' of Renee by men posing as doctors or therapists in order to make Renee terrified of cooperating with professionals who might initiate an investigation into her abuse in the future. Renee explained how, if she or other children resisted the abuse, they were subject to torture techniques better known in military contexts, including the use of stress postures and the stretching of limbs that, whilst agonising, does not leave a mark on the victim.

So whilst Renee's experiences of organised abuse had many parallels with her other experiences of physical and sexual abuse, it involved a degree of sadism and premeditation that marked it as particularly painful, confusing and traumatising. On the one hand, it is important to recognise both the similarities between organised abuse and other forms of child abuse and gendered violence, but on the other hand it is clear that organised abuse has unique characteristics with particular implications for victims and survivors, and indeed for investigators, therapists and others concerned with preventing, intervening in and treating child sexual abuse. The following sections seek to maintain this 'dual vision' of both the common and uncommon characteristics of organised abuse as a form of gendered violence, with a particular focus on the spectrum of abuse disclosed by participants in the home, school and other institutions.

Power and abuse in the home

Research has found a common group of family characteristics associated with both incest and extra-familial abuse, particularly a lack of emotional support and closeness (Gold et al. 2004, Yama et al. 1993, Gold 2000). Loose or tenuous emotional relations between family members were a dominant theme in participant's accounts of family life. Some of the parents described by participants clearly wanted the best for their children, however, they often lacked the solutions to the problems that characterised their everyday life, whether it was poverty, family violence, mental illness, or substance dependency. Other parents, and particularly fathers, were characterised as violent, abusive, and unconcerned about the wellbeing of other family members. Smart (2007) highlights 'how grim families can be' (p 155) and her notion of the 'everyday unhappiness' of children (p 154) was in evidence throughout these participants discussions of their family life.

Of all 21 participants, only Helena and Sarah indicated that they grew up in homes without any physical or sexual violence. All other participants reported witnessing or experiencing physical or sexual abuse at home. Sixteen female participants reported being sexually abused by their fathers, as did a transgendered male participant who was born and raised as female. Their family structures were highly authoritarian, where roles within the family were strictly defined by paternal power. These interviewees often spoke of their role in the home as 'little mothers' (Herman 1981) or 'little wives' for their fathers; cooking, cleaning and raising their siblings. Throughout their childhood, they learnt that sexual coercion was part and parcel of the gendered division of labour that fell to girls and women. Incest took place in the context of severe emotional abuse and neglect.

> It was after she [Mum] died that my father started, well, basically, I replaced her as far as he was concerned … He made the decision to turn her life support off. And he came back to us to tell her she was dead. And that was the first night that a part of me shared his bed. That's it. 'You are taking her place'.
>
> Rhea

Jane recounted how, at the age of eight, her mother was hospitalised with a major depressive illness, and Jane was instructed to 'take over' from her. She says, 'And I bloody well did!' In addition to raising her younger sibling and doing the housework, Jane was subject to sexual abuse by her father through-out her childhood and adolescence.

> Daddy was a monster, when it came to his sexual orientation. He was a paedophile, a rock spider. And he was a *bad* one.
>
> Jane

A number of participants reported witnessing and/or being subject to their father's domestic violence in the home. In their accounts, the police refused to intervene when men battered their wives, and their battered mothers were provided with no alternatives by family, friends or the authorities. Most participants grew up prior to the advent of domestic violence services and no-fault divorce in the 1970s and hence their mothers had few options available to them if they sought to bring their abuse, or the abuse of their children, to an end. Even where abuse was absent in their house, participants indicated that, if they wanted, fathers could, and did, impose silence when faced with distress, ignore and invalidate unwanted opinions, withhold healthcare if they did not view an injury as deserving of attention, and control the flow of economic resources in such a way as to curtail the freedoms of their wives and children.

> I get the impression that Mum was totally powerless with Dad. She was totally reliant on him for money, I guess, she was repeating lots of messages she must have gotten from her family – she said things like, 'There's no divorce in our family.' She had been instructed not to leave him, there was no back-up for her if she did. And I don't think there was support for single mothers at that stage. But she definitely acted as though she had no choice. That she wasn't going to leave, she was going to stay with him for the money, and that he had to support his children.
>
> Anne

Some participants in this study came from middle-class families, in which family problems were concealed from outsiders by a well-maintained facade of respectability. Other participants came from working-class families in which their parents struggled to work long hours and raise their children. The financial and emotional pressure on their parents was often of such magnitude that, even where parents were ostensibly protective or nurturing, the needs of their children came second. Participants often described themselves, or their siblings, being forced to shoulder adult responsibilities as children. Says Colleen: 'We acted like adults, I never felt like a child. When I was a little girl, I was always an adult'. That was a common sentiment amongst

research participants. Whilst their parents worked, or were otherwise incapacitated through illness or substance dependency, some participants described
raising infant siblings whilst still children themselves.

> Being the eldest, in a family with an alcoholic father, um, my mother
> shoved me into the parent role. With, ah, the younger kids, much younger.
> And would talk to me as if I was an adult, and confide in me. Ah ... I didn't
> like it, and, ah, so, in my later teen years, I avoided involvement in the
> family at all. Ah. It was noisy, it was often violent, when it wasn't violent,
> you were waiting for it to break out, and there's this very awkward posi-
> tion I was put in, in being responsible for supervising the other kids, but
> no authority over them, and certainly no experience. And so on.
>
> Seb

Participants described families facing a range of challenges in which
parents and children engaged in a range of strategies in order to craft a more-
or-less cohesive and functional family environment. These efforts were often
complicated by the informal dynamics of gender and power that structured
the relations between parents and between parents and children. Helena
was one of the few participants in the study to describe a caring father who
was not violent or neglectful. Her family was poor, and whilst both of her
parents worked long hours it was her mother who was forced to accept what
Hochschild (1989) called the 'double shift' of paid labour and domestic labour.
Helena's mother rose at three each morning to work as a cleaner, returning
home at 11 in the morning in order to attend to the domestic labour of childrearing and house keeping. Her father enjoyed time away from the family
whilst his wife laboured at home:

> Mum did all the cooking and cleaning, you know, the old way. Mum
> did the cooking and cleaning, dad, you know, was down at the races, he
> liked to back a horse. Um, he ... yeah, that was dad, they had very defined
> processes in the house.

Through their control of the material and subjective conditions of family life,
fathers were in a position to establish and enforce what Smart (2007) calls the
'rules of remembering'. That is, they were able to determine and enforce what
their wives and children were permitted to acknowledge occurring in their
daily lives, and how they were to understand those occurrences. This had particular implications in those homes in which fathers were engaged in physical
and sexual abuse. Jo described her father as a sexually abusive 'woman and girl
hater' who forcefully imposed his view of her thoughts and feeling upon her:

> He would tell you what you were thinking and what you were feeling,
> and you had to agree. 'You did that because you are insolent'. My mum

used to despair because I used to want to try and stand up to him and say, 'No, it's really like this'.

Sometimes there would be arguments, and sometimes it would be going on for ages, but eventually I would just have to back down and say 'Yes, you're right, I was thinking this, I was feeling that, blah blah blah'.

Eventually, even when I got older, one time, I was trying so hard not to cry, but I couldn't help it, and then I would start crying, and it'd be 'Oh, you see, now you are turning on the water works, trying to be manipulative'.

Families are, in Misztal's (2003) terms, 'mnemonic communities' that shape what children remember about their lives, and how they understand those memories. For many participants in this study, their families were places in which their identities and recollections were 'storied' in ways that conflicted with their own direct experiences. Abusive fathers used their position of authority to deny the presence of abuse, obfuscate responsibility and silence their children and partners. In such an environment, participants were frequently required to silence their own opinions or suppress their needs in order to meet the requirements of their parents, who had their own complex investments in viewing their families, and their own competency as parents, in a favourable light. May commented how, in her family, it fell to her to meet her mother's need for validation and support, and not the other way around:

She wants to be really loving, she wants to be the perfect mother. She wants her kids to be the best. In a lot of ways, but in other ways, she's very needy. It's almost as though we have to validate her need to feel perfect, in a lot of ways. But she's very sincere about all that.

Participants became aware at a very young age that discussing their experiences of abuse at home was not possible, either due to likely reprisals or denials from parental perpetrators, or due to the fragility of non-abusive parents who were struggling to meet their own needs, let alone the needs of their children. The similar descriptions provided by participants of families involved in organised abuse, and families not involved in organised abuse, were striking. It was rare for participants in this study to describe a nurturing or protective home environment. If abuse of some variety was not present at home, and it usually was, then their parents' capacity to provide care and supervision was often limited by life stressors outside their control. In this regard, participants in this study fell into two categories: those participants raised in highly regimented families in which their fathers exercised power in harmful ways, including physical and sexual abuse, and those participants raised in struggling and sometimes chaotic families in which children were often forced to make sacrifices from a young age.

Abuse in schools, churches and residential care

In this study, extra-familial abuse usually occurred in an institution such as a school, church or children's institution. Outside the family environment, a few participants described opportunistic sexual abuse by strangers, however it was in institutional settings that such abuse was prolonged and severe. Burman (1994) suggests that dominant notions of the 'proper' child prescribe normal routes of development that rely, as reference points, upon hegemonic values of gender, class, sexuality and ethnicity. One of the central goals of adult strategies of surveillance and control over children is not necessarily the child's wellbeing, but rather the progressive constitution of the child into prescribed modes of adulthood. In Parkin and Green's (1997: 76) research into residential care in the United Kingdom, they found a 'high emphasis on surveillance and discipline and little evidence of caring for children', concluding that in an institutional setting 'issues of control and containment take precedence over care'. Whilst the official discourses surrounding schools, churches and other children's institutions is one of pedagogy and care, a 'second' or hidden curriculum is often in operation in which child wellbeing is subordinate to the requirements of normalisation and discipline.

In this study, participants recalled how institutional regimes of power had the effect of constraining their agency and intensifying adult control over them to such a degree as to exacerbate their vulnerability to abuse and violence. Reports of sexual abuse by teachers were common in this study, with almost half of participants reporting sexual abuse at school.

> Teachers grabbed you – I had a teacher come after me, and I fought it off, and then he turned on me and encouraged everyone to bully me. It was – I just called school 'jail', it was awful. I wasn't safe at school as well as home.
>
> Sky

> The priests were supposed to take us for some sort of leisure activity, and I can remember they would try to sexually abuse – we were very young, only about five, kindergarten! You just want to kill them when you think about it.
>
> Jane

> Later on in high school, there was a chaplain who was sexual towards me. And there was another teacher who was sexually abusive.
>
> Kate

In participants' accounts, the emphasis on surveillance and discipline in children's institutions simultaneously enabled sexual abuse but it also led to an institutionalised disinterest in children's wellbeing or safety. Participants'

narratives of school foreground the unresponsiveness of regimes of adult surveillance to behavioural indicators of child abuse. Virtually all participants
described institutional environments in which staff were, at best, incurious
when faced with evidence of child distress and trauma. More often than
not, the child's abuse-related problems were misrecognised as evidence of
slow social development or a learning disability. The normalising judge-
ments of families and schools then constituted the child's symptoms of
abuse as evidence of a moral or intellectual flaw, thus consigning them to a
diminished status that enabled sexual abuse to continue.

Sarah described how her victimisation in organised abuse, through a
babysitter, coincided with her transformation from a bright and gregarious
child to a shy and confused little girl. Her behaviour at school began to change
as she became more and more withdrawn.

> I was feeling really different and unable to connect and that sort of
> thing at school. My school work was still – I still did well with that – but
> even in earlier years, from an adult's perspective, they identified that some
> of my behaviours were a bit strange.

Sarah's teachers noticed this transformation and repeatedly contacted
Sarah's parents about 'a whole lot of things whereby teachers said that
they were concerned about my social interactions and behaviours and social
development, I suppose'. Whilst her parents and teachers observed this transformation, and were clearly concerned by it, they did not consider that it
could be the result of sexual abuse. Instead, Sarah was labelled as socially
underdeveloped and erratic, and subject to an array of sanctions designed to
correct her behaviour. Her shyness and lapses in memory and concentration
were interpreted as evidence of an innate flaw within Sarah that her parents
and teachers became increasingly frustrated in their efforts to change. Sarah's
sense of helplessness as she tried to live up to their expectations, whilst still
enduring increasingly severe levels of organised abuse, reinforced the message
that she was receiving from her abusers; that is, that there was something
wrong with her, and hence that she was deserving of abuse and harm.

Most participants went to school during the 1960s and 1970s, and it is
tempting to suggest that there are now more controls in place to prevent
institutional sexual abuse. Nonetheless, it is evident from ongoing reports
of harassment and abuse in schools, churches and children's institutions
that the male sexual prerogative remains intact from many adults in institutional environments. In children's institutions, in which children's lives
are subject to extraordinary degrees of adult oversight and regulation,
the prevalence of physical, sexual and emotional abuse of children in care
has been frighteningly high (Hawkins and Briggs 1997). A survey of over
2,000 American high school students found that 6.7 per cent of all children
in years 8 to 11 reported contact sexual abuse by a teacher (Shakeshaft 2003).

Jenks (1996) notes that child abuse remains an enduring feature of adult-child relations despite the emergence of new forms of adult surveillance over children that were supposed to render it impossible. She wonders whether the emergence of the disciplinary apparatus, far from heralding a new era of child welfare, has instead 'rendered child abuse less visible, or considerably more subtle' (Jenks 1996: 97).

The continuum of abuse and powerlessness

The powerlessness of children is commonly accepted as a biological fact and necessity. After all, an infant or a young child is physically, emotionally and psychologically dependent upon adults. However, whilst children are necessarily immature in physiological and psychological terms, their dependency on adults is shaped by and mediated through social structures that situate children within power relations (Jenks 1996). Children's powerlessness does therefore not take a 'natural' or 'inevitable' form but rather it is mediated by, and formed within, social structures. In this study, the spaces of childhood – particularly home, church and school – provided the geographic locus of profoundly unequal relations between adults and children. In participants' accounts, their diverse experiences of sexual abuse in different sites shared an important point of commonality: namely, the largely unchecked power of adults at home and outside to coerce them into abuse. The abject powerlessness of children faced with organised abuse was a consistent theme in participants' accounts. This was graphically illustrated in the following quote by Neil:

> Now, I spent a lot of my time absolutely black and blue from these people. They'd butt out their cigarettes on me, they'd use me as an ashtray, they'd piss on me, they'd shit on me, they'd belt the fuck out of me, kick me around the room if I didn't do something properly. But nobody in my family noticed it. Nobody noticed my distress on that first occasion. Nor any other time. It was just put down to me being a clumsy kid.

Neil was the only participant in this study to be sexually abused by a group of strangers who were not affiliated with his family, school or some other institution. However, neither Neil's family nor teachers inquired into the injuries Neil sustained during abuse nor his withdrawn and distressed demeanour. The two men that Neil was closest to as a child were his uncle and a teacher at school, both of whom were sexually abusive. When Neil disclosed his organised abuse to them, they used it as an opportunity to normalise and minimise their own abuse of him. Other participants described how their attempts as children to disclose their abuse generated shock and disbelief by adults, who appeared to be paralysed by what they had heard.

I [often] went over to the convent and had a hot lunch. And I can remember sitting in the sun, and trying to – one of the older nuns, in her long habit, was talking to me, and I just said – because I was the sort of kid that was very 'in your face' – and I think she was trying to talk to me about Mum, and what was wrong. And I must have told her about Dad. Because she sat in her chair screaming and flittering, and ran screaming into the convent. And I, I think I must have just said, 'My father gets into my bed and shows me his penis' or something. [laughs] The poor woman!

Jane

As these excerpts from Jane and Neil demonstrate, participants were not simply the passive recipients of harm. They exercised agency and resistance in relation to their abuse, however it is notable that no participant reported an effective intervention in childhood into their experiences of abuse. To the contrary, the actions that adults took when confronted by their distress was often counter-productive and harmful. This led to a pervasive sense of helplessness and powerless was captured perfectly by Darren when he said:

Because there's just – there just was nobody. I tried going to the police as a kid, and got laughed out of there. I tried everything. I tried writing letters to the prime minister. Tried all sorts of things as a kid. And nothing happened. And there's just that feeling that there's not a real hope. And there wasn't anybody.

In effect, participants became entrapped in social life as the pervasive conditions of childhood simultaneously rendered them vulnerable to victimisation whilst preventing them from protecting themselves. Throughout this process, participants became sensitised to their subordinate and powerless status, although they did not experience it as such; instead, they blamed themselves for the experiences of humiliation and marginalisation that they felt so vividly. The ways in which they internalised responsibility for their abuse had serious consequences for their subsequent health and wellbeing. Shame and self-blame led many participants to a state of complicity in relation to their own abuse, which they described facilitating in a range of ways, including meeting their abusers at prearranged times and places, remaining obedient during abuse and silent afterwards. In the following excerpt, Jo recalls her internal dialogue during an incident in her mid-teens in which she had been told to meet the abusive group after school.

I remember thinking 'I don't want to go, I don't want to go, I don't want to go, oh, but I have to go, but I have to go'. Because my parents worked after school, and, so I would go off, walk off.

The conundrum of 'I don't want to go, but I have to go' articulated by Jo was evident in many participants' accounts of organised abuse. Gaspar and

Bibby (1996: 50) observe that it is often difficult for investigators of organ-ised abuse to understand 'why children keep going back to be abused, some-times in the most degrading manner, and why, when away from the offender, they do not disclose'. In this study, children's obedience was not simply a product of the coercive strategies utilised by abusive groups, although the threats, violence and emotional manipulations of the abusive group certainly exerted a powerful influence. Rather, the acceptance that 'I have to go' was the product of a process whereby participants became enmeshed within a larger cycle of abuse, invalidation and powerlessness, as their attempts to disclose were ignored, their symptoms of abuse were misunderstood, and their escalat-ing need for intervention and support went unmet.

Participants' lives as adults had been marked by violence and physical and mental illness. For seven female participants, organised abuse continued into adulthood and three participants spoke, with great difficulty, about the fact that their children had also been victimised. Rhea and Isabelle described how, in the early years of their children's lives, they were still struggling to extricate themselves from the abusive group and as a result their children were also abused. Anne's son Jimmy was subject to organised abuse by Anne's parents when she left him with them for babysitting. It was only after Jimmy began describing sadistic sexual abuse by his grandparents that Anne began recalling her own childhood abuse (Anne's case is discussed in more detail in Salter 2011). Anne immediately reported Jimmy's disclosures to child protec-tion services and the police, and moved away from her parents, however she lived for many years with feelings of guilt at having placed her child in the care of her parents in the first place.

> The denial – for ages, I had the guilt. How can you be forty and not know this about your dad? I still idolised dad. And then, when these facts came out [Jimmy's abuse], then eventually I was just hearing things [about sexual abuse and traumatic amnesia] on the radio at the time. And I think the guilt must have lessened enough for me to hear it [information about sexual abuse and traumatic amnesia]. They said [on the radio program], 'The more trauma you've experienced, the less you are likely to remember it.' But it took me years [to accept that], even after hearing hints like that, and doing counselling courses. I felt so guilty that there was no way I could accept that I didn't, somehow, know that this was the family I came from.

Achieving a sense of personal safety and autonomy was a project that took some women years or even decades of struggle, and some participants reported that they were still not safe. Members of abusive families and groups used a range of strategies to coerce them into abuse, including threatening phone calls and emails, violence against pets, and even home invasions. Sarah reported an incident in her mid-20s when the abusive group sent an envelope of pornographic magazines to her employer with her name attached to them in an attempt to disrupt her employment.

> All the stupid discrediting sort of stuff that the group did. Things that set me up. In the mail, when they sent – oh my god – they sent those porno magazines in the mail to my boss. With a note saying they were returning them to me. It was so full on.

Rhea described how her friends and supporters were targeted by the abusive group during a period in her 30s.

> They made threats against my friend's daughters that they were going to bring them in, they were going to be raped, they were going to be brood mares, they were going to be sent overseas to live with people over there. All that stuff. Really scary stuff.

Sky moved a number of times to maintain his safety, and he stated that he was still receiving strange emails, letters and phone calls. He reported a recent phone call in which he was told he had only a few days to live. His anxiety and fear escalated with each passing day until a group of men showed up at the front door:

> And on the last day, at twenty past ten at night, a car pulled up. And there were three guys outside my house, with someone else still in the car – the engine was running – and they just kept knocking on the door. And it was like – are they just going to grab me?

Participants actively resisted attempts to revictimise them and they worked hard to establish a safe and stable life as adults. However, this was dependent in many respects on their capacity to afford mental health care and the level of support they could find from partners and friends. With their employment and their relationships severely impacted by their abuse and ongoing mental health concerns, they were often unable to find the necessary levels of professional or personal support. For many female participants, their intimate relationships as adults had been characterised by patterns of financial abuse, coercive control and domestic violence. Male participants also spoke of their difficulties in interpersonal relations but when they encountered violence and abuse, it was primarily in the context of public brawls and street fights. There were intimations of domestic violence in the accounts of two male participants and another had spent considerable time in prison for serious child sex offences. Early experiences of chronic abuse set the men and women in this study onto a troubled trajectory through life, with women evincing a high level of tolerance for abusive behaviour and/or an inability to trust themselves to make safe choices in sexual relationships, and men tending towards displays of aggression and sometimes abuse.

It is important to recognise the ways in which the powerlessness that participants confronted as children persisted in myriad ways for them as adults through victimisation in interpersonal relationships, the disability and poverty associated with serious mental illness and the disinterest shown in their plight by a range of authorities. Participants discussed at length their struggles to find accessible, effective mental health care, and their attempts to notify the authorities of ongoing abuse against themselves and others. However, as people with mental health problems and other psychosocial issues, such as alcohol or drug use, their narratives were often discounted by professionals. The opportunity to document their histories and voice their opinions freely in the context of the interview was a rare and welcome one for participants, many of whom had become so accustomed to being invalidated that they rarely spoke about their history of abuse. The efforts of perpetrators to silence their accounts through threats and violence was in many ways perpetuated by institutionalised forces of disavowal and disbelief that actively undermined their efforts to seek care and support, and prevented them from finding justice for the crimes committed against them and witnessed by them.

Conclusion

Whilst the specifics of their life circumstances varied widely as children, in each case participants' enmeshment within organised abuse arose out of the 'fit' between the power of adults to identify and manipulate vulnerable children, and the gaps and contradictions within adult regimes of control and surveillance at home and school. This introduces one of the key paradoxes of child abuse more generally: in a culture in which gender-based violence is widespread and frequent, adult regimes of control and surveillance have both protective and harmful aspects. Some participants were subject to organised abuse because their parents, teachers and others were unable or unwilling to provide adequate care and support. However, there were also participants whose organised abuse was made possible by a high degree of control and surveillance enabled by disciplinary regimes at home, school and church. Whilst it may be that 'childhood is the most intensely governed sector of personal experience' (Rose 1989: 123), it seems that this governance has not ameliorated the inequities of adult-child relations and indeed may have exacerbated them. The impacts of abuse followed participants throughout their lives, and the consequent physical and mental illness limited their capacity as adults to protect themselves from ongoing abuse or pursue fulfilling relationships or employment. Where they sought external assistance, they often found that their complex needs undermined their credibility in the eyes of health professionals, police and other authorities.

Child-care strategies of control and surveillance are often legitimised as being in the child's best interest. In this study, however, it seems that children's interests are frequently defined according to the adult imperatives and interests rather than to the child's wellbeing. Within the disciplinary apparatus operating at home, school and other institutions, the principle of adult control was pre-eminent, and abusive adults were provided with a range of opportunities and strategies through which they could identify vulnerable children, and manipulate them into abuse. Simultaneously, children faced an uphill battle in making their needs known and urgent to authority figures, who were accustomed to determining the child's needs in their own terms. Whilst adult scrutiny of children can be extraordinarily intense, its goal is the reproduction of children as prescribed kinds of subjects, which has traditionally necessitated a certain level of physical or emotional coercion. Discomfort, confusion or distress is considered a 'natural' part of childhood; that is, a necessary by-product of the pedagogical or parenting process. Hence families and institutions can foster a culture of indifference to children's wellbeing which, in the accounts analysed in this chapter, effectively silences abused children and forces them to accept abuse as their lot. The following chapters will consider this paradox in more detail by analysing the experiences of participants subject to familial, institutional and network abuse.

Chapter 7

Living in two worlds
Familial organised abuse

It is well recognised that some abusive families contain multiple members who are active in the sexual abuse of children to the point where a familial 'culture of abuse' begins to flourish. In their research and clinical experience, therapists Bentovim and Tranter (1994) have found that families harbouring cultures of sexual abuse are of two types: openly dysfunctional and well known to welfare agencies, or closed systems unknown to the authorities and isolated from their surrounding communities. Whilst both kinds of families place a high premium on loyalty and secrecy, abuse within openly dysfunctional family types is more likely to be detected due to their contact with police and health and welfare services. In contrast, organised abuse within apparently 'normal' families who are not dependent on government assistance can go unnoticed for many years if at all. The children of these families are afforded few opportunities to disclose their abuse or to seek external intervention. Some have taken to the streets to protect themselves, disclosing their abuse to crisis services (Scott 1998) whilst others may report their victimisation in therapy following years or decades of abuse (Sinason 2002). The frequency of brain injury, developmental delays and mental illness amongst victims of familial organised abuse (Bentovim and Tranter 1994) suggests that many victims of such abuse are unlikely to ever disclose and others are silenced through suicide (Salter and Richters forthcoming).

The life stories analysed in this chapter provide an important insight into the closed and isolated family regimes of organised abuse that rarely attract the attention of the authorities. Interviewees described highly regimented families that were enmeshed within abusive networks of extended kin and family contacts in which sexual abuse was normative, widespread and expected. Their families formed a nodal point within a larger system of abuse, in which their parents had obligations to provide their children for abuse to relatives, friends and other associates. These obligations structured all of family life so that the directives of abusers, and the defence mechanisms and adaptations of the abused, constituted the primary family dynamic. In these participants' accounts, the involvement of their parents varied by degrees from passive acquiescence to active participation and facilitation. Some participants' parents grew up within a familial culture of organised abuse, whilst other participants indicated that their parents became voluntarily involved with a sexually abusive group. In either case, organised abuse transformed the family environment into a training ground and holding pattern for sexual exploitation. Faced with parents who they couldn't trust or depend upon, the challenge that faced participants was summarised by Sky, who described his realisation as a young child: 'Alright, I've got to keep myself alive'.

Participants described a range of benefits accruing to adults who participated in organised abuse, including professional, social, financial and sexual benefits. However, it was clear that organised abuse was neither a free nor voluntary system of exchange. Like other forms of organised crime, familial organised abuse occurred within strictly observed hierarchies of men who maintained control through blackmail and the threat of injury and death. Participants indicated that parental involvement in organised abuse was a source of fear for both parent and child, who could both be subject to serious sanctions if they did not comply with the requirements of the sexually abusive group. Fear of more senior or powerful men within the abusive network loomed large in the minds of abusive adults as well as children, and the act of providing a child for abuse was a mechanism through which an adult could defer or displace the violence that was an ever-present threat within the abusive group. This chapter will explore the relations between family members trapped within organised abuse, and the manner in which children and adults adapted to a situation that was simultaneously intolerable and inescapable.

Private abuse, public facade: dissociation and the public-private divide

Participants subject to familial organised abuse described their childhoods as bifurcated into 'two worlds': there was the 'everyday', in which they went to school and maintained the pretence of a happy family, and 'night-time', which represented the unpredictable and dangerous reality of living with organised and (often) ritualistic abuse. Rhea encapsulated this perspective when she said:

> There were two lives. It wasn't like living in a cult where you were kept segregated from the outside world. It was nothing like that. I think that's so extreme, and we hear about those now. What we don't hear about are the kids that are just living absolutely normal, middle-class-type lives, where nobody's able to open the door and get behind to see what's happening. The group always talked about people being outsiders, you never speak to outsiders. Ever. You don't tell outsiders about what happens in

the home, you don't talk to outsiders. And what we learnt to do was not to talk to anybody about what was happening.

Lily and Darren spoke in similar terms:

> Y'know, there's the two worlds. There is the normal, everyday world, and there is the ritual abuse world.
>
> Lily

> [S]o much of my life is just sectioned off. And it had to be while I was a kid. I mean, I couldn't be going to school and remembering all that stuff. Y'know, there was two worlds.
>
> Darren

It is notable that participants lived in households that maintained (to greater or lesser degrees of success) a veneer of normalcy. Despite the abuses contained within them, their families did not attract the attention of the authorities, since family life was carefully structured around a collective denial and disavowal of organised abuse. Participants' parents maintained a strict distinction between the 'private' world of organised abuse and a 'public' facade that was employed in interactions with those outside the family.

> They [parents] portrayed themselves as decent law-abiding, working-class citizens. Which, of course, then – it was just a big front. A pretence, anyway. And they would make sure that they would follow all day-to-day laws, and look good, and respectable. And it worked, because nobody dug underneath, and had a good look at them. Took the mask off their face. But they were hiding a great deal.
>
> Lauren

> A neighbour had come to our house, and Mum said to her, 'I don't hit my children'. And I distinctly remembered being hit by her a few days earlier. So, again, this is what I mean about the way we were fed certain stories about our family, which was different to what was really happening. But it wasn't until I was older, and I remembered that conversation, and I thought, 'But that's not true'. But we were all taught to bury the truth.
>
> Anne

> I think, I recall, a lot of my childhood life not making sense because what happened during the day was very different to what happened at the night, or on weekends. What was happening was the total opposite to what was being portrayed during the day, you know, the whole Brady

Bunch thing. Mum, Dad, kids, everything looks hunky dory. It was the opposite to that.

Isabelle

For many participants, this divide between 'day' and 'night', and 'public' and 'private', was so stark that it was internalised and became manifest through psychic structures. Specifically, many participants developed psychological adaptations, such as dissociation and amnesia, in which the lived experience of schooling and life outside the home was 'split off' from the fear and terror of organised abuse in domestic contexts. Scott (2001) argues that, in circumstances of organised and ritualistic abuse, children develop multiple personalities because their roles in abusive family contexts are incompatible with their roles at school and outside the home. Such an argument finds support in this study, where participants subject to organised abuse described in detail the contradictory roles that they were expected to adopt inside and outside the home, and the multitude of rules and regulations that demarcated this divide. The child was placed in an impossible situation by organised abuse: under pain of death she was to deny (even to herself) that any abuse was taking place, nonetheless she was expected to conduct herself at all times according to the code of secrecy and loyalty imposed by the abusive group and enforced by her parents. Jo described the strict policing of her 'everyday life' by the group, who stipulated a set of requirements to Jo that, she felt, she must obey or else risk being killed.

> It wasn't only a question of telling, you had to not draw attention to yourself ... You're not [allowed to be] a trouble maker or having problems, but you're not [allowed to be] drawing to attention to yourself the other way as well [ie excelling in any way]. You've got to be fairly average, particularly not be noticed, and not just in terms of what happened [ie organised abuse]. If you were in any way drawing attention to yourself that there might be something funny [there would be consequences].

Trapped by irreconcilable demands to 'not know' about their own abuse but to 'know' not to tell anyone about it, participants described themselves inhabiting an in-between space of awareness during 'everyday life', as they avoided any stimulus that might remind them of their abuse whilst simultaneously maintaining semi-awareness of the rules against disclosure and disloyalty. As children, their response to this life-threatening paradox was to dissociate, which participants described as 'flying away', 'going inside' or going to the 'deep dark'. This 'going inside' was described by participants as their only available response to a totalistic and life-threatening environment in which other options for resistance were unavailable. Says Anne:

> That's the only safe place, your own brain. Because, definitely, your body has been invaded, your body is not your own.

Dissociation enabled the child to enact the multiple, contradictory roles demanded of her whilst also maintaining the illusion of control and order in her life. Over time, the child came to identify herself according to these multiple roles; she develops DID, in which her social interactions and practices are mediated by multiple, alternating self-states. Fittingly for a last-ditch psychological defence mechanism, participants' descriptions of DID emphasised its functional quality, and the manner in which it enabled them to perform adequately within life-threatening and unpredictable circumstances. Rhea described how she generated new personalities and identities according to the respective dispositions demanded of her in sexual exploitation:

> Cult was separate to our day-to-day life. Me, Rhea, was there just for the day-to-day things that were happening. If cult stuff was happening, it would be other parts that were involved. I guess there were a few things that were happening around a few people that knew cult, knew we were involved, um, but they were very careful – a lot of them, they were very careful. As I said, we were just leading ordinary, normal lives. And only cult parts – cult parts would be activated if certain triggers were being used.

Rhea described her multiple personalities in almost mechanistic terms: when a different 'part' was necessary for a particular function, that 'part' would 'switch' in and fulfil its role. The maintenance of two separate lives was achieved, for Rhea, through the amnesia that comes with dissociation. Nonetheless, she also indicated that maintaining the distinction between these 'two worlds' required explicit instructions by her father at times, and her conscious obedience:

> There were marks after some rituals, I did have – I remember, we had marks on us, physical marks of the abuse, and our father told us that we were not to get undressed, we were not to get changed [at school].

Jo had also been diagnosed with DID and, like Rhea, she also indicated that her 'two worlds' were kept separate not only by amnesia and dissociation, but also through semi-conscious effort. This gave rise to considerable anxiety.

> I did sometimes lie in bed and wonder, and worry that I would have enough … left to live in the day. So much was being taken up with coping with everything that was going on, I was worried that I would have actually enough resources to actually go about my everyday life and put on a facade of everything being fine.

The literature on trauma and dissociation is written almost wholly by psychologists and psychiatrists, and hence it maintains a primary emphasis on the psychopathological impacts of violence for the individual victim. However, it is important to note the political nature of dissociation, and how the spatial distribution of relations of gender, age and power can organise children's lives in ways that generate an intolerable contradiction between their 'public' and 'private' roles. In this study, participants described how they responded to the contradictory roles demanded of them at home and elsewhere by generating a multiplicity of identities that corresponds to specific configurations of power in particular circumstances. Over time, dissociation may become the child's primary response to a world that they experienced as unpredictable and violent, resulting in the proliferation of identities until, as Darren put it, 'you are so splintered, and so divided, that you have no particular strength left in your compartments – no compartment is particularly big or strong'.

Paternal domination

For the majority of these participants, their fathers were their primary abuser who subjected them to incest as well as organised abuse. Fathers featured in their histories as the 'perfect patriarchs' that have been noted throughout the literature on incest (Herman 1981, Williams and Finkelhor 1990, A. Morris 2009). They were the arbiters of family life to the point where it was unusual for participants to report domestic violence by their fathers; the suggestion was that such violence was unnecessary. In many participants' accounts, their fathers' capacity to dictate the terms of family life was so entrenched that it went largely unspoken, and was expressed and reinforced through subtle displays of control and coercion.

> There was no physical stuff [domestic violence]. Occasionally, I can remember them having an argument or two. But – nah, there was no need for it. Because what he said went. Nobody ever questioned it. As soon as he walked into the room, everyone knew what their place was, and what they were allowed to say, and what they weren't allowed to say.
>
> Isabelle

> I didn't see any violence [between Mum and Dad] – I'm not saying it didn't happen, but it was never in front of us. No, it was psychological, looking back on it to see what the relationship was, and looking at domestic violence in those terms. It was total, y'know, it was financial dependency, it was psychological, emotional abuse. He didn't need to hit her.
>
> Rhea

> I think she [Mum] must have been very defined in her role as mother and wife, I think. But it wasn't the sort of house where there were any kind of arguments or disagreements. Everyone agreed with everybody. Um. And you didn't get angry, and you didn't cry, and you didn't complain, and you had perfect manners. And those things were kind of unspoken, rather than actually spoken.
>
> Felicity

In this study, the dominant position of abusive fathers in these households was constantly reaffirmed through a regime of discipline and control embedded within the everyday routine of family life. Participants' families adhered rigidly to the traditional sexual division of labour. Most of their mothers were involved in full-time housework and childrearing, or else in low paid service or administration roles. In contrast, most fathers were engaged in higher status, better paid professional work. A number of authors have remarked on the alienation between mothers and daughters which seems to prevail in incestuous families (Herman 1981, Laing 1999, A. Morris 2009). This was a noticeable feature in participants' accounts of familial organised abuse. Participants often described their mothers as weak and helpless and unable to nurture or protect them. This characterisation of their mothers was most frequently reflective of the fathers' treatment of them, which was both implicitly and explicitly disparaging.

> He was scathing [of my mother] in his cynicism, on the one hand, and he'd put her down. So much so that, when I was a teenager, I didn't think much of her, I thought she was a stupid woman with no brains – which is terrible, really. On the other hand, at other times, he would show a sort of – it was almost a borderline personality type switch there – he'd go into 'Oh, if it wasn't for you I wouldn't have any friends come to visit' and 'Oh, look at you, Madam, you do such wonderful things here in the house, making this beautiful meal.' He'd be so effusive in his praise, but you knew it could drop any second. He could go into a temperamental rage in a moment, and then switch it off at a moment's notice if someone unexpectedly came by or the phone rang.
>
> Kate

Typically, participants' descriptions of their mothers were richer and lengthier than their descriptions of their fathers, since their mothers were largely responsible for childrearing and featured more frequently in their lives as children. Nonetheless, it was clear that fathers and grandfathers loomed over participants' families as powerful figures in a totalistic regime of coercion and exploitation. Many participants described their fathers' alarming and unpredictable oscillations in mood between aggressive violence, cold aloofness and sexually inappropriate or abusive affection. These mood swings were all the more terrifying because of the seriousness of the crimes that participants had witnessed their fathers engaging in within organised contexts.

Maternal complicity

In autobiographies of familial organised abuse, survivors often refer to their mothers as being actively involved in their organised abuse (eg Lorena and

Levy 1998). Scott (2001: 106) has documented the claims of survivors of ritualistic abuse that women are 'as bad' or 'worse' in abusive contexts than men. In this study, it was rare for participants to describe an incident in which their mothers were enthusiastic participants in organised abuse. Sky was the only participant who spoke of his mother as a regular and proactive participant in organised abuse alongside his father. Sky remembered his mother as 'the boss' in family life. His parents formed a tightly-knit unit and he suggests that, together, they manipulated their children with great skill.

> I think I have three memories of my mother hugging me as a child, and they were all – even as a 12-year-old – I was thinking 'You are faking it.' I'm bawling my eyes out and thinking, 'You don't even know how to hug.'
>   [...] It's almost clinical, the day-to-day relationships with my parents. At least, when you are in class with your mates, you say, 'Are you having a decent day? What's going on for you?' But I knew more about the emotional life of my next door neighbours than I did about my family. In my family, sentences never start like 'I feel ... blah blah blah.' It was very odd.

Other researchers have documented incidents of severe sexual abuse by women in families that participate in organised abuse (Sarson and McDonald 2007). Such accounts were not unknown in this study. Polly described 'bizarre, sadistic, hideous' abuse by her mother and her grandmother, who would threaten to chain Polly outside like a dog if she did not acquiesce to sexual abuse. Nonetheless, these women had subordinate roles in their families and they often took a secondary role in organised abuse, assisting male abusers while trying to balance the demands of their violent husbands with their own needs. This was a juggling act that could involve sacrificing the wellbeing of their child in an effort to ameliorate their own abuse. Whilst Lauren expressed great antipathy for her mother, who had facilitated Lauren's sexual abuse by her grandparents and others, she acknowledged that her mother was subject to ongoing victimisation as well:

> I have to admit, I have come to realise that all these mothers – I hate them – as young girls, they went through all this shit themselves. And they are victims themselves, I do recognise that. But it's still hard to cop, that the women are assisting the men all the time, and can be the main perpetrator.

Trauma, violence and other factors, such as alcohol and drugs, often featured in narratives of maternal collusion or participation in organised abuse. Many participants grew up in the 1950s and 1960s in which their mothers had few opportunities to protect themselves or their children from abuse. However, younger participants also described the captive lives of their mothers who were petrified of leaving their violent husbands, whose paternal authority was bolstered by the looming threat of the abusive group. Furthermore, none of the mothers described by participants had the skills or experience that would have made independent survival a realistic option.

In the absence of alternatives, women appeared to have employed a range of psychological mechanisms, such as denial, suppression and rationalisation, in order to maintain the integrity of the family unit whilst attempting to ameliorate the harms that were befalling themselves and/or their children. This placed them in the contradictory state of 'knowing-but-not-knowing' about organised abuse, a paradox sustained only by frantic attempts to push from awareness any stimulus that might bring to light the contradictions inherent in their lives. When evidence of their children's abuse became unavoidable, some mothers responded with physical and emotional abuse.

> I still know that I came home one time [from organised abuse] and she [Mum] beat me up, probably because of she was just, all her anger about the cult getting to me, and that sort of tells me to dissociate further. So obviously you don't sort of have any, you are in that typical situation where you don't have support anywhere.
>
> Jo

> And if I dared to try to communicate to her that I was traumatised, and try to seek some soothing or some comfort from her, she would turn into this monster, this shrieking monster – that I wanted it ... Like it's all my fault. 'Don't you come crying to me!' You know. She was just crazy with me.
>
> Polly

> Not only are you taking all the abuse, but whenever aberrances occur because of the abuse that's going on throughout the family, then it's blamed on you. Y'know, you're the reason why everything is falling apart, or why we are all arguing. And it was just constant.
>
> Darren

Cara described her mother's consistent denial and minimisation of the extent of abuse in her family, even as she was dressing and bandaging the injuries inflicted on Cara by her father and the abusive group.

> [Mum would say] things like, 'This is just the way it has to be.' 'It's not as bad as you think.' Just minimising stuff.

Whilst the behaviour of these women can be conceptualised as complicit, it can also be understood as protective, in that it facilitated the long-term well-being of the family.

In denying the seriousness of organised abuse, these women were able to maintain their attachment to an abusive husband, thus ensuring the social status and financial security of their family, and ameliorating the escalation of violence against themselves and their children. The lack of options available to victimised children and women was a material condition of life that these women had to adapt to, due to the systemic neglect of the needs of abused women and children by the health and welfare services and by the government more generally. This prompted a kind of learned helplessness that was reflected in their dispositions and parenting practices.

> Her [my mother's] biggest message to me was always 'Don't get your hopes up.' And she acted as if she was doing me a favour by squashing everything I ever wanted to do, because it was like, 'No, just don't get your hopes up.'
>
> Anne

Some mothers did attempt to protect their children from organised abuse but to no avail.

> Mum did try, I've got to admit, Mum did try a few times to get us out of it. But she was very much under his control. And on one occasion, she did take off, she was — I was probably about eight or nine, and my brother — she was actually pregnant again, and she took off with us. And it was very hard at the time to, when it started coming back, and I had to talk about it — because a part of me rang my father and told him where we were. So it wasn't me, it wasn't Rhea, but it was certainly a part of me, a [different personality], and he and a few of his cronies showed up and brought us back. And due to what they did to her at the time, she miscarried, so, she lost that baby. She was punished very severely for that.
>
> Rhea

> I remember lying in bed, being really sick, and hearing them in the next room, and my mum saying 'I don't know what you are doing, I don't know what you've done to her, but you have to stop.' And then just hearing this thump, thump.
>
> And what the hell could she have done? She had two kids, and was incredibly conscious of her position in society. And divorce was just not done.
>
> Lily

When considering participants' descriptions of maternal complicity in organised abuse, it is important to be mindful of the constrained choices available to their mothers. Most participants indicated that their mothers' involvement in organised abuse was leveraged through threats and abuse, or else their mothers were not directly involved. Regardless of their level of involvement, it seems that these women had few choices available to them if they sought to protect themselves or their children from abuse. It is also pertinent to consider how years or decades of exposure to the household gender regime described in the previous section (and, indeed, the gender regime of the abusive groups within which these families were embedded) may serve to undermine the autonomy and agency of women and delegitimise individual resistance to sexual abuse or organised abuse.

When one parent doesn't know: the complexities of deceit and denial

The complexities of complicity, deceit and denial in families involved in organised abuse are well illustrated by the life histories of those participants who had a 'non-involved' parent; that is, a parent who was unaware and uninvolved in the organised abuse of their child. In interview, May and Felicity reported being subjected to organised and ritualistic abuse by their father whilst their mother was unaware of this behaviour. In their life histories, 'not knowing' about organised abuse emerges as a situated accomplishment for non-involved parents. It seemed that the non-involved parent was unaware of the organised abuse, not because they had failed to 'put the clues together', but because the circumstances of their life were such that inquiring further into the distress of their abused child would have placed them in an intolerable position. As such, the division between the 'non-involved' parents described by these participants, and the 'coercively involved' parents described by other participants, was somewhat indistinct.

These families shared a great deal in common with families in which both parents were aware of their organised abuse. At home, their fathers were distant, unavailable and unpredictable, and their mothers struggled to raise their children without partners who provided emotional support or assistance with childrearing and domestic labour.

May characterised her mother's state of 'not-knowing' as an ongoing process constituted by a complex array of defensive techniques, ranging from denial, minimisation and dissociation to insults and angry outbursts. She described her mother's efforts to maintain the ideal of a 'happy family'. This ideal was all the more valuable for its fragility. As her father subjected her to incest and organised abuse, May became a troubled child, with frequent migraines, nightmares and inexplicable phobias. She describes 'switching off' as a child, dissociating in the family home and being unable to recall daily events or participate fully in family life. In her home environment, May's symptoms of trauma were rationalised away. May says her family 'seemed to think that the way I was being and acting was very normal, and that was the way I was expected to act'. May was frequently tearful at home, and her mother viewed May's depression as a personal affront:

> It was almost as though she felt that she had failed as a mother if I was upset. And I had to validate her then. 'Perfect mother'.

Maintaining a relationship with her mother required May to fulfil her mother's emotional needs whilst denying her own. In her early teens, however, the scale of her distress became impossible to hide.

> She would often find me – I was often crying, but I wouldn't know why I was crying? I didn't know why I was upset. And she would always be digging and needling me, 'Why are you upset?' Questioning me and trying to get to the bottom of it.
>
> And anyhow, this particular time – I really couldn't tell her, I didn't really know – but I think the only way I could describe what I was feeling was, like, 'I don't think Dad is loving me right. I don't think he's loving me right. When he's hugging me, he's not hugging me as a daughter.' And Mum was most offended. And she said, 'Aren't you lucky that I'm not the jealous, vindictive type of mother who would believe this type of stuff.'

This pattern of disclosure and invalidation was repeated a year later when, at the age of 15, May attempted to kill herself.

> *What was your family's response to that?*
> Oh, my mum was angry. 'We gave you everything you need, why would you try to kill yourself?' She was the only person I told [about the suicide attempt]. I don't think she took me very seriously anyway.

May demonstrated a great deal of insight and empathy regarding her mother's inability to acknowledge her distress.

> It was very hard for me. But, I think about how it must have been for her – being the type of person, with the emotional neediness she had, to be in the situation in which all hell was happening to her daughter, and she felt she couldn't do anything about it. Really, she had no option but to turn off. And dissociate from it.
> *So do you feel that she was aware of your distress?*
> Umm ... yeah, I do, I think she felt that there was something not right. But I think she felt that it wasn't safe to pursue it any further.

Felicity's descriptions of her mother are in contrast to other descriptions of parents who were unaware of their organised abuse. At the time of interview, Felicity was still putting together an image of her childhood and life in the family home. Nonetheless, she describes her mother as a protective and involved parent, although she suggests that the family home was somewhat devoid of spontaneous displays of emotion or affection.

> I think she was a pretty amazing sort of woman, really. She was very family oriented ... She had a great sense of humour, I remember her

laughing a lot. I remember her being at home, I can remember her cleaning, doing things.

But I don't ever remember anything much in the way of physical touch. I don't remember her hugging me. Possibly that's how it was at that time, I'm not really sure. But I don't remember physical touch within the family happening at all.

Felicity recalled her father subjecting her to organised and ritualistic abuse within an abusive group that met at the local church. Like May, Felicity spoke of her need to 'protect' her mother from this knowledge, and she tried to compensate by being the 'perfect child'. Unlike May, however, Felicity's mother acted decisively when she was confronted with evidence of her child's sexual abuse.

[M]y mother discovered him [my uncle] abusing me one day, and then he was thrown out of the house, I assume, that night, and I never saw him again ... I was too scared to ask her about things for a long time – this was about my uncle – because there were things that I remembered but I didn't know how much she knew. And when I asked her about it, she said she believed that it started when I was a baby.

Felicity's account suggests that, in the gender-divided world of the 1950s, an otherwise protective mother could be deceived by an abusive spouse as he sexually exploited their child. Felicity's father was a distant man who was home only infrequently, and Felicity suggested that there was little communication between her mother and siblings, and her father.

I'd have to say that I don't think I ever really knew him. He wasn't part of our lives. The only conversation I remember having with him – 1952, I think it was, the morning the king died – he was having breakfast, because he started early, and I could hear the national anthem playing. And I asked him what that was, and he said the king had died. And I think that's kind of ... about the only conversation we had.

[...] And he was always out a lot at night, and saw the family, I think, as Mum's responsibility. She brought us up, she took us to church, and, um, he didn't see that as part of his – which is probably what happened in those days, a lot. But I don't know much about him.

The colonisation of family relations by organised abuse

For those participants with a 'non-involved' parent, the encroachment of organised abuse into the family home was somewhat limited. The abusive parent often had to wait for their spouse to be absent from the home, or else find excuses to take their child from the home, in order to expose the child to organised abuse. These boundaries and constraints upon organised abuse were not in place for those participants whose entire household was aware of, and active in, organised abuse. The nuclear 'units' of these families were often embedded within extensive networks of abusive kin within which incest and violence was widespread and normative. The abusive group was an unspoken, although powerful, factor in family life. Organised abuse was rarely openly acknowledged in the home and participants described parents who were at pains to conform to conventional family norms. Nonetheless, participants indicated that the sadistic violence of the abusive group was a silent but powerful threat that permeated the family home.

> But then there was this kind of reign of terror of my father, and my mother, and what they would do in a ritual context. It took over everyday life too. It was just keeping us in check with fear. I don't know if you would call that discipline, but it kept us in line.
>
> Sky

> Everything that I did, somehow, had a link back to sex and candles and dark places, religion and basically, if I didn't do what I was told, I was told it would result in something happening to me, something happening to the people that I care about. You know, there were times where I had something that I did care about, like pets, they never stayed around.
>
> Isabelle

Many participants were kept in a state of isolation by their fathers, who controlled and monitored all aspects of family life. In Isabelle's family it was considered a male prerogative to supervise and restrict the activities of women.

> I was kind of my father's property. He sort of saw me as his second wife. So everywhere he went, I did. If he was at home, I was at home. If he went shopping or something, and it wasn't a school day, I would be with him. There was no space to go on your own. It was kind of, 'I'm not letting you out of my clutches, because if I let you out of my clutches you might start talking to people, and things might start making a different sense.'
>
> Isabelle

Many participants were deterred from establishing any social contact outside the family. Their fathers and grandfathers consolidated their power by isolating their wives and children from the outside world. For some participants, the women in their family were just as active in policing their conduct as men. As a child, Lauren and her mother lived in her grandparents' home, and it seems that all adults in the home took responsibility for the micro-control of children.

> Growing up with my family, they wanted to control every aspect of my life. They want to know everything you do, every conversation you've had, because you are never allowed to speak about what's going on. So it's to keep this tight control, tabs on you.

Lauren lived with her three siblings and her mother in her grandparents' house and was expected to engage in regular sexual activity with her grandparents as well as with her uncles and other family members and friends. The participation of children in this activity was coerced by withholding food. Lauren reported that she and her siblings were often hungry and were given small amounts of money for sex acts. They used the money to buy food.

> We were all constantly abused. And also the involvement of other family members from a very early age. [...] In particular, one uncle would come to the house, and ... any one of us would have to perform oral sex or whatever with this uncle. Whoever he wanted. And that's where money would start changing hands. [...] Because there was major food deprivation and all that, you would accept that money and just use it so you could buy some food.

This excerpt demonstrates how, in circumstances of familial organised abuse, sexual abuse can become one of the organising principles of family relations. Lauren's mother lived with her parents, and in lieu of rent and board she provided her children for sexual abuse to her father. In turn, when Lauren's uncle came to visit his parents, he would regularly abuse Lauren and her siblings, providing payment to his parents as well as small amounts to the children. In this way, lateral and intergenerational relations within Lauren's family were expressed through the medium of child sexual abuse. Adult male family members acted as abusers whilst adult female family members acted as facilitators, a division of labour that reflected, more generally, the relative status of women in Lauren's family.

In participants' histories, their abusive families and kin networks overlapped substantially with religious, fraternal and other male-dominated organisations. Their families maintained involvements with churches, Masonic groups and other institutions in which they had close linkages with other sexual abusers. The patterns of sexually abusive exchange outlined above were therefore not limited to intra-familial relations; they included relations with family 'friends' and contacts across a range of institutions and social contexts. The abusive group could include members of mainstream institutions who, by acting cooperatively, were able to create systems of patronage and favour for others within the abusive group. A number of participants suggested that, through organised abuse, their fathers were provided with professional connections and opportunities that would otherwise have been closed to them. For example, May's father rose from humble beginnings to become a senior business executive in a relatively short period of time. May noted that his rapid advancement coincided with his 'association' with a group of wealthy men who subjected her to organised abuse.

> He [Dad] didn't have a lot of education. And he didn't have a lot of money. But somehow, he had all these rich people in his life. And there was this group of people that he used to be associated with. And they are all quite wealthy. I always thought he started associating with them when he started getting wealthy himself, and moving up in the business world.

Anne also described her father's swift promotion from a relatively low-paid and unskilled position into a very senior position in the public service. Cara charted a similar path for her father from impoverished beginnings, to participation in organised abuse, to a managerial position. Isabelle noted a general relationship between her father's sexual exploitation of her and his ability to obtain social and economic advantage.

> He [Dad] always knew prominent people in the community – lawyers, solicitors, doctors, police officers – he could always manage to get out of something, or make excuses for something. He always had people coming to the house – males. Always. Every night there was always people chit-chatting and stuff, and I had to be his ... I don't know, prize possession thing. Like, let's show off the daughter thing, let's put her on display. It was almost like you were a part of this meat market, being checked out for possible ... whatever.

Both Lily and Rhea commented on the affluent and professional status of the men who participated, with their fathers, in organised and ritualistic abuse.

> I think, in a lot of ways, ritual abuse is an upper class crime. It's your solicitors and QCs and surgeons and academics and all those professions.
>
> Lily

> Dad was a partner in a large firm. The people who were members of the cult were all professional people. And some of the names, as I said, I mean, the names are all very well known. Oh, gosh, yes.
>
> Rhea

For these participants, organised abuse was linked directly to their family's socio-economic status and their father's professional standing. In these contexts, children were assets or objects. There was little emotional investment by parents in their relations with their children. Lily described her father as 'incredibly aloof' and her mother as 'cold'. As a child, she felt her most sympathetic attachment figures were her pet and her teddy bear.

> We had a dog, and I have memories – like, a couple of very clear memories of sitting on the back step, talking to the dog, and sitting on the back step, and talking to the teddy bear. They were the two that were going to listen.

Isabelle described her father as a 'mask' for a man whose primary obligations lay outside his family.

> I don't know if I've ever seen him as my father. I have a birth certificate, in that sense. But I'm not sure that I ever put it in that context. I saw him connected to something outside the family, as opposed to … He played the role of being the, you know, figurehead, and I'm sure there were times where there were some nice things that he did just so that you knew he wasn't 100% horrible. But I'm not sure that I even related to him that way. It's kind of, 'I have to do that at home, because that's the game we are playing'.

The subjection of children within these families to organised abuse became linked not only to their father's financial wellbeing but to their physical safety, even their lives. Parental involvement in organised abuse appeared to be a product of interlocking disincentives as well as incentives. Cara describes how her grandfather's fear of the abusive group effectively hollowed out and colonised all relations in her nuclear and extended family, as he sought to ensure the compliance of his wife, children and grandchildren to the demands of organised abuse and thus avoid any 'trouble' for himself.

> Even though Poppy was still a 33rd degree [a senior role within the abusive group], it felt like he was still being controlled from above too. If he didn't do what he was meant to do, it was like he was going to be in trouble. It felt like he was acting from a place of fear. I know that Nanna definitely was. She was totally dominated by Poppy. And it just went down, of course, Dad was dominating Mum and Mum was very scared. So I think it was all about control.

Kate's father became involved in a sexually abusive group whilst overseas on missionary work. He pursued his interest in organised and ritualistic abuse when he returned to Australia although the abusive group became increasingly violent towards him as well as his children. Kate witnessed her father's physical and sexual victimisation in the organised group, and she spoke of her belief, as a child, that he would be killed if she didn't 'go along with this'.

It was almost, though, as if he [Dad] was scared for his life. He was both a victim and a perpetrator. I had the sense that I had to go along with this, or else father would be killed. So I was kind of protecting him.

As the violence escalated, Kate's father found it difficult to extract himself and his family:

We kept moving all the time. Father kept us moving, and I presume now that it was to get away from them. We could be gone at a moment's notice. But it was sort of a love-hate thing with father. He was a weak man, and I guess he loved the money [that he gained from organised abuse], too, although he didn't need it by that time. He was making good money. But I guess he just loved that, you know, they would tie you up, and they'd hurt you, and then they'd assault you, and it'd be on film, and then he'd get paid.

Smart (2007: 45) describes family relationships as 'sticky', suggesting 'it is hard to shake free from them at an emotional level and their existence can continue to influence our practices and not just our thoughts'. Within organised abuse, the 'sticky' quality of family relationships took on over-whelming and life-threatening dimensions, as men viewed them as pro-prietary links that justified their exploitation of wives, children and grandchildren. In participants' accounts, these relationships were enduring and extraordinarily difficult for women, in particular, to extract themselves from. For example, Jo's mother had been subject to organised abuse by her own family as a child. Although she had escaped ongoing abuse by marrying Jo's father, and moving away from her family, the original abusive group threatened the safety of her infant son if she did not permit them regular access to Jo.

The first thing that happened was when I was about three these men appeared during the day at our house, and I had a brother who was about eighteen months at the time. So they came and basically threatened my mother and I, and said that they would kill my brother if we didn't comply and I had to go with them. And my mother, I think, also having been pre-programmed … um … uh, didn't resist and I can remember her standing there kind of shaking, like almost in anger, kind of shaking like this and pointing to me [mock voice] 'Get in the car', so I basically had to go with them.

Frankel and O'Hearn (1996) used the social dynamics of the Jewish ghettos in the Holocaust as a metaphor for the intra-psychic processes of people subjected to severe abuse, highlighting simultaneous patterns of strategic complicity, victimised coping, and underground resistance in victimised people as well as victimised communities. These patterns emerge in participants' accounts as characteristic of both the intra-psychic processes and familial relations that dominated their home environments, highlighting the constraints that organised abuse imposed upon parents as well as children. In a system of exchange regulated through threats of violence and death, the decision to participate – enthusiastically or otherwise – is neither simple nor free. These participants described their parents' complicity occurring contemporaneously with their compulsive denial of the abuse, and sometimes their frantic efforts to escape.

Nonetheless, parental involvement in organised abuse cannot be reduced to a simple pattern of incentives and disincentives. The significance of sexual abuse in the lives of the families described by participants in this project was not a simple matter of economic gain. As children, participants occupied the lowest rung of a hierarchy of abuse and victimisation that structured their immediate family environment, and children were objects of sexual exchange that regulated relationships between their nuclear family, their extended family and other family friends and contacts. Within these networks of relationships, fathers, grandfathers and other male authority figures used the bodies of children to establish their status *vis-à-vis* one another as well as to gain professional advantage and other forms of prestige. Mauss (2000) argued that systems of reciprocal obligation and exchange give rise to, and organise, mutually affirming relations between men, however he notes that exchange can also be part of brutal and destructive competitions between men in the establishment and maintenance of social hierarchies. This system of exchange described by participants arguably created the context in which groups of men could generate a sense of self and status through practices of sexual abuse. However, once they began to engage in organised abuse (and, for some participants' parents, it appeared they had little choice as they were born into familial organised abuse) they could not disengage without the threat of violence or death. In participants' childhoods, this process was experienced through the depersonalisation and objectification of children that characterised their home lives.

'It's all a bad dream': parental facilitation of abusive incidents

Participants subject to familial organised and ritualistic abuse generally reported an abusive ordeal at least once a week, most often on Friday and/or Saturday nights. Their reports of the transition from the family environment to abusive ordeals followed a common pattern. A number of participants reported their parents providing them with a drink before bed-time, and they would either quickly fall asleep as though sedated, or become aware of changes to their perceptions.

I would get this horrible drink before I went to bed. It must have had something in it. And then we'd be in the car and I'd be taken out somewhere, I'd be semi-conscious type of thing.

May

We were given juices and milk drinks before going to bed, and waking up an hour or two later. And then we'd be taken off later.

Cara

My mum would say, 'Kiddies, I've made you all a hot chocolate.' For my brothers and sisters, she would use any old cup ... but they would always bring out a particular cup and make sure they gave it to me. And they'd say to me, 'This is your special cup.' And sometimes they'd put cinnamon on the top. I don't know if the cinnamon was about disguising the taste, or if it was meant to be a trigger or something. But it was primary school, and that would happen, and then I'd get all the symptoms – I realise now – of being drugged.

Sky

Anne reports a similar pattern, in which she was lying in bed as a child, and she would begin to see 'black and yellow swirls' behind her closed eyes. This was the inevitable precursor to a 'nightmare' of organised and ritualistic abuse. Her parents had assured her that these experiences were just 'bad dreams', and she believed them as a child. It was very common for participants to report being told by their parents that a recollection of abuse was a 'bad dream'.

If it had been a really bad night [of organised abuse], I would always be told the next day that it was nightmares. That it wasn't real.

Lauren

I'd be put in my bed, and sometimes I'd open my eyes and see these men in robes in my room, and I'd close my eyes and I'd try to wake myself up – because I'd been told they were a dream – I'd open my eyes, and they were gone, and I'd scream for my mum. And she'd come in and say, 'It's all a dream, it's all a dream.'

Sky

And my father would even say, if I questioned something, 'No, that was just a dream. That was your imagination and it wasn't real.' So you could never piece anything together.

Isabelle

Participants maintained differing levels of awareness of the physical transition – that is, the travelling – from their family home to instances of organised abuse.

Although they sometimes 'woke up' from sedation in the car, there were incidents in which they woke up at an abusive ordeal. For Isabelle, home life seemed to cease when she went to bed, giving experiences of organised abuse a dream-like and unreal quality.

> There were a lot of times in life where you'd be doing your normal daily school activities and stuff and you'd go to bed asleep, and all of a sudden you'd wake up in the car. Going on these long drives into the bush and things would happen where you couldn't figure out, 'Was I dreaming? Did I have a nightmare? Was it real? Am I crazy?'

Most participants who experienced familial organised abuse indicated that, during childhood, they were not always aware of their experiences of abuse; that is to say, in the periods of time between abusive incidents, they did not necessarily recall that abuse had occurred. They were not entirely unaware of the abuse and yet their capacity to recall it was intermittent. Freyd (1996) argues persuasively that such forms of forgetting are a logical response for children abused by a parent or caregiver, since forgetting the abuse enables the child to maintain their relationship with the person(s) upon whom they are dependent for their basic needs. However, for these participants, abusive parents appeared to reinforce the amnestic process by assuring the child that the abuse was a bad dream. In Lily's case, she was instructed not to remember her abuse. In this excerpt, Lily describes her father's use of a strategy of 'directed forgetting' in the immediate aftermath of an abusive ordeal.

> We are coming home, and my father saying, 'You know that I love you. It didn't happen. You don't remember. You know that I love you. It didn't happen. You don't remember.' And it's like ... um, and it still just completely fogs my head.

This strategy of directed forgetting may well be an effective one. Cognitive research has found that people are less likely to remember information that they have been told to forget (Sahakyan and Kelley 2002). Sivers, Schooler and Freyd (2002) have identified that the encoding of memory by children may be inhibited by a lack of discussion and validation for the event, and the threats or denial of perpetrators. In this study, it seemed that abusive parents placed great faith in the child's capacity to forget traumatic events. Anne's father was able to sexually and ritually abuse Anne's children because she had not, at that time, recalled his abuse of her. In interview, she recalls a telling slip-of-the-tongue.

> Before I knew what Dad was up to, at a conscious level, he said something that has stayed with me. He was talking about something innocuous, like, he said, 'Do you remember when you were little we used to say this

little rhyme?' It was something about Mickey Mouse. And we'd have to answer, making a squeaking noise like a mouse. It was in regards to that. And he said, 'You don't remember that? We did it all the time?' And he made a little laugh, and he said, 'For some reason, when they grow up, kids don't remember.' And then he caught himself, and it was as if, 'Oh, I've just said something I shouldn't have.' And that's precisely how he got away with abusing my children.

The mind-bending and incomprehensible nature of the abusive ordeal was often taken advantage of by fathers and abusive adults, who encouraged victimised children to forget what had happened to them. Nonetheless, adults frequently utilised processes of amnesia and dissociation to compartmentalise their own involvement in organised abuse. Levi (1986: 24) notes 'A person who has been wounded tends to block out the memory so as not to renew the pain; the person who has inflicted the wound pushes the memory deep down, to be rid of it, to alleviate the feeling of guilt.' Lily, whose father's soothing mantra after organised abuse was 'you don't remember', would repeat similar words to himself just prior to his death.

A friend of mine was a priest and he decided that he wanted to go and visit my dad. [...] And my friend just said who he was, and that he was a friend of mine. And Dad just sat there, saying, 'I don't want to know. I don't want to remember. I just want to forget. I don't want to remember. I don't want to know.' And my friend said it was the most heartbreaking thing. And so my friend left.

Conclusion

The violence unfolding around and within families described in this chapter was of such magnitude that it prompted last-ditch psychological defence mechanisms, such as denial and dissociation, in parents as well as their children, in abusive men as well as their victims. Family life was structured according to a system of obligation in which parents provided their children for abuse to other family members and family contacts, who in exchange provided access to other children as well as financial and professional advantage. This created a strong inducement for some men to enter into organised abuse but it was a system of obligation enforced by blackmail and threats that locked members of abusive groups into ongoing compliance. Participants described how their parents, usually their fathers, could sacrifice the wellbeing of their children in order to meet these obligations, thus maximising access to the benefits of organised abuse, whilst minimising the risk of serious harm to themselves. This created a family environment fraught with danger in which any form of power or authority represented a means to ameliorate the threat of violence. A number of participants described how their mothers became allied with the abusive group, or acquiesced to the abuse of her children, out of fear of the potential repercussions of resistance or disobedience.

Given the prohibitions against and consequences of breaking the silence, children and women were forced to accept and cope with organised abuse as a condition of their lives. Treated as 'objects' by the very people designated as their caregivers, participants described creating spaces within themselves through which they could craft alternative identities and self-histories, which enabled them to maintain their attachment with abusive caregivers whilst dissociating overwhelming emotions and memories. For participants, simply maintaining a memory of their abuse, however dissociated, was an act of rebellion in an environment with so many directives against remembering or disclosing. Through the gender regime controlled and maintained by their fathers (and/or other abusive relatives), participants' familial environments were organised in such a way as to inhibit the formation of alliances with their mothers or other potentially protective individuals. They described homes in which they were on their own, unable to trust their parents or siblings, from the youngest age. The very space that has been idealised within liberal democracies as the locus of paternal love, care and protection – that is, the family home, which must be veiled from state oversight in an act of respect for the sanctity of the relations therein – thus becomes the space through which serious and life-threatening crimes against children can be coordinated and camouflaged.

The sadism evident in these accounts will be examined in more detail in the next chapter, which draws on life histories of network and institutional abuse to map out the relationship between control, violence and pleasure in organised abuse. In circumstances of familial organised abuse, the child is constituted as an 'object' of sexual exchange through an ongoing process of abuse and neglect by a parent(s). Chapter 8 will examine the functional and symbolic dimensions of this process.

Sadistic abuse

Control, violence and pleasure in organised abuse

Psychoanalysts have long argued that fantasies of control and domination are integral to psychic life. Feminist theorists have identified the gendered dimensions to these fantasies, suggesting that common childrearing and socialisation practices lead to rigid psychic formations in boys and men that predispose them to differentiate themselves from girls and women in aversive ways (Benjamin 1990, Chodorow 1978, Dinnerstein 1978). This literature suggests that archaic fantasies of control and domination are experienced by both sexes, however through processes of socialisation and sexualisation these fantasies become intertwined in the efforts of boys and men to establish a sense of masculine selfhood by distancing themselves from feminised 'Others'. These efforts can become manifest in social institutions and cultural patterns, however they can also be manipulated by social agencies in ways that give rise to 'highly irrational and affectively charged social processes' (Bohleber 2010: 161–2). This is particularly the case in group environments, which can involve the delegation of individual authority in ways that enable the expression of aggressive and violent urges.

This chapter will examine the ways in which organised abuse creates a symbolic matrix in which fantasies of control and domination can materialise and thrive, giving rise to sadistic abuses that seek to reduce victims to compliant and dehumanised objects. Sadism is a defining characteristic of many victim's experiences of organised abuse, to the point where some commentators have dubbed organised abuse 'sadistic abuse' or 'organised sadistic abuse' (Goodwin 1994b). This chapter argues that, in organised abuse, sadism is a collective performance of eroticised violence that takes the child quite literally as its object, since the child's status as agent is effaced and her subjectivity is denied. Such processes were central themes in the accounts of familial organised abuse discussed in the last chapter but they featured somewhat differently in the histories of those participants whose abuse was predominantly or exclusively extra-familial, and it is these histories that will be the focus of this chapter. For participants subject to network or institutional abuse, the work of ensuring that they remained silent, obedient and compliant during organised abuse was undertaken by abusers from outside the family.

This involved a process of sadistic abuse to prepare the child for entry into a sexually abusive economy, in which the status of the child was primarily that of an object exchanged between perpetrators in order to generate status and prestige within cultures of violence.

As the discussions of institutional and network abuse in this chapter will show, these cultures emerged as extreme configurations of the masculine hierarchies operating in a range of licit and illicit contexts, ranging from schools and churches to illicit brothels and drug-trafficking networks. The sadism described in this chapter eludes explanation in terms of either profit or pleasure. Instead, organised sexual violence emerges as a kind of 'participatory theatre' (Franklin 2004) within which men establish their collective claim to a masterful and dominant subject position by performing the reduction of the victim to a passive, compliant object. In this manner, sadistic abuse is a powerful method through which profoundly unequal power relations can be erocitised, intensified and imposed within a group culture of sexual violence.

Grooming and processes of control

The preparation of a child for sexual abuse has been called 'grooming' in the literature on child abuse, which has emphasised how perpetrators can use inducements and emotional manipulation to coerce a child into sexual abuse. However, this section argues that so-called 'grooming' behaviour has symbolic as well as practical dimensions, and can be more accurately identified as a process of objectification through which a perpetrator can seek to ensure that the child's behaviour during abuse affirms a view of her as an object: compliant, obedient and without a will that contradicts his own. This can be achieved through promises and entreaties, however the sadism described by research participants suggests that processes of objectification can include more forceful strategies such as threats, violence and drugging. The reduction of the child to object is particularly important in organised abuse since the child is then to be incorporated into larger systems of sexual abuse in which the child's silence and compliance is paramount. The availability of the pliant child 'object' serves as the precondition for the embodiment of a perpetrating subjectivity and the associated fantasies of domination and control that bind abusive groups together.

For extra-familial abusers, selecting and manipulating a particularly vulnerable child was a key strategy for ensuring that abuse and exploitation would go undetected by others. Perpetrators often capitalised upon crisis points in the child's life to initiate sexual and organised abuse. This is a common tactic amongst sexual abusers generally, who specifically target children with family problems and/or children who lacked confidence and have low self-esteem (Elliott et al. 1995). In this study, Jane described how she was targeted by a neighbourhood priest for organised abuse after her mother was hospitalised for major depression. Helena and Seb also described being subject to organised abuse at school once their teacher became aware there was a serious illness in their family:

> She [Sister Beryl] knew that my mother had a heart attack, she knew that my mother was sick – and it took me a very long time, even as an adult, when I found out what had happened to me, to tell Mum – I only told my parents a year and a half ago. Because I was still so frightened that my mother would die. Because she [the Sister] told me that my mother would die if I ever told anybody.
>
> Helena

> At the time, when this started, my father was in hospital. He spent six months, I think, in hospital. A very long stay, anyway. So, yeah, the family was very vulnerable, I was very vulnerable. And it was open season.
>
> Seb

Seb was targeted for sexual abuse by a teacher, Father Grenham, who taught at Seb's school and slowly ingratiated himself with Seb's family. According to Seb, Grenham initially acted like 'a big kid' or an 'older brother', buying him presents and cigarettes whilst sexually abusing him under the guise of 'tutoring'.

> Somewhere along the line, he started buying me plastic models, first of aeroplanes, then military aircrafts and ships, military ships. He was mad keen on military stuff. Um. They were OK, but they didn't fascinate me. After a while, he realised I was really interested in cars, so he used to by me these – at the time, very expensive and elaborative – plastic, stick-together model cars.

In the experience of other participants, the onset of organised abuse was also marked by small gifts and compliments from perpetrators. Renee, whose history of organised abuse was also discussed in Chapter 6, described how the local proprietors of a photography studio lured her and other children to participate in the production of child abuse images with compliments and sweets.

> So they basically befriended us and started saying things like, 'How pretty you are!' and that they took photos of pretty children and, y'know, like, you are this chosen, special one.
>
> It sort of went from talking outside, from opening the studio doors up, and there were photos of children on the walls ... And that's how it started, with, just, 'take pretty pictures'.
>
> And, look, I can't remember the exact step from being in the studio to, one day, lying on this mattress with another kid just in our underwear on, and simulating sex. But we had been shown, by Frank and Amy, and we were being filmed.

... It was always – we were always told it was love. Our games after school were called S and L, which was 'sex and love'.

These attempts to establish a rapport with victimised children through friendly and reassuring behaviour conforms with other research on abusive 'grooming' in sexual and organised abuse (Burgess and Lindeqvist Clark 1984, Elliott et al. 1995, McAlinden 2006). Evident throughout Renee's experience of organised abuse were the efforts of perpetrators to appeal to, and manipulate, her childish sensibilities, but over time, the 'games', lollies and ice creams began to blur into increasingly serious and disorientating abuse. She described abuse by men dressing up as television characters such as 'Fat Cat' and a skunk from a popular children's cartoon:

And there was one guy, 'Fat Cat', there was actually dress-ups, and he used to dress up like Fat Cat. There was dressing up, there was a skunk, um, it all sounds crazy ... And this skunk used to omit an odour, and things became smoky ... And, like, a game, but there were lots of older men there. And it was almost like a, like a pick the child thing ... Because it was always, it was 'a smartie' they called it, and they had a smiley face on it. Saying, you know, 'Have a lolly, pick your smarties'. And always, we were always waking up, coming out of a sleep, hair stroked, 'It's alright, it's just a terrible dream'.

Participants suggested that, as children, they became aware fairly quickly of the seriousness of their situation once organised abuse had begun. The initial niceties and compliments typically associated with 'grooming' dropped away quickly and victims were confronted with the enormity of their abuse and their powerlessness to defend themselves, a point that was often reinforced and emphasised by the perpetrators themselves. However, costumes, uniforms and other staged performances remained an important feature in the control of children in organised abuse even where the pretence of 'fun' and 'games' had been left behind.

Shortly after telling another victimised child that she was thinking of disclosing her abuse to another adult, Renee was driven by her stepfather to see someone she was told was a counsellor. This 'counsellor' asked her questions about her abuse, who she had told about it and the extent of her disclosures. Once he had ascertained that Renee had not disclosed her abuse to an outside party, the counsellor suddenly 'turned' and began threatening her with violence if she spoke about her abuse to the authorities.

It must have been pretend, a psychologist or something like that [cries] getting all this information out of me. Right, even though – it was like, 'OK, she's spoken up, how much does she know?' And then came all the mental games, which were worse than anything. The person who played the counsellor role, being oh, so nice, and all 'You poor thing, what happened to you' and then just turning on me. And [I was] being threatened with violence. All these mind games because I spoke up.

Following the ordeal with the 'psychologist', Renee received a visit from a man and woman in police uniform:

We were latch-key kids, and I came home from school one day, and the police knocked on my door. And there was a man and a lady. And I can't remember word for word but it was basically, 'We've been told to come and see you because you've been telling stories.' Now. I truly don't ... believe they were real police. They may have been, I don't know, but they took me for a walk up the street and back home and that was *it*.

In reflecting on the role of uniforms in ten cases of ritualistic abuse, psychologist Hudson (1991: 15–16) states: 'It is obvious that the costumed perpetrators tried to destroy the child's trust in law enforcement and in the medical community', resulting in 'noncooperation during investigation or trial'. In Renee's account, costumes and uniforms were part of a larger strategy to undermine her capacity to distinguish between her abusers and potentially helpful authority figures. Through drugs, 'games' and costumes the perpetrators sought to dissolve the boundaries between reality and deception so that Renee's fear of torture and punishment became all-pervasive, and every adult loomed large in her world as a potential abuser.

Perpetrators used a range of strategies to inhibit disclosure and ensure the compliance of children in organised abuse, including blackmail. Neil described, at the age of eight, being abused by a neighbour who had lured him into his home, promising to give Neil pocket money if he undertook some household chores. However, he instead took indecent photos of Neil and violently sexually assaulted him.

And then he became really really apologetic. You know, 'I'm sorry, mate, I shouldn't have done that, I don't know why' ... Anyway, he, um, you know, 'be a good boy and I'll give you a whole dollar. And please don't tell anybody'... And he said, 'Come with me, I'll get you some money now.' Anyway, when he looked in his wallet, he showed me that he didn't have any small notes there. And he said, 'Come back here tomorrow, and I'll give you two dollars. I promise I won't do anything to you. And I'm really sorry for what I did.'

At the age of eight, these promises made sense to Neil. His mother had also oscillated between fits of rage and burst of affection, and through a sexually abusive uncle Neil had become accustomed to the intertwining of abuse with apologies and promises of affection. When Neil returned the next day for his money, which he reasoned was rightfully his, the man blackmailed Neil with the photos he had taken of him the previous day.

> He said to me, 'How would you like me to put some of these photos in the school grounds for your friends and teachers to see – they'll see what a little shit you really are.' And he said, 'I can put them in the milk bar window.'
>
> And I didn't know at that stage that he couldn't put them in shopping windows and all of that. And he made the whole thing out that it was my fault, I caused him to do it, all that. And he said to me, 'You've got a choice, boy. You can either come here and do what I tell you, when I tell you, how I tell you. Or I'll send one of these photos every week to your mum and dad, and put them in the school.' And everything. And I believed he would do that ...
>
> And at that stage, I was just trapped, I knew I was. And he took out some photos, he'd obviously followed me home to make sure I'd given him the right address. And he'd taken photos of my two sisters, and my dad. And the housekeeper we had at the time. He would have thought she was my mum. Anyhow, that was that. I mean, I was just completely trapped.

All participants reported that child abuse images were made of them, and the shame and fear associated with the potential distribution of these images to family and friends was a powerful factor in preventing them from disclosing their abuse. Whilst some child sex offenders appear to experience their abuse of children as an expression of love, affection or a 'special bond' between them and their victims (Elliott et al. 1995), the perpetrators described by these participants were brutally instrumental in their manipulation and silencing of their victims. Even once they were assured of the child's compliance, drugs were often used to sedate or render the child unconscious prior to abuse. The clear implication is that the inner world or subjective experience of the child – the child's status as a living subject and agent – was of little or no relevance to perpetrators, who sought to reduce the child to an entirely passive, silent body.

Sadism and internal colonisation

In participants' accounts, perpetrators of organised abuse were willing to acknowledge and engage with the subjectivity of children insofar as compliments, sweets and 'games' could be used to manipulate them into placing themselves at risk of abuse. Once organised abuse was underway, threats, blackmail and reality-distorting techniques were employed to cement the control of the abusers over the child and minimise the risks of disclosure and detection. What is striking in survivors' accounts is that the natural emotional responses of children were of interest to perpetrators only where they could be utilised to subordinate them to abuse. The perpetrators engaged with the child's subjective experience in an effort to inhibit disclosure but otherwise their wellbeing was of no interest to them. Interviewees described groups of perpetrators who were prepared to inflict considerable degrees of harm upon their victims in order to accomplish their aims. Violence and threats of death were common techniques of control and domination:

> Brainwashing stuff, y'know, that 'If you do tell, we'll kill you, and there are people out there that will find you' and the threats, y'know, with knives held at throats and that kind of stuff.
>
> Renee

These threats were often substantiated with torturous practices designed to inflict agony upon the child whilst leaving little if any detectable mark.

> If you want to take a person to death and back again, all you need is a bit of gaffer tape. Y'know. Wrap around their hands, put it over their mouth, two fingers [pinches nose] over the nose, that's as scary as it gets. And afterwards, there isn't a mark on their body. There is nothing to say that anything happened. That's how vulnerable human beings are.
>
> Darren

> They had me stripped off, and they put stakes in the ground and tied me to the stakes ... And he lifted me up around my middle, and pushed away the dirt there, and there was a bull ant's nest beneath me. And I had to lie there, with bull ants crawling all over me. And he said, 'If you don't want to get a mouth full of these things, keep your fucking mouth shut.'
>
> Neil

> ... As a child, in the studio, as part of the punishment, it's like this stretching, like, lying on the floor with your hands and legs outstretched, one person each side, and lift you, stretch you, until you feel like your arms are popping out of your sockets.
>
> Renee

'Mentalisation' is a term that is used in psychotherapy to refer to the phenomenon in which, 'whilst interacting, each person remains attentive to mental states, holding the other person's mind in mind as well as their own' (Allen 2006). In contrast, 'mindblindness' refers to failures of mentalisation in which the inability or unwillingness to acknowledge the subjectivity of others leads to a largely behaviourist style of engagement (Allen 2006: 11). However, Allen (2006: 12) acknowledges that mindblindness can be dynamic in that it is possible to acknowledge some aspects of the subjective experience of others whilst denying or ignoring other aspects, and this balance can shift depending on circumstance. In their reduction of the child to an object, the perpetrators shifted strategically between mentalisation and mindblindness, engaging with the child's subjective experience in order to entrap them in organised abuse before eliciting abject terror and agony in an effort to negate their sense of agency and identity altogether. The victim did not exist for them as an agent or subject but rather as a body in which a range of responses could be stimulated. The mental activity therein was acknowledged by them insofar as it could facilitate their aims, otherwise the subjective experience of the child was ignored or torture and brainwashing could be used in an effort to actively deconstruct the agency of the child and reconstruct it according to the needs of the abusive group. This amounted to a form of internal colonisation, in which the body of the child was harmed and invaded in an attempt to transform and ultimately annihilate any impulse towards self-determination and autonomy.

This phenomenon is illustrated by Colleen who described being subject to organised abuse by grounds staff at the children's institution where she had been taken into care. Colleen's parents were poor immigrants and her father suffered from an acute mental illness that contributed to his violent and erratic behaviour at home. Out of desperation her mother was forced to place Colleen and her siblings in care until she could find more stable living conditions. The day after Colleen was first admitted to the home at the age of seven, an older boy, Hugh, offered to show her around the home, however, he then took her to meet the abusive group.

> Hugh said that he would show me around the home, and then he'd take me to [my brother]. Well, he showed me around the home, but he took me down to the dairy. And I remember there were men at that dairy, and I remember they were very interested in me. And it wasn't long before I was being raped in that dairy.

The men who sexually abused Colleen were a group of labourers led by a violent and sadistic man who was a gardener at the institution. Colleen recalls the manner in which this primary abuser regulated a clandestine network of abused children and abusive staff members. He forced the victimised children to 'police' one another by threatening to harm them all if one of them disclosed their abuse.

> On Saturdays, the man would take the older children that he had under control down to the dairy. He'd make me go around, and tell all the older children, certain children, that they had to go down to the dairy. And then he would take a chicken, break its neck, throw it and shoot it. And then he would say, 'If you tell your parents, or anyone that comes tomorrow' because Sunday was the day where we had visitors, 'you will be the chicken.' And you didn't want to be the chicken. On Sundays, he would hide and watch us. You always knew he was watching.

In Colleen's account, former wards and abusive staff cooperated in the sexual and physical abuse of children in the home within a culture of exploitation, violence and fear. This institutionalised culture of abuse was camouflaged from view during government inspections, as the nuns who ran the orphanage threatened to beat the children if they disclosed any maltreatment or violence. The primary abuser pursued a degree of control over Colleen that can only be described as obsessive. The practice of sexual abuse was not only a strategy of power through which he sought to realise his capacity for control and domination. Rather, sexual abuse was the foundational practice of a fantasy of omnipotent control in which Colleen's body was also the doorway to her mind. She described how, during sexual abuse, he would bite sensitive areas on her body with such force that she recalls 'blacking out' from the pain. His campaign of terrorisation was so extensive that Colleen would follow his punishing injunctions, even in his absence:

> Once he told me, as punishment, that I couldn't drink any water. He told me all the places I couldn't drink water – the tap, the bubbler, the water tanks, the dam, the pool. But he didn't tell me I couldn't drink from the toilet. So I had to go to the toilet to drink water.

Colleen described how she sought to forget the extent of her abuse whenever she could. Over Christmas she would leave the home to stay with relatives, and she described the ways in which she 'blanked out' her abuse during this time in order to be 'healthy and normal'.

> When I went on holidays, I just blanked out what was happening at the home. I saved myself for that time – I would just be healthy and normal and do what normal kids do. When that man was abusing me, I used to go to my bed at night. Do you know what I used to do? I used to cry, and I used to say, 'Me. Me. Me.' Every now and again when I'm self-soothing, I say the same thing. 'Me.' Because I lost my whole self.

The ways in which sadistic abuse performs the reduction of the abused child to a 'thing' or dehumanised object was experienced by Colleen as a total loss of selfhood and identity. The utility of sadistic abuse as a gendered performance may rest upon its capacity to destroy or annihilate the victim's sense of agency and thus reinforces the abuser's sense of dominance and control. Mollon (2001: 216), a psychologist specialising in treating sexually abused people, notes that, in the act of abusing a child:

> a significant part of the motivation of the abuser may be to evoke projectively in the child the unwanted negative images of the self – to make the abused one feel utterly helpless, humiliated, shamed, violated and abject – and to bring about a near annihilation of the true self of the abused.

In this process, a kind of splitting is observable whereby the child is constituted through abuse as a container or holder for despised aspects of the self: vulnerability, powerlessness, helplessness and so forth. Through acts of sadistic abuse, deMause (1990: 4) argued that children are reconstituted by perpetrators into 'a receptacle into which one can project disowned parts of one's psyche, so that one can manipulate and control these feeling in another body without damage to one's self'. By forcing the child to occupy a subordinate subject position defined by intolerable degrees of exposure to abuse and intrusion, the perpetrators appeared to craft a corresponding fantasy of power that bestowed a collective sense of impunity and supremacy. Darren suggests that, for the victimised child, the overwhelmingly intrusive nature of this abuse causes psychological trauma of such magnitude as to render resistance almost impossible, a state that he labelled as 'slavery'.

> Slavery can be as simple as – if you take someone up to what I call a 'crisis mind', if you take someone up to a crisis mind, it's like – When people have a car accident, they hardly ever remember the actual accident. They remember up to it, and then the actual moment, or whatever, is just blanked out – it might even be ten or fifteen minutes beforehand.
>
> And that's the same sort of thing that they utilise when they break you. Because you don't actually remember the trauma. The mistake that most people make is that they don't inflict *enough* trauma, because then people can remember, and come back from it.
>
> These guys, they will go so hard on you that you just never want to go back there. You will block it out of your mind. Y'know, if you have to remember, relive all that, it will just be too much for your sanity. So you stay where you are, trapped.

Critical masculinity theories have typically emphasised the importance of conformity to hegemonic ideals in men's performance of gender. Even typically 'transgressive' acts of criminality or delinquency tend to conform to a script that preserves heterocentric gender norms. However, Darren's interview emphasised the utility of radical transgression as a resource for 'doing gender' (West and Zimmerman 1987) in organised contexts. This is not the 'oppositional masculinity' of disenchfranchised men and boys, as described by Messerschmidt (1993) and Connell (1987). Darren's account suggests that the attraction of child sexual abuse in the context of organised abuse is its illegality and immorality. It is not simply in the commission of these acts that perpetrators find pleasure, but also in orchestrating these acts in order to *get away with it*.

> It's taboos. What you are not allowed to do is the greatest thrill. Y'know, crossing the gender line is one thrill, and crossing the age line is another thrill, and crossing the pain line, and, y'know – what can you do that is

more horrible and nasty and taboo than killing a child? Well, I'll give you an answer. You eat it. So they did that.

They were always looking for the next thing. [...] You see, other people have a sexual lust, but these people, they thirst for pain. They want to degrade and it builds up. Whatever a person can't do this month – after successive steps – they'll do the next month, y'know. And once again, they are just leading them through the paths, the people who have already been there.

In this excerpt, Darren situates the sadistic abuse he experienced within the culture of the sexually abusive group, detailing the ways in which perpetrators overcome one another's inhibitions over time. 'The group gives the rapist protection through loyalty and support, but also puts pressure on the man to imitate his peers and live up to or even exceed their expectations with his actions' (Hague 2007: 57). The objectification of children through the act of sadistic abuse served as a form of patriarchal bonding between men, for whom collective sexual violence served as the crucible for the transformation of individual and collective identity. Sadistic abuse therefore has both intersubjective and collective dimensions, as the psychological changes wrought through sadistic abuse serve as the foundation for a subculture of sexual violence.

Conclusion

Sexual abuse is frequently explained in the psychological literature in terms of the perpetrator's pursuit of sexual pleasure. Indeed, the bodily experience of pleasure in sexual abuse may have a powerful role to play in the symbolic affirmation of the perpetrator's gender identity (Liddle 1993). However in this study, an act of sadistic pleasure was also a strategy of control and vice versa. In this context torture is simultaneously practical and expressive: the measures that the abusive group used to silence and control children were the same behaviours that they revelled in. Through this violence, the emotions, responses and behaviours of children are shaped to correspond with profoundly unequal and violent relations of domination. The self-legitimising quality of sadistic abuse is similar in many regards to political torture, which Scarry (1985) observes crafts a 'spectacle of power' that legitimises abusive regimes and beliefs. 'The physical pain is so incontestably real that it seems to confer its quality of "incontestable reality" on that power that has brought it into being' (Scarry 1985: 28). Similarly, sadistic abuse was a manifestation of ideologies of masculine sexual aggression operant within groups of abusive men, and means whereby violence against children was infused with pleasure and fantasies of absolute domination over others.

In participants' account, abusers appeared to find a particular pleasure in inhibiting or preventing the child from exercising any agency to shut out the persistent efforts of the abusers to invade both physically and mentally.

Participants described being continually, and it seems quite deliberately, exposed to overwhelming and intolerable intrusions from which they were prohibited from defending themselves against: any show of resistance was simply met by even greater excesses of psychological invasion. The child is forced to accommodate and absorb the excessive force produced by masculine fantasies of omnipotence and control. The harm that is caused by this intrusion goes largely unrecognised by perpetrators who engage their victims with strategic forms of objectification and 'mindblindness', or else the pain that they incite is then woven back into a fantasy of power and control.

These fantasies could at times take on a metaphysical or pseudo-religious significance, giving rise to ritualistic practices and occult beliefs. Neil's account demonstrates the overlap between sadistic and ritualistic abuse. Whilst most of the perpetrators who harmed him were engaged in organised and sadistic abuse, there was a subset of abusers who orchestrated ritualistic ordeals that Neil stated were quite distinct from the other abuses he had suffered.

> They used to get really, really – revved up [during ritualistic abuse]. I can't think of the right word, but they used to get to such a state where they were frantic ... It was totally different to ordinary group days.

The escalation of sadistic abuse to ritualistic abuse will be discovered in more detail in the following chapter. It will emphasise in particular the ways in which ritualistic abuse represents an intensification of the efforts of perpetrators to symbolically distance themselves from their victims, who are constituted as defiled or dehumanised 'objects'. This intensification can at times give rise to calculated acts of life-threatening aggression which will be examined in the Chapter 10.

Chapter 9

Ritual and torture in organised abuse

In the 'psy' professions, the ritualistic practices of abusive groups have been a cause for alarm and uncertainty for over 100 years. Confronted with a client who described recollections of ritualistic abuse, including bloodletting and genital cutting, Freud stated in a letter to a friend: 'I dream, therefore, of a primeval devil religion whose rites are carried on secretly, and I understand the harsh therapy of the witches' judges' (quoted in Masson 1985: 227). Masson (1984: 105) states: 'Freud is implying here that the Sabbats were real events (part of a ritualized religion in which sexual perversions were acted out). He seems to be saying: The torture and the murder of witches are understandable, for the judges were attempting to curtail a heinous cult.' However this chapter will argue that, in the context of organised abuse, ritualistic abuse is not a form of perverse cultic activity but rather it is part of a range of legitimising practices whereby abusive groups express, intensify and justify the sexualised subordination of women and children.

The connection between sexual violence, irreligiosity and masculinity was described in detail in Chapter 3, and this chapter will expand on this linkage by examining contemporary accounts of ritual abuse. In the context of organised abuse, sadism is a mode through which children are dehumanised and objectified, and through the exchange of these 'objects' abusers experience and affirm one another as masterful subjects. However, ritualistic abuse serves as a way of drawing clearer boundaries between 'master' and 'slave'. Benjamin (1990) suggests that a paradoxical dynamic is at work for the 'master' who constitutes himself as dominant through his dehumanisation of the 'slave'. In this process, he brings himself into close proximity with a person that he views and treats as subordinate and contaminated, which threatens the sense of superiority he has established through his perpetration. This chapter argues that ritualistic abuse serves to evade the threat of pollution through symbolic performances that seek to affix, for the perpetrator and the victim, the distance between the two. In doing so, perpetrators establish a fraternal solidarity based on a symbolic relation between masculinity and femininity, and power and powerlessness, expressed through the extremes of dehumanisation and degradation. In such an environment, victims are at risk of severe and life-threatening abuse.

A smaller subset of participants also reported a range of 'mind control' experiences, in which they were tortured by abusive groups with the apparent intention of inculcating a dissociative and amnestic reflex in the child. This chapter will explore the ways in which abusive groups adopted scientific *as well as* religious ideologies to legitimise their abuses and to mystify the relations of gender, age and power that formed the basis of their power and control. In subcultural environments structured around narcissistic fantasies of omnipotence, sexual violence can take on florid and bizarre forms that seem to evade comprehension. This chapter suggests that the seemingly bizarre content of the ideologies espoused by ritually abusive groups can be understood by relating them to the contexts and practicalities of child sexual exploitation, and the efforts of perpetrators to realise and embody impossible ideals of control and domination.

Ritualistic abuse and deviant scripturalism

Those participants subject to ritualistic abuse reported that their abuse included references to a range of religious mythologies, particularly Christianity, Satanism and occultism. Kent (1993a, 1993b) described the misuse of ritualistic practices within organised abuse as 'deviant scripturalism', noting that abusive groups draw from a range of ritualistic traditions in the course of harming children. Participants' accounts of organised abuse were replete with examples of 'deviant scripturalism' in which abusive groups appeared to adopt and parody many of the traditions of the Christian churches. Allegations of 'satanic' abuse have been particularly controversial but some participants pointed to an indistinct boundary between 'Satanism' and a perversion of Christianity.

> I think what they did centred around Christian, I can't say ideals, can I, but Christian symbols and worship. You know, I'm sure it wasn't Satanistic stuff, so I think it was some kind of, abomination, perhaps, of Christianity.
>
> Felicity

> I wonder whether the inverted Christian stuff is just … if you have an extreme Christian background, and you want to have sex, and you are raised not to have a lot of empathy for women and children – maybe that's how you justify it to yourself, that's how you form your sexuality, that's how you justify it to the kids. And then you come to believe it? I don't know.
>
> Sky

Other participants were unequivocal about the Satanic or occult ideology that informed their abuse, however these ideologies often had mainstream

origins, since abusive groups often emerged from within ostensibly benevolent religious and fraternal organisations. There was not a consensus between
participants in this study regarding the motivations of their abusers in engaging in ritualistic abuse: some argued that their abusers were following a perverse religious creed, but others suggested that a significant degree of cynicism
and manipulation underlay their abuser's incorporation of ritual and iconography into abuse. These two positions are not mutually exclusive. Bourdieu
(1977) has observed that social agents often legitimise their conduct through
mytho-poetic logic that they subsequently become 'enchanted' by; that is to
say, an individual or group may believe in the ideologies that they use to
rationalise their conduct. The emotional and socio-practical dimensions of
ideology are therefore important in understanding its descriptive content.
Ideological statements about the supremacy of Satan, for example, were
common in the experience of participants, but these claims were not simply
enunciations of religious conviction. They were linked to the perpetrator's
sense of entitlement to abuse others, their efforts to terrify children into obedience, and their attempts to outdo one another in performances of sadism
and violence. Polly argued that, in her experience of ritual abuse, references to
Satan featured mainly as a tool for controlling young children through fear:

> I think Satan gets brought in because he's very handy for terrifying small
> children. If I was brought up in a Hindu country, they wouldn't use Satan,
> they'd use whatever their religious bad guy is.

In contrast, May suggested that her abusers had some conviction in the 'quasi-
religious' gnosticism that they practised. However, she suggested that their
belief was functional since it operated to engender a sense of superiority and
to legitimise the abuses that they engaged in:

> It seemed a very elitist type of gnosticism. Stuff like 'We are God, the
> masters of the universe, so we are entitled to do whatever we wish. We
> need to overcome our petty moral human standards which the world has
> imposed on us.'

May emphasized the practical dimension to the ritualisation of her abuse,
which she felt had enabled her abusers to engage in extreme forms of abuse
that they might otherwise have felt inhibited to.

> I have often wondered why they did that [the rituals] as they didn't actu-
> ally seem particularly religious at all. When I think about, I see that,
> psychologically, the ritualisation made people feel like they didn't have
> to stay in their little moral boundaries – they could go across them,
> become capable of doing anything. Become detached from their own
> personalities.

Participants' accounts of ritualistic abuse suggested that ideology and ritual practice were interlinked in ways that legitimised their exploitation to their abusers. Ritualistic abuse can be understood as a form of praxis whereby the discourses of supremacy and entitlement espoused by the abusive group was acted out and experienced at a group level. A number of participants described the ways in which ritualistic ordeals were orchestrated to assist men in overcoming their hesitation and to initiate them into the abusive fraternity of the organised group. Sky said:

> When new people came, there was an induction process. And often the men would be quite unsure. They would be hesitant. Sometimes they would be put in groups together, like, three of them, and they would all have to 'perform' together. There would be themes, someone would say, 'Alright, everyone today is doing this particular act to this kid'.
>
> And then they would get up the front, and heaps of other people would do it, and they wouldn't. They'd freeze a bit. And my dad would come over, and be like 'OK, this is what you do, this and that and that.' And everyone is watching, of course. Not necessarily directly at them, it wasn't necessarily a direct pressure, but I can understand that they would be feeling it. It was definitely, it's like – you start a new job, and here's the policies and procedures, and you've got to know it.

Ritualistic abuse is a behaviour that is often explained as a technique for inducing dissociative and traumatic symptomology that inhibits disclosure and increases the control of perpetrators over victims. However, it seems that the role of ritual abuse in cultures of sexual abuse is more complex than this. Sky's account emphasises the transformative qualities of ritual abuse for perpetrators as well as victims. He describes a scenario in which children feature as little more than passive objects to be acted upon by men within an abusive pedagogical process, as 'new' abusers are taught the rules of appropriate abusive conduct and, through open displays of sexual violence, establish their status in the eyes of other men. Whilst these ritual performances incorporated florid occult mythologies and symbols they served an important practical function that has been noted in the anthropological literature on ritual practice: affirming the hierarchy of the group, encouraging a sense of loyalty and belonging, and ushering disparate individuals into a shared worldview.

In participants' accounts of ritualistic abuse, ritually abusive groups overlapped with cultural institutions of masculine hegemony, such as Christian churches or Masonic groups, from whom they drew on symbols, iconography and rituals that were incorporated into child sexual abuse. Ritualistic abuse is clearly at odds with the ethical principles of such mainstream institutions as Christianity and Freemasonry. However, in this study ritualistic abuse shared a *practical* and *experiential* logic with the gender regime of religious or fraternal groups. For instance, Kate was raised within a strict evangelical Christian sect.

Several local men of the sect, including her father, participated in a group that sexually abused children in satanic rituals. In Kate's childhood, her father's 'dual practice' of fundamentalist Christianity and abusive Satanism was fraught with contradictions.

> It [Satanism] would have been something consciously abhorrent to all of us. We consciously were all – certainly, Mother was – talking about the goodness of God, and trusting him, and everything we stood for was against that. We were against anything of the occult, or the bad. Mum broke apart an LP of a singer who was maybe from some New Age group, because we thought, 'Oh, that's maybe demonistic'. In the belief, things could be demonistic, and they had to be wiped out, which was rather ironic. There was … ambiguities everywhere.

At a superficial level, the evangelical sect and the abusive group appear irreconcilable in theological terms, although both groups maintained a belief in Satan as an active and influential force in daily life. At the level of practice, however, both groups shared a power structure in which male authority was supreme and unquestioned. Sexual abuse was endemic within the sect, and the sect's professed ignorance of sexual matters enabled the ongoing violence of male sect members against women and children. Kate notes:

> If you did get some men who were abusive in there [the sect] – like rocks under the water – they could have one hell of a time. A lot of people have sexually abused me, in my life. The pattern started early. And of all those people, probably forty per cent were of the original religious group, although the beliefs were against abusing children. Nevertheless, it happened within them, and some from the leadership.

In the context of ritualistic abuse, Kate described torturous and gruelling ordeals of sexual violence that mirrored, in many respects, the power differentials that were perpetuated in her day-to-day life in the evangelical sect. The sect was dominated by male 'elders' who, whilst sometimes physically and sexually abusive, were considered above reproach since it was their shared responsibility to administer justice within their communities. Without a male witness to vouch for them, the value of women's and children's testimony was negligible, which reflected their marginal and subordinate status in the community as a whole. Whilst the sect was ideologically opposed to the kinds of beliefs espoused during ritualistic abuse, such abuse revelled in the power differentials between men, women and children that formed the power structure of the sect itself.

On a practical level, the overlap between ritualistic abuse and male-dominated institutions provided a power base that amplified the capacity of abusive men to maintain their control over victimised children and women. Acting collectively, and utilising existing systems within the institutions they controlled, these men could exponentially increase their control over a victimised child to the point where organised abuse was, in Sarah's words, 'present in all aspects' of the child's life. Sarah grew up in a small township, in which a number of sexually abusive men held prominent roles in local organisations, schools and churches.

> It sort of encroached into all aspects of my life, in a very concrete sense. Because of how the group ... you know, basketball was another significant area of my life. And sometimes these things [organised abuse] would occur at school, sometimes at basketball, sometimes in parks close to my home. And so it was just there, even physically, it was present in all aspects.
>
> ... I don't know if it was facilitated in living in the place that I lived – it was a small community anyway. One of the men involved was a key organiser of the local basketball club and things like that. But that's easy to do when everyone in the town either plays basketball or joins Scouts or whatever.
>
> ... One of them was a local priest, one of them was the president of the basketball club who was also the local GP [general practitioner]. Yeah. Let's just say they were influential people, definitely. Everyone knew and respected some of these people.

Participants generally felt that the involvement of their abusers across a number of different institutions meant that they had the capacity to coordinate their abuse of children and to camouflage their activity. As May said, 'these people know how to cover their tracks and have the resources to do so'. Anne connected the power of her abusers to conceal their activities with a socio-cultural environment that invalidates and stigmatises victims of sexual violence.

> They are ahead of the game. I think they were set up and organised a long time ago. I think they are aware of the system and they've been co-existing in it for much longer than the victims. We still live in a culture where it's much better to be an abuser then to be a victim.

From object to abject: dehumanisation in ritualistic abuse

Crossley (2004: 39) notes that 'the value of the ritual' is 'its capacity to "condense" meaning and circumvent verbal negotiation'. In ritual, the exhaustive lists of rules that govern acceptable conduct do not need to be articulated or discussed, because '[t]he ritual brings them to pass' (Crossley 2004: 40). The indisputable finality that is implicit in ritual practice was an important feature of participants' experiences of ritualistic abuse. In participants' accounts of ritualistic abuse, the abusive group integrated sexual assault and taboo substances into ceremonies of degradation that resulted in the victim internalising a profound sense of shame and dehumanisation. For example, Kate describes how vaginal, oral and anal rape were part of a continuum of sexually abusive practices in the abusive group that included bestiality, the mutilation of animals and the forced ingestion of animal faeces, blood and flesh.

> So they would hurt their own children, then they would hurt the others' [children] as well. And they would use vaginal and oral and anal entry. They also forced – they would force – they did it to me – your face onto the genitals of the black dog. And then they tried to make you eat the faeces of the dog. And when they killed the chicken, they tried to get you – they would put it into the bowl, and they'd push your face towards it – and they tried to make you drink it. Which I refused. And when they killed the goat, the flesh was warm and they tried to make you eat it. It was horrible.

Previous chapters have described the strategies that perpetrators use to symbolically reduce the child to the status of a pliant and passive object, who is then provided for abuse to other men as part of a sexually abusive economy of status, pleasure and profit. However, in ritualistic abuse the process of objectification becomes in effect one of 'abjectification', as the subordinate position of the victim is inscribed upon them through increasingly horrifying acts. Kristeva (1982) described the 'the abject' as all that is 'radically excluded' from the symbolic order and the world of social relations, comparable to taboo substances such as corpses, sewage and vomit. Kristeva argues that the construction of meaning and relations are premised upon the extrusion of knowledge of such phenomena from awareness:

> A wound with blood and pus, or the sickly, acrid smell of sweat, of decay, does not *signify* death. In the presence of signified death – a flat encephalograph, for instance – I would understand, react, or accept. No, as in true theatre, without makeup or masks, refuse and corpses *show me* what I permanently thrust aside in order to live. These body fluids, this defilement, this shit are what life withstands, hardly and with difficulty, on the part of death. There, I am at the border of my condition as a living being (Kristeva 1982: 3, emphasis in original).

During ritualistic abuse, the child is forced to take into herself an array of taboo substances and objects, and in doing so, she experiences herself as synonymous with those substances. In this process, all that is extruded from the symbolic order is made synonymous with the selfhood of the child, who becomes, to herself as well as to her abusers, the embodiment of all that must be quarantined from the social order. Anne spoke powerfully and disturbingly of the 'sewage cesspool inside myself'; May had felt she was 'this corrupted, violated, horrible person'; Lily learnt that 'if I loved somebody, they died' because 'I'm poisonous, and if people touch you, if they love you, if you love them, the poison that is within you will kill them'. Through violent degradation and ritualised exposure to taboo substances, the child is assigned to a non-place beyond the hope of comfort or love. She is treated as a vessel and source of contamination, and she comes to share the view of her abusers that she must be extruded from the social compact between persons.

Indeed, it seemed that it was through collective participation in the extrusion of children that abusive groups constructed and affirmed the 'sacred' bonds of their masculine fraternity. The accounts of participants show that abusive groups embody a gender order in which maleness is synonymous with personhood, and this relation could only be maintained through the constant ritualistic cleansing of 'abject' feminising contaminants (that is, children and women) from their idealised body politic. In his account of the portrayal of sexual violence in Western cultural production, Kramer (1997: 259) observed:

> At a visceral level, misogyny expresses itself by identifying femininity with filth. Stray, formless matter, oozing liquids and the stains they leave behind, become both the signs that betray the true character of the feminine and the traces that women accordingly seek to cover or erase. The feminine is that which has to be cleaned up. If necessary, it has to be scoured.

In participants' accounts, this 'cleansing' of the feminine took symbolic and literal forms. Kristeva (1982) suggested that the corpse is the paradigmatic example of the abject: it places us 'at the border of my condition as a living being' (p 3), it is 'death infecting life' (p 4). It is telling that, in this study, a number of participants recalled being forced into prolonged contact with dead bodies. This contact was disturbingly intimate; the child did not simply witness a corpse, but was forced into the subject position of a corpse. For example, Jo recalled an abusive ordeal in which she was placed in an open grave and told she no longer had a soul:

> They also did various rituals, I can remember one where, they had, this one scared the hell out of me, I think they dug up a grave, and put me in it and stuff and started putting dirt on me and said 'Jesus is killing your soul' kind of anti-Christian type things ... just rituals that they did ...

Polly was subject to a similar ordeal by her grandfather, in which she was required to accurately mimic the properties of rigor mortis:

> My grandfather, there was some ceremony where he had to place me in the ground and bury me. And he trained me for it – and I remember, I was quite little, just three or four, and I remember trying to make him proud of me. Trying to do it right. To not struggle, to keep my body limp

but not totally limp, to go through it all according to how I'd be trained. To make him look good.

Polly lived with her mother and sister on her grandparents' property, where they ran a nursing home. When a resident died, her grandmother would force Polly to share a bed with the deceased for a night:

> So if one of the residents died, which happened fairly often, because they were very old and frail – hopefully, they weren't assisted on their way – but one of the things my grandmother would do, is she would come and get me from my bed, and take me into the room where they kept the dead body. There was one particular bedroom in the room where they would place the body until the undertaker came. And she would make me sleep with the dead body, naked, skin on skin. And when the nursing home closed down, that room was given to me as my bedroom. Of all the bedrooms they could have given me, that was the one.

Through these ordeals, abusers disrupted the child's sense of belonging within the social/symbolic order and effected an enduring transformation in the child's sense of self. They crafted an alternative subject position for the child in which she was a non-subject, synonymous with a corpse, an exile from both the social order and the subcultural hierarchy of the abusers. Polly's non-status as a child who was also a living corpse, having undergone both burial and disinternment, was reflected in the treatment she received living under her grandparents' roof. She was treated not only as a defiled object but as a source of defilement. She was not allowed to sit on the furniture within the house. She was frequently denied a bed at night and forced to sleep on the floor, or else collared and chained up outside the house. In her words, she 'wasn't even a little girl' to her family but something else entirely, something non-human and untouchable.

> Even when we were sitting in the lounge at dinner time, watching television, I was not allowed to sit on the furniture. I had to sit on a wooden box. So I had this role in the house, where I wasn't part of the family. And I've never felt like I had a family. The group has become my family. And if I was upset or hurt, as a child, I had no one to turn to for comfort or reassurance. Or anything.

Anne described how the abusive group enacted a range of ordeals that were designed to craft a subject position for her at the symbolic borderline of life and death. She was brought into contact with murder and death and the possibility of her own death was made vividly real to her:

> I also have a memory of being held over an acid bath. The reason why I know it was acid is because they put things in it – bones – so that you knew that there was no way you could survive.

The abusive group frequently terrorised Anne with a black dog and sat her in the midst of a writhing pile of snakes. Anne recalls her father's anger during an incident in which she failed to display any fear of these snakes, possibly due to the effects of the sedatives she was given prior to organised abuse. Anne's son Jimmy, who began disclosing victimisation by Anne's father when he was three years old, also spoke of being terrorised with snakes.

> Jimmy brought it up, and he said it like I should already know – 'Grandpa uses snakes, and he always tried to tell me I was poisoned.' And Jimmy did say to me that he felt sick after some events like this, so maybe Dad does try to make the snakes bite you.

It seems that Anne's father employed non-venomous snakes as part of a performance in which the child's very nature was purportedly transformed into a venomous poison. In this sustained process of abjectification, Anne's parents employed their faeces and urine, and mimed murdering their grandchild in an oven:

> And that night, Jimmy said to me, 'They didn't give me anything to eat or drink. They peed and pooed on me. They scrubbed me in hot water to get the poo off. The shower was too hot. Grandpa put my head in the oven. Made me scared. I got nearly an asthma attack.'

Rationalising ritual abuse: coercing victim consent for their own abuse

Within these traumatic ordeals victims came to experience organised abuse as an inevitable and natural extension of who they were; that is, they internalised their non-status as objects or property who can only achieve value through abuse. However, an ideology that functions solely to distract victims from gross inequality and injustice is unlikely to win their consent for very long, and sexually abusive groups utilised a range of strategies to encourage victims to become invested in the discourses and practices that rationalised their abuse. Sagan (1988: 12) notes the ways in which the Nazis blurred the boundaries between morality and immorality by promoting genocide through the invocation of concepts such as 'purifying, healing, curing, oath, community, the Volk, social usefulness, ideal society, sacrifice, dedication, ideology, idealism and morality'. Similarly, participants described how their experience of dehumanisation in organised abuse was inflected with ideological tropes to rationalise their abuse and torture. For some participants, ritual abuse was presented to them as a form of purification from some undefined 'original sin'. Says Sarah, 'It fitted that I was the one who [was abused] … It was like a comic book. I was the evil that the rest of the world is trying to fight'. Other participants were told that 'sacrificing' themselves to organised abuse was a form of penance that would ultimately redeem them.

> ... I always grew up with this sense of: 'Our body's a sacrifice, and we're just there for their pleasure. And somehow, we're evil, and the only way that we are going to get some form of repentance and get our soul back, because we don't have one, is if we comply and do what is expected of us.'
>
> Isabelle

Some participants were told that that their abuse was a form of 'training' that they required in order to fulfil their 'destiny'. Sky said 'I was brought up to fervently believe that the apocalypse was coming' and hence his abuse was framed as an 'honour' in preparation of the end of time: 'It's an honour to do things for them, it's an honour to die for them, it's the greatest honour to be picked for them. It's my destiny'. Polly referred to the farm where she was often taken for ritual abuse as the 'training ground' in which she was not only abused but subject to tortures that, she was told, would strengthen and prepare her for the future.

Rhea described how as a 'first-born girl' in her family she was told she had a 'privileged position' within the abusive group, and hence she needed to be taken for 'training' which involved rape and torture. Abused children were promised positions of authority within the abusive group such as 'high priestess' and 'occult queen' for girls and 'assassin' or 'warlock' for boys. From Lily's point of view, such promises are so ubiquitous in the testimony of survivors of ritual abuse that she wondered if it was just another strategy of control:

> And I was always told that I was in training to be a high priestess. But I also know of a few other ritual abuse survivors who say the same thing, so I'm never sure if that's a line that is used regularly, and it's just a lie.

In ritualistic abuse, girls and women were constituted as degraded objects before being offered a specifically crafted subject position as 'priestess', 'queen' and so forth, the sole preparation for which was rape and torture. The socialisation of boy children within the abusive group took a somewhat different route. Abusive groups often became disinterested in victimising boys once they reached adolescence, but for those boys who continued to be victimised they were often socialised into perpetration rather than forced to acquiesce to continuing victimisation. Sarson and MacDonald (2008: 429) comment that, in their interviews with survivors of ritualistic abuse, '[s]ocialized sexual victimization and aggression was frequently spoken of as being central to the enforcement of gender-based roles'. Whilst 'perpetrators tell a little girl she needs to be taught "How to be a woman", justifying her rape', a boy 'is socialised to be an aggressor; forced into sexual acts with another child, he is taught "how to be a man"'. Within abusive groups, it seems that abusive men conceptualised their 'true' nature in terms of an unmitigated right – indeed, a duty – to sexually abuse children and women. In the same context, women and children are expected to find expression of their 'true' nature through subservience to, and complicity with, men.

Nonetheless, the gender order that emerges from participants' accounts of organised abuse is not a totalistic or inflexible one. Participants described perpetrator groups that were diverse in structure, and it is clear that some women could, and did, achieve a sense of power and status in the context of sexual exploitation. In organised abuse, women could engage in a variety of strategies in order to ameliorate their subordinate status. However, their opportunities to exercise power within the conditions of organised abuse appear to have been limited to facilitating their own abuse or participating in the abuse of others. All these actions ultimately reaffirm representations of women and children as maleficent and deserving of abuse and harm. For example, Rhea described how, whilst women's role in the abusive group was largely restricted to being 'victims', they took an active role in 'managing' children throughout abusive ordeals. They could then leverage the information they gathered in this role in an attempt to curry favour with abusive men:

> Then there's also the times when there are groups of kids who are waiting, um, for rituals to be performed. It's often women who are looking after, um, and it's women who will trick, it's women who will get close and make you start to trust them, and then report that you've actually trusted, or acted in some kind of faith, and so then there's the brutality or the murder that comes as a result of that.

Both Sky's parents were actively involved in his organised and ritualistic abuse, much of which took place in the family lounge room. He describes his parents' relationship as close and affectionate, and he describes his mother as 'the boss' at home, as well as in organised contexts.

> I still get really confused about my mum's role in this. So much of what I've read [about organised abuse] is about the woman being enslaved and captive. I think my sister is in that position. But my mum – I thought, very recently, does she have any symptoms of a battered woman? In terms of being grateful to the perpetrators and so forth? But she didn't have any of that. She's the dominant one in day-to-day life.
>
> But I do remember one event where – I don't know, there were guys on her, and I was next to her, and there were guys on me. But I just wonder, if for her it was an S&M type thing. I don't know.

Sky's memory of this scene in which there were 'guys on her' just as there were 'guys on me' clearly troubles him. It contradicts his perception of his mother as 'dominant' and in control of her life. His example highlights the complexity of ritualistic abuse, and how difficult it can be to neatly assign categories such as 'victim' and 'perpetrator' to individuals whose lives have been 'permeated with abuse and its legitimations' (Scott 2001: 130). Nonetheless, the life histories gathered in this study illustrate the iterative relationship between the gender regimes of abusive households and abusive groups, and the gender order within which these groups and families are embedded. The patterns of violence within ritual abuse overwhelmingly have women and children as their objects, and they are forced to accept and adapt to this violence to the point where 'the most intolerable conditions of existence' are 'perceived as acceptable and even natural' (Bourdieu 2001: 1).

The use of torture to inscribe and trigger obedience

Of the 15 participants who stated that they had been subject to ritualistic abuse, nine described a continuum of pseudo-medicalised abuse in which 'doctors' or other abusers used a variety of techniques, usually incorporating hypnosis and/ or electro-shock, to induce dissociative or hypnotic states. For some participants, this activity appeared to be designed to inculcate or induce a dissociative reflex, possibly with the intention of disrupting the child's capacity to accurately recall or report her abuse. For example, May described her father taking her to a 'doctor' who hypnotised her and taught her to 'float away' in the year prior to the commencement of organised and ritualistic abuse. May said that this 'treatment' only occurred a few times, and ceased once her ritualistic abuse began.

> I used to have these nightmares, when I was a very young child. Of being taken to a doctor, and he would hypnotise me, and tell me to leave my body. And I didn't know what to make of this for a very long time. Not so long ago, I realised that this was part of the abuse. And that's how it all started ... when I was a toddler.

Other participants reported more intensive, prolonged, structured kinds of experiences. Participants described these ordeals in terms such as 'mind-bending' or as a 'mind fuck' in which perpetrators systematically undermined and invalidated the child's sense of reality. Of the nine participants who reported these pseudo-medical experiences, five reported that they believed they were subject to a programme of torture designed to induce DID. They claimed that this programme had been carried out by a particular person, or group of people, within the abusive group who were trained in the inducement of DID. Such descriptions of torture and hypnosis are recurrent themes in disclosures of ritualistic abuse around the world (see Becker et al. 2008). In cases of organised abuse, clinicians have suggested that traumatic and dissociative psychopathology may be deliberately induced by sexually abusive groups in order to inhibit victim disclosure and reduce the likelihood of detection (Sachs and Galton 2008, Epstein et al. 2011, Miller 2012), resulting in what

Chu (2011: 263) has described as 'massive devastation of the self'. In the literature on organised abuse, such ordeals are frequently referred to as 'mind control'.

Unsurprisingly, accounts of 'mind control' have contributed little to the
credibility of narratives of organised abuse as a whole. As Bell et al. (2004)
point out, claims of 'mind control' are common themes in the clinical presen-
tations of people with schizophrenia. Nonetheless, the majority of adults
with histories of ritualistic abuse do not meet the diagnostic criteria for schizophrenia (Ross 1995), and indeed there are a number of differences between
their reports of mind control and those of people with schizophrenia (Lacter
and Lehman 2008). In fact, whilst some observers have dismissed such disclosures as evidence of delusion in cases of ritualistic abuse (Richardson et al.
1991), there are a number of criminal cases in which complainants have
reported mind control and hypnosis in relation to their claims of sexual abuse
and sexual assault. In these cases, 'women were sexually abused while in trance
states that were induced powerfully and quickly caused the women to lapse in
their normal, self-protective behaviours' (Noblitt and Perskin 2000: 82). In
Australia, hypnosis and brainwashing have featured in child sex prosecutions
(Petraitis and O'Connor 1999, Grant 2005). In these cases, child victims
reported amnesia for their sexual exploitation as a result of hypnosis.

Sky described how his organised abuse transitioned from a focus on rituals
and the supernatural into pseudo-medicalised sexual abuse as a teenager.
When he was a young child, he recalled that his abuse predominantly involved
what he called 'the ghosts' – that is, men and women would come to his
house, and they and his parents would dress in robes, and subject him to ritualistic abuse. In his early teens, the emphasis of the abuse began to change.
Rather than wear robes, the abusers began to wear medical outfits, or suits,
and claim to be 'the government' engaging in 'experimentation'. However,
Sky maintains that these were the same people as those who had previously
worn 'robes' and told him they were supernatural 'ghosts'.

> And then there were the 'doctors'. And, again, as a kid I didn't under-
> stand. I guess, when I hit about eight or nine, I remember trying to figure
> out what was going on. But I couldn't understand why I couldn't move, I
> was just paralysed with drugs, and didn't know where I was. But they'd
> all be dressed up in white, I'd be put on this table – I remember them in
> the same marching pattern, the same number of people as the supposed
> 'ghosts'. And then tortured with electricity.

Initially Sky's abusers told him that they were abusing him in preparation for
the coming apocalypse, but later they claimed to be abusing him for the 'government'.

> I was brought up to fervently believe that the apocalypse was coming.
> And a lot of the theme was to do with the end of the world, blah

blah blah. [...] Then, when I hit 13, 'the government' theme appeared in my day-to-day awareness. And my understanding of it, I was just confused out of my head. I was like, 'Why is the government interested in me? Like, seriously, I'm a kid, what do they want?'

By connecting his abuse to the 'government', Sky's abusers crafted the impression that they could locate and harm him if he attempted to escape or evade them. In interview, Sky was still very fearful of the abusive group. Whilst he was uncertain that they were connected to 'the government', he was nonetheless terrified of the potential consequences of resisting or disobeying a direct order from the abusive group, since they claimed that the FBI or some other government agency would track him down if he did not do as he was told. This account raises the possibility that ritualistic abuse and 'mind control' are two sides of the same coin – practices that employ different ideologies (one religious, the other scientific) to mystify the relations of domination in abusive groups and make the abuse appear both inescapable and inevitable.

Polly's account of her 'mind control' illuminates the complex emotional dynamics that survivors of organised abuse may have in believing, and adopting, particular explanations for their organised abuse. In Polly's description of her childhood, she had been 'sold' by her family to a psychiatrist called Christian who then engaged in 'mind control' research upon her. This 'research' involved sadistic sexual abuse, however by accepting that it was 'research' Polly was able to preserve a sense of attachment to Christian in a life that had often been devoid of opportunities to experience love and support:

> When I was sold into that [mind control] program, or given into that program, or whatever it was – there was never any love or care in my family – and any approach that I made to a member of my family was rejected. I was rejected. I was pushed away. And forced to bond with this man. And I did. And he was, you know, compared to everyone else in my life, he was the best of a bad lot.
>
> There was nothing sadistic about him. Mind control was a science. And there were all these distasteful things he had to do as part of his work. But he didn't enjoy them, he didn't get off on them. And so I have this really strong sense with him that these were necessary evils to try and achieve what he was trying to create.

Through the frame of 'mind control', Polly was able to minimise Christian's rape and torture of her as 'distasteful things he had to do as part of his work', and thus maintain her sense of affection for him. Nonetheless, her conceptualisation of Christian as a 'scientist' with no personal investment in his 'work' of rape and torture was frequently disrupted by her own narrative. Despite her repeated insistence that Christian 'wasn't sadistic, he wasn't violent, he wasn't awful', she also described the pleasure he found in watching children fight and struggle:

> I remember him saying to me once, that nothing interests him about broken people. He wants people who still have something intact and will fight him. He wants the challenge. And so I've got lots of memories of him, when I was a kid, because I'm fairly feisty, and I've got some feisty alters, where there would be this active resistance in the middle of a session – and the smile would come on his face and his eyes would twinkle, and this little chuckle, and this genuine enjoyment of this feisty child ... that would present a challenge to him.

Polly's conceptualisation of her sexual abuse as a form of scientific 'research' was contradicted by her admission that Christian appeared to be sexually attracted to children:

> But I think, with Christian, when I look at how he was with adults, he really had a thing for kids. And I'm aware of a lot of grief about losing him, about him losing interest in me as I got older. By the time I was seventeen ... I would still see him – whenever I went home – but the relationship wasn't the same any more.

The pseudo-scientific trappings of 'mind control' may function much like the religious overtones of ritualistic abuse, legitimising the abuse and enjoining the victim to participate in her own exploitation. This practical but symbolic relation may explain why the two forms of abuse frequently co-occur, and why it is frequently unclear where ritualistic abuse ends and 'mind control' begins. Polly's description of Christian's 'mind control' programme includes references to prolonged confinement, sensory deprivation, and torture with snakes, spiders and insects, and possession by 'the beast', all of which are also well-identified features of ritualistic abuse.

> There was a lot of electroshock. Of all sorts of different voltages. Confinement in small, dark places with creepy crawlies. Which is always revolting. I can remember one session that happened, when the two overseas visitors were there, and it was a session about silencing. One guy had a huge insect that he kept putting in my mouth. And I was strapped down with my mouth strapped wide open. With all these references to 'I can see the beast right inside you' and 'My my, you have a big mouth' and all this stuff. And he killed a spider and I had to swallow it. Using a lot of those archetypal things that humans are instinctively terrified of. Spiders, snakes. A lot of that kind of thing. Sensory deprivation, isolation. There were drugs used. And some of the programming just went on and on and on. It was this real, progressive activity, wearing me down. This prolonged torture.

Many of the 'mind control' ordeals described by participants had similar themes to other sadistic and ritualistic ordeals. This observation disrupts the 'scientific' justification of 'mind control' as a functional method of control and instead highlights its similarities with ritualistic abuse and other practices that serve to legitimise organised abuse. Indeed, in the broader social context, just as religion is a domain within which masculine domination is simultaneously sacralised and mystified, so too has scientific authority traditionally justified men's dominance over women and children. It may be that, in abusive groups, religious and pseudo-medical/scientific ideologies serve to inform the abusive practices of the group and thus serve as an ideological framework within which abusive men craft and enhance experiences of domination and superiority.

Conclusion

Understanding the origins of ritual practice, Bourdieu (1977: 114) argues, 'is not a question of decoding the internal logic of a symbolism but of restoring its practical necessity by relating it to the real conditions of its genesis'. In a similar vein, this chapter has sought to contextualise ritual abuse and 'mind control' within the practicalities of child sexual exploitation. Through symbolic practices such as ritualistic abuse and 'mind control', the abusive groups generate a symbolic universe of domination and subordination that has experiential validity for victims as well as perpetrators, grounding the practices of organised abuse within a primordial 'nature'. This 'nature' is the metaphysical pretence that abusers give to their shared interest in inflicting harm on children and women. Within traumatic rituals in which they were forced into contact with death and blood and human waste, participants' views of themselves ultimately came to accord with the view of their abusers. The embodied experience of ritualistic abuse involved such overwhelming trauma that it became the basis for the development of a subordinated and obedient disposition amongst victims that predisposed them to ongoing compliance with sexual exploitation. In turn, it seems that such abuses also transformed the worldview of abusers, enabling them to view victimised children and women as dehumanised and shameful, and thus legitimate objects of hatred and sexual violence.

In the experiences of participants, perpetrators of ritual abuse and 'mind control' adopted florid titles for themselves (eg 'kings', 'warlocks' and so on) and imposed similarly florid labels on victims (eg 'priestess', 'assassin' etc). They generated a complex vocabulary of abuse to the point where the real relations that enabled abuse (eg parent-child) becomes veiled by mythological or 'scientific' roles and symbols. The totality of the abusive system is fragmented by this logic and becomes difficult for the victim to grasp as a whole, let alone communicate effectively and coherently to 'outsiders'. The mundanities of sexual exploitation and abuse are transmuted into a set of self-referential signifiers with little meaning to those who have not been socialised through the cycle of victimisation and perpetration. Through ritualistic practices, organised abuse becomes, in effect, a closed system that is less vulnerable to resistance by victims and inscrutable to 'outsiders'.

When faced with such extreme abuse, it is easy to lose sight of their relation to the 'micro-practices' of power in operation throughout in the more mundane circumstances of victims' lives. Whilst 'mind control' and ritualistic abuse are processes that dehumanise and degrade victims, this degradation is all the more powerful because it intensifies and legitimises the normative structures of power, as discussed in Chapter 6. It is the reproduction and intensification of the gender order within organised abuse, through practices of rape and torture, that lend the relationship between abuser and abused its concrete and inescapable quality. This relationship between the gender order and organised abuse explains why, whilst investigators may experience organised abuse as 'grappling with smoke' (Gallagher 1998), victims experience organised abuse as, in the words of one survivor, an 'almost unbreakable circle' (Carli 1998). It is in the context of this abject captivity that children and women are vulnerable to the extremes of sexual violence, and survivor accounts of murder and mutilation in organised abuse will be discussed in the following and final chapter.

Chapter 10

Sexual murder and reproductive harm

The outer limits of organised sexual abuse

I am always amazed when people are so staggered by the atrocities committed during war. Have you noticed they are always perpetrated by the 'other' side?

Lily

It is not uncommon for survivors of organised abuse, and particularly ritualistic abuse, to describe witnessing crimes so serious that they are better described as atrocities. Card (2002) suggests that atrocities have two defining characteristics: (a) culpable wrongdoing by perpetrators, and (b) foreseeable intolerable harm to victims, whose lives, if they are not ended, are likely to have been forever marked. Whilst the term 'atrocity' is usually reserved for serious violence in political or civil conflicts (see Chapter 3) the two dimensions of Card's definition are often present in the context of early and repetitive child abuse, in which children are repeatedly subject to levels of violence that are likely to have serious and life-long impacts on physical and mental health. Shengold (1979: 556) has described the 'deliberate traumatisation or deprivation' of children by a parent or authority figure as a form of 'soul murder'. In this process, '[t]he victim is robbed of his identity and of the ability to maintain authentic feelings' (p 556). This process is often attended by 'brainwashing', since the child is forced to turn to her abuser for relief of the distress that the abuser has caused, who in turn compounds this distress by insisting that the child's abuse is normal and no harm has taken place. The resulting delusion that the 'bad' adult is in fact 'good' (a point that is often actively reinforced by the perpetrator/s') leads to a splitting of consciousness that profoundly comprises the child's mental and emotional wellbeing.

This enmeshment of 'brainwashing' and coercive control with repetitive and deliberate abuse is a characteristic of organised abuse. The dependency and powerlessness of children is turned against them by abusers who seek to craft a grandiose image of themselves through the negation of another's agency. Previous chapters have examined the intensification of this process through processes of objectification and ritualisation. This chapter will explore the ways in which this logic extends beyond ritualisation into desecration and to the 'outer limits' of organised abuse: sexual murder and reproductive harms such as non-consensual impregnation, termination and infanticide. Such horrors have been linked to the organised and ritualistic abuse of children in high-profile investigations including Fred and Rosemary West's 'House of Horrors' in Britain and in the Belgian organised abuse scandal that centred on the sex offender Marc Dutroux (Kelly 1998). Less well-known cases of organised abuse have also included evidence of child torture, rape and murder. American psychotherapist Lenore Terr (2003) has documented her long-term psychotherapeutic work with 'Cammie', who was removed from her parents as an infant after her 25-day-old sister was found dead in the family home from fatal brain injuries. The child's corpse was covered in teeth marks and so too was Cammie, who had internal injuries from rape requiring surgery. During the subsequent investigation, Cammie's relatives described satanic rituals and the torture and slaughter of sheep and stray cats in her family home. Whilst there was strong evidence of multiple perpetrators in the torture, rape and possible ritual abuse of Cammie and the death of her sister, there were no sex offences or murder charges laid, with Cammie's father imprisoned for the death of his infant daughter 'without malice'.

Sceptics have been at pains to exaggerate the numbers of deaths reported in cases of ritualistic abuse and to suggest that such deaths could not go undetected. For example, Bromley (1991: 56) alleged that survivors of ritualistic abuse collectively report 'tens of thousands' of child murders a year in North America. He offers no source for this claim, nor do other sceptics who refer to the 'thousands' or 'hundreds of thousands' of murders that they suggest would be taking place if allegations of ritualistic abuse were factual. In this study, participants did not report the mass or random murder of children or adults by abusive groups. Instead, some participants described witnessing the carefully orchestrated and planned murder of vulnerable infants and adults. Rhea offers a reasonable explanation for the deaths she witnessed, deaths which she suggests were neither a common nor indiscriminate aspect of her experience of organised abuse.

> And people say, 'Oh, how can people be killed, and not be found?' Now, I hate to say it, but there's a lot of missing people. And they stay missing. And it didn't happen all the time. It didn't happen on a regular basis. But it did happen.

A small proportion of people reported missing are not found and they are likely to be homicide victims (Cameron and Frazer 1987). However, accounts of homicide in organised abuse often pertain to children who are never listed as 'missing' because they were born, raised and killed without being registered. Whilst such accounts may appear far-fetched, it is clearly possible to bear and raise children without attracting the attention of the authorities. In 2005,

American police found that multiple children had been born and raised in a cult that routinely sexually abused them. Press reports stated 'many of the children in the group have no birth certificate, Social Security number or any type of documentation' (Brady 2005). Where such children 'disappear' they may never be found. In Australia, at the time of writing, a coronial inquiry is ongoing into the disappeared child of Kate Hutchinson, a mentally ill woman with a suspected history of involvement in ritualistic abuse (O'Neill 2009). It was two years before the authorities detected that her two-year-old child was missing, and they uncovered the disappearance inadvertently in the course of investigating another child protection issue. It has since been suggested that the woman may have given birth to another missing child (O'Neill 2009).

Even where the bodies of children murdered in the course of organised abuse are found, the specific circumstances of their deaths may go unacknowledged. In her autobiography, Owen (2010) described secretly giving birth at 11 due to incest and organised abuse, and the subsequent murder of the infant by Owen's mother in order to cover up the abuse. It was over three decades before the Dublin coroner's court confirmed that the murdered infant, whose body was found by the police immediately following the murder, was Owen's child. When reflecting on the cases of torture, murder and infanticide that have been linked to organised abuse, it is notable that they were often detected inadvertently rather than through systematic police work. In this regard, murders in the context of organised sexual abuse have important similarities to serial and sexual murder, where cases of repeated rape, torture and murder have gone undetected by the authorities because victims are vulnerable and easily overlooked (Cameron and Frazer 1987, Caputi 1988).

In light of the evidence of torture and murder in the course of organised abuse, this chapter will take seriously the descriptions of atrocious violence recounted by participants in interview. These atrocities were intimately bound up within the gender regime of the abusive group, who were already engaged in the sustained processes of dehumanisation and degradation associated with the ritualistic abuse and torture of children. In acts of atrocity, the abusive group engaged in acts of intensive and homicidal aggression towards girls, women and their reproductive capacities in ways that were designed to either end or deform the lives of their victims. The aim of this chapter is not to offer a comprehensive explanation for these acts but rather to open the dialogue around them and point to future areas for inquiry and exploration. The available data on atrocity in organised abuse is fragmented and uncertain, involving the testimony of survivors and some substantiated case studies as described above. Emerging from this evidence is a compelling picture of atrocity within the 'private' confines of abusive groups who orchestrate the lives and sometimes the deaths of others in accordance with an ideology of masculine supremacy and sadism. In these performances of murderous violence, the perpetrating 'subject' seeks to extend the logic of objectification and abjectification (as discussed in previous chapters) to the point of desecration. The foul and unclean 'object' that is represented by the victim is physically and symbolically entered by the masterful 'subject' who destroys her utterly, and in doing so seeks to finally embody the transcendental subjectivity that animates much of organised, sadistic and ritualistic abuse. These acts generally fell under the two general categories of (a) sexual murder and (b) reproductive harm and infanticide, which will be discussed in turn.

Sexual murder

A number of participants described the sadistic and sexual murders of infants, children and adults, followed by acts such as necrophilia and cannibalism. The instinctive response to such acts has been to 'banish them from consciousness' (Herman 1992: 1), either by denying that they could occur, or else by symbolically quarantining them as the pathological aberrations of a select few. The atrocities described by participants have parallels with the crimes studied in the literature on 'sexual murder' or 'sexual homicide', the 'intentional killing of a person during which there is sexual behaviour by the perpetrator' (Meloy 2000: 1). Cameron and Frazer (1987) define 'sexual murder' as those acts of murder in which 'killing is *itself a sexual act*' (p 17), the 'eroticisation of the act of killing in and for itself' (p 18). In the act of sexual murder, the moment of death does not demarcate the end of the rape and torture of the victim. The murderer engages with the body of the victim in a manner that erases the victim's subjectivity in life *or* death. Such acts are generally considered to be symptomatic of a deep-seated psychological pathology, however psychological screenings of sexual murderers find that the majority of perpetrators do not have psychotic or delusional disorders or some other mental illness that might predispose them to such violence (Meloy 1988, Meloy et al. 1994, Warren et al. 1996). In their analysis of a sample of 42 mass and serial killers, Levin and Fox (1985) found that sexual murderers are not mentally ill but rather they are motivated primarily by the desire to control and dominate others.

This desire for control and domination was closely associated with a hatred of women and a history of violence against women (Revitch and Schlesinger 1981, Beauregard and Proulx 2000, Meloy 2000). Dietz and colleagues (1990) studied 30 men convicted for murders that were sexually sadistic and included acts of torture. They found that the men had carefully planned the murders with the intention of causing and witnessing the victim's fear, pain and the realisation of impending death. These research findings support Cameron and Frazer's (1987) argument that sexual murder is motivated by the pursuit of *masculine transcendence*. This is a transcendental subjectivity that can be claimed by men through the destruction and desecration of 'Others' who symbolise the feminine, corporeal 'nature' from which men (according to this sexual ideology) must free themselves. This explanation of sexual murder accords with the accounts provided in this study, in which sexual murder featured as the culmination of the efforts of perpetrating 'subjects' to claim a position of unassailable domination and prestige by utterly destroying victimised 'objects'. This act of negation was strongly gendered, with Seb the only participant to report witnessing the murder of an adult man in organised contexts:

> There was one young man who was definitely in his twenties, probably late 20s, who was beheaded by Doherty. And … I had my, ah, Doherty brings the axe down on his neck, and rushes around to the front, and there's this gushing blood. And he's drinking it, he's just wild with excitement. Then he comes over, grabs me by the hair and pushes my face into the severed neck. And I'm told to drink it.

Such a description is unusual in this study. Where participants reported the sexual murder of teenagers or adults, the victim was almost invariably female. It is notable that, in Seb's report of this man's death, he does not describe any sexualised component. In contrast, where participants reported that teenage girls or women were murdered, the victim was subject to a range of sexualised tortures. Such tortures were present, for instance, in Seb's description of the murder of a teenage girl, which was attended by the cannibalisation of her body:

> She – she's flailing around, she's naked, and [the abusers] are trying to grab her and get her up onto this table. And she's resisting it. Presumably, she knows what is going to happen. And in the next instance, she's lying quite motionless, so I presume they've drugged her.
>
> But I'm watching this, quite helpless. And then, um, I'm brought around to the side of the table, the dagger is put into my hands, and Doherty's hands over my hands, and it's placed on her throat. And her throat is cut, very quickly, quite deeply … And the next thing, I'm on the other side of the table, there's Grenham and Doherty on the other side, her body in between. And they've cut her breasts off, and they're eating them. Y'know, this is great for them, they're happy as Larry.

During acts of atrocity, perpetrators expressed a sense of god-like or omnipotent selfhood. During abuse, Lily's father would tell her 'I am God, I am the God you must worship. I am the God you must adore. I am evil'. Other participants reported that their abusers called themselves 'gods', 'the masters of the universe', 'warlocks' and 'kings'. Participants described perpetrators wearing robes, hoods, medieval ruffs and other paraphernalia designed to designate a special and superior status. According to participants, some perpetrators even claimed to have magical powers. It was acts of ritualistic violence and murder that appeared to most powerfully activate these fantasies of transcendence and omnipotence, in which the victim's personhood is denied as they are literally and symbolically reduced to a violated and eviscerated body. In other contexts such as serial murder and war crimes, perpetrators of atrocities also report a feeling of 'godlike' power and manhood (Caputi 1988, Warren et al. 1996, Kelly 2000).

In acts of ritualistic atrocity the subjectivity of the 'other' is not simply negated but utterly obliterated through symbolic enactments of all-consuming masculine sexual aggression. Neil described an occasion of sexualised murder followed by necrophilia, in which the sexual assault of a young girl before and after death constituted a joint performance between two men who characterised the child solely in terms of 'a fuck'.

> On one of these occasions, there was a young girl, only about three years old, that had been raped. And she actually died there. And one of her abusers looked and said, 'What a waste of a fuck. Fucking little shit just died on me.' And another man came over, and said, 'Can I have my turn now?' And the other guy is still going aggro that she'd died. And he's saying, 'Fucking little bitch, she's dead.' And the other guy just looked and said, 'Well, she's still warm, she's still fuckable.' And he dragged her away and, you know, did what he wanted to her. And over the years there were many children who were killed, maimed and very badly injured. You know. And I can say that because I was there, I witnessed it.

In psychoanalytic theory, the wish to destroy or obliterate others is not only common across the human lifespan but crucial to psychological development. Benjamin (1995: 39) argues that in 'the mental act of negating or obliterating the object, which may be expressed in the real effort to attack the other, we found out whether the real other survives'. That is, the fact that others continue to exist even where rage gives rise to a wish to harm or negate them establishes that they exist outside and independently from the subject, and hence they are not just a mental object of subjective experience. This is a realisation that leads away from narcissism and towards a more fully integrated and meaningful engagement with others as subjects rather than objects. It is the *survival* of others in spite of the destructive impulses of the subject that establishes them as entities in their own right and thus constrains the force of primary narcissism (Benjamin 1995). However, in some sexually abusive groups, the sadistic impulse of narcissistic fantasies are given free reign, and participants described how acts of torture, murder and desecration induced 'ideal states' in perpetrators who appeared captivated by a sense of beatific/ horrific transcendence and masculine supremacy.

This quest for transcendence is a noted feature of other criminal practices, including armed robbery, car theft and joy riding, in which going over the 'moral edge' delivers intense experiences of power, control and supremacy over others (Katz 1988). However, transcendence is essentially an imaginary and perpetually out-of-reach state, and the inevitable failure to realise this ideal can prompt 'painful, sometimes frenzied, attempts to drag an unwilling psyche into line with the unwanted social expectations' (Jefferson 1994: 13). In this study, the cultures of abject violence that prevail amongst sexually abusive groups serve as the backdrop to escalating acts of group violence up to and including the sexualised destruction of the 'Other' – that is, women and children, who are represented often enough in a patriarchal culture as embodying all that is 'split off' from masculinity and despised accordingly. Within the symbolic order of the abusive group, women and children are symbols of powerlessness and base corporeality that men must destroy from within and without if they are to realise their 'true' and transcendental self. Practices of ritualistic violence and sexualised murder were the embodiment of this logic, through which perpetrators could grasp at a 'supreme' masculine subject position. However this state is inherently unrealisable and perpetrator groups were locked into a cycle of carefully planning and staging the deaths of others in order to reproduce the momentary experience of transcendence arising from abject destruction.

Reproductive harm and infanticide

The forced murder and cannibalisation of children is a widely reported feature of organised and ritualistic abuse (Rutz et al. 2008, Young et al. 1991, Scott 2001), dating back to the earliest attempts to prosecute organised abuse in the United States. The allegations of organised and ritualistic abuse in Jordan, Minnesota made by a number of children in 1983 included reports of the murder and cannibalisation of an infant (Hechler 1988). In this study, some of participants recalled incidents in which they witnessed infanticide, and were forcibly engaged in the murderous act. The abusive group typically orchestrated the murder in order to inculcate a deep sense of culpability in the child.

> I remember, once, I was made to hold a knife while an adult held a baby. And, to me, it was a feeling that they were trying to make me feel guilty, so that I would never speak. They tried to make the child – and I knew, at the time, I wasn't strong enough to do what they did with that knife – but they try and make you feel involved, make you feel like you are in it. But that was one of the most traumatic times.
>
> Anne

Participants' accounts of infanticide and cannibalism parallel recent reports from Africa in which militia groups abduct children and, as part of their 'initiation' as sexual slaves and child soldiers, force them to participate in the ritualistic rape, murder and cannibalisation of adults and other children (for a newspaper report, see Judah 2004). Through such a process, the child experiences a symbolic transformation of the 'traditional system of meaning' resulting in 'cultural and mental destruction' (Medeiros 2007: 500). The resulting internal sense of anomie then binds the child to the abusive group, since they have lost their sense of communion or belonging to a wider social order. In Lauren's experience these acts were considered to have magical or supernatural significance by perpetrators:

> The sacrifice of babies. The eating of their flesh, and the drinking of their blood. That is – the purpose of that, they believe, they believe it is the eternal fountain of life. And by eating new life, they will live forever.

In participants' accounts, and in the literature on ritualistic abuse, infanticide and murder tended to be referred to as a 'sacrifice' or in similarly religious terms, with perpetrators readily appointing themselves 'gods', 'kings' and 'warlocks' with the power of life and death over their victims. Such delusions of grandeur are not limited to ritualistic abuse. In their study of serial killers, Warren and colleagues (1996: 974) noted that 'This sense of being godlike and in control of [the] life and death of another human being … is reported by some of the men as one of the most exhilarating aspects of the sexual experiences and of their crimes'. Claims to immortality and omnipotence frequently attend acts of sexual murder, which somewhat obscures questions of gender and power in relation to the commission of the crime (Caputi 1988).

In this study, such acts were heavily gendered and formed part of a cycle of reproductive harm and infanticide. Through this cycle, the specifically female work of gestation and child-bearing was not only integrated into organised abuse but it was annihilated through acts of reproductive harm. In participants' accounts, women's and girl's bodies and their reproductive capacities were the targets of many of the atrocities enacted by abusive groups. These acts seemed designed to establish male dominance over the female body in the most atavistic and primal way possible.

> They actually managed to get a pregnant woman from somewhere, they abducted a pregnant woman. And, I kind of think, um you know, you think that … um … you know, I know that she was terrified and you'd might think actually think if I was making this up, you'd think if I was making this up … but I remember that he, he pulled her apart with, with his bare hands … it was terrible and I actually had, I had to eat parts of the baby.
>
> Jo

The infants and children subject to sexualised murder were the children of captive teenage girls and adult women who had fallen pregnant through rape. Such pregnancies were rarely carried to full term. Participants stated that these pregnancies were typically aborted in the second trimester, or induced early in the third trimester, and these procedures were undertaken at home by members of the abusive group.

I've read all this 'How ridiculous, the idea that they could have "baby breeders" where girls could get pregnant and walk around to term and have a baby and no one will notice.' And I'm thinking, 'You *stupid* idiots, what makes you think that they let us carry it to term?'

Jo

Two male participants, Darren and Neil, identified that pregnant teenage girls were frequently targeted by the abusive group, and their children removed from them after birth.

It's so easy for them, the actual killing of infants, they would just get one of these addicted women, removed her from society – and when that child is born, there is nothing, no records, nothing to ever say that child has been born. And so they can do what they like.

Darren

For their 'breeding purposes', as they called it – [they used] runaways. People who had stained the family name, back in those days. They put these people into places where, you know, to have the child and whatever.

Neil

These descriptions accorded with some female participants' descriptions of having been sequestered in the latter stages of pregnancy and giving birth to children who were subsequently murdered. For example, Rhea recalls being pregnant as a teenager, and being taken in her final trimester to a remote house where she gave birth to a child who was later murdered.

There were a number of early pregnancies which were hidden. The only one that I remember was up in the house, in the forest, where we were kept up there for must have been for about three months until we delivered.

Rhea recalled a number of secret pregnancies as a teenager and young woman. Some of these pregnancies were carried to term and she believed that some of these children may still be alive, although she was uncertain. As an adult, Rhea was still being victimised in organised abuse and she gave birth to a child in the apartment of the group leader, Peter. In the following excerpt, in which Rhea refers to herself in the third person, she describes how one of her personalities, Leah, agreed to allow Peter to keep the child in his apartment, and the subsequent murder of the child. She also reflects on her uncertainties over the fate of other children born in secrecy.

She [Leah] even had a child at that stage that he kept there for a while. The child died ... I mean, I've got one son, who's very much alive, well and kicking, but, um, there were others, I, I don't know, some, some I know are alive, but others, others I don't know what may have happened to them. But this one certainly I saw her when she was about two months old, and he decapitated her, so I saw her die – Leah saw her die.

Rhea characterises Leah as a willing, if duped and coerced, participant in organised and ritualistic abuse. However, it seems that this was a period in her life in which Rhea was employing a dual strategy of overt obedience and covert resistance against Peter. After witnessing the murder of the child described above, Rhea terminated a subsequent pregnancy without Peter's knowledge, and found some safety by initiating a relationship with her now-husband. Peter responded to Rhea's emerging autonomy with increasingly brutal and terroristic measures, including stalking, home invasions and sexual assaults. Throughout this prolonged and terrifying ordeal, any act of self-determination in which Rhea exercised her right to control her body and her reproductive capacity was viewed by Peter as an intolerable affront. In this excerpt, Rhea describes how she again fell pregnant following a sexual assault by Peter, and his violent response when she terminated the child.

We were raped, we were almost killed. He found out we'd terminated the baby, that he knew was his, and he wanted it, that was one he did want. It was gone, and, um, he abused us physically – he really got stuck into us for that.

It is telling that Peter responded violently when Rhea took it upon herself to decide the fate of a foetus whom she knew she could not keep safe from harm. It may be that, in organised abuse, the act of impregnation of a girl or non-consenting woman is a performative act that establishes the virility of the abuser, and this act of pride can only be undone by an equivalent or greater demonstration of masculine control and domination; non-consensual abortion or induced birth and infanticide. Arguably, Rhea's termination was an act of self-determination and therefore a slight against Peter's masculine prestige, which he maintained by subjugating Rhea and utilising her reproductive capacities, in effect, as a form of literal and symbolic colonisation. This is similar in many regards to the reproductive control exercised by domestic violence offenders who coercively impregnate their partner with the intention of demonstrating masculine potency and establishing control over her and their offspring (Miller et al. 2010).

A number of female participants alluded to violent and non-consensual abortions and/or the murder of their children. The ongoing grief associated with these ordeals prevented them from speaking further about the conditions under which these abortions and infanticides took place. For example, Lily referred in passing to two pregnancies conceived through rape when she was a teenager, their violent termination and the incorporation of the foetal tissue within ritualistic abuse:

How far advanced were your pregnancies permitted to go?
Enough … month wise I don't know, but enough so that when it was terminated there was enough for there to be a pretty graphic ritual. And very identifiably …

Lily was not able to speak in detail about these events. Nonetheless, these were ordeals that stayed with her throughout her life, impacting upon her life choices and how she negotiated issues relating to her body, reproduction and sexuality. She situated the violent impregnations and terminations as the culmination of a series of ritualistic abuses that had become progressively more intrusive and soul-destroying throughout her childhood. In interview, she felt that these terminations had destroyed her capacity to willingly have children, emotionally if not physically.

I remember as a very young child being dedicated to Satan, then at another point I had to pledge allegiance, and then later on was impregnated by, and married to, Satan. So those things, whilst at an essence, they are the same, each one is more complex, each one takes more from me, and then, with the, the impregnated and married to Satan, there was also an abortion, as a result of that. And that, still, is kind of one of the absolute worst memories of the whole, the whole thing. Not just the abortion, but the way it was done, and what happened. And I still think that still has a huge amount to do with why I don't have children. I was going to say 'why I chose not to have children' but I'm fairly sure that was never a free choice.

Lily's description of the phased escalation of her abuse over time is driven by what Benjamin (1990: 58) called the 'dialectic of control'. It is through the process of objectification and dehumanisation that the perpetrator extracts recognition from the victim of his dominant status, and so 'the struggle to possess her must be prolonged' (p 58). Therefore, sadism proceeds 'piece by piece', with perpetrators seeking out 'new levels of resistance' so that the victim can be 'vanquished anew' (p 58). Lily described how desperately she wanted to keep the pregnancies, and her father's promises that she would be permitted to keep, at least, the second pregnancy: 'Of course you will be able to keep this child. Yes, this will be your baby. Yes, it's special, nobody can take this away. You know you can trust me, you know that I love you.' She called the violent termination of this pregnancy 'the final death of hope':

Because that was the point, I think, where I really just gave in. And that was really the point where I moved into being a perpetrator. Because of the despair. It was like there was no point any more. And the hope, that, as a perpetrator, you'll get treated better.

The manipulation of children's reproductive capacities was a strategy of power that could be extended to entrap captive boys as well as girls and women. After Seb had witnessed the murder of a child, and was forcibly engaged in the murderous act, he was told that the child was his. Like Lily, Seb describes this incident as a moment of 'collapse'.

> After the baby had been killed, there was another occasion after that, I'm told that the infant was mine. That I'd fathered it with [a teenaged girl who was also being abused by the group]. And it was quite impossible because I hadn't reached puberty. But I didn't quite understand that at the time. I must have understood puberty and all the rest of it, but, still, I believed them, or I was at least confused by it. And she is wailing and she just falls over me, and, y'know, saying 'You killed my baby, you killed my baby'. And then I started, I just collapsed onto the floor.

Participants employed a range of strategies to protect themselves and others from the emotional and physical harms of the reproductive harms they had witnessed. In Rhea's case, she utilised abortion not only to protect herself, but to protect the foetus. As she wrote in her diaries after she found out she was pregnant after a sexual assault: 'It must be taken gently, nor not at all. It must not die in terror and pain but gently on its way, towards the light.' Lauren utilised anorexia as a strategy to disrupt her menstrual cycle, prevent pregnancy and thus gain a sense of control over her body. As a child, Lauren witnessed the devastation wrought on her older sister through the murder of her children and she grew to adolescence seeking to forestall the horror of an induced birth and infanticide. She reported witnessing her sister haemorrhage to death in the family home after the early inducement and murder of her newborn by the abusive group. Lauren believed that, in order to staunch her bleeding following the home birth, her sister was administered a high level of a blood clotting agent and died the following day of a blood clot.

> ... One of the drugs that they used to use, after the girls or women in the group gave birth, they'd give them a blood-clotting agent. So they wouldn't haemorrhage, and bleed, and continue to bleed ... I didn't see them administer her the drugs, but that's what I believe happened to her. She was given a blood clotting agent.
>
> And the next day, she had this pain all up through her leg and into her groin. And she was just getting sicker and sicker. Something was really wrong. And she said she had to go lie down. I was getting really concerned, she was only 22 but she had this look on her face, a look of death. That was when I said to the mother, 'You've got to call an

ambulance, there's something wrong.' She wouldn't, so I went and called an ambulance.

And the next thing, I went back into the bedroom, and there's my sister, and she can't breathe. And I'm watching the mother thumping her chest, giving her CPR, but she's full on with it – like she's going to break every rib in her. So I went back to the phone again, to call for an ambulance again. And this all went on in the space of 40 minutes, before she died. It was horrific ... I rang for the ambulance three times, but it was too late.

After her sister's death, Lauren utilised anorexia in a strategy to prevent herself from falling pregnant. She says:

The primary reason for anorexia was the total paranoid fear of not wanting to get pregnant. I had heard that anorexia throws out your periods. And nothing – because, they [the abusive group] kept count of everything, even your periods. You had to tell them when you had your last period, and when you'd be fertile. So anorexia was my way of fighting it – 'I'll do whatever it takes, you are not making me pregnant'. Because I'd seen my sister go through that, and it totally destroyed her.

In her study of ritualistic abuse, Scott (2001: 121) also noted that starvation was 'practised by some survivors as providing some measure of control and experience of personal power. One woman claimed to have been able to keep her body weight so low in her mid-teens that she ceased menstruating and could not fall pregnant'. In Lauren's case, the struggle over her right to reproductive control became central to her survival, both emotional and physical, and she employed starvation as the only method available to her.

Connell (1987) notes that sexuality is one of the central structures through which relations of gendered domination are eroticised, acted out and reproduced. In organised abuse, the pursuit of unobtainable fantasies of omnipotence demands relations of domination so totalising that they can only be sustained by the expansion of the terrain of sexuality into the realm of the atrocious. In this study, the bodies of girls and women were the primary objects upon which abusive groups wrote what Scarry (1985) calls their 'fiction of power', as fantasies of transcendence and supremacy were made corporeal through acts of mutilation, murder and desecration. These acts were staged progressively across the childhood of the victim in ways that were designed to intrude further and further into the body and mind of the victim until the victim is finally 'possessed' by her perpetrators, and experiences herself as an emptied-out object or abject vessel without agency or hope. In truth, this 'final' point may never actually be reached, with perpetrators repeatedly re-staging the surrender or submission of their victims for their own pleasure. However, the abjectification of the victim, who is constituted as a dehumanised and contaminated object, can find final and definitive expression through murder and desecration. Such acts are powerfully symbolic for abusive groups, as the culmination of the sadistic narcissism that animates much of their activity, however they are not engaged in indiscriminately. Rationality and the maintenance of control are central to the dynamic of masculine sadism (Benjamin 1990) and in this study perpetrators orchestrated their most sadistic and atrocious crimes with great care and forethought.

Conclusion

In patriarchal settings, women's bodies are defined as the property of men, and their sexuality and reproductive capacities are the medium through which men established their self-identity as potent masculine subjects: husbands, fathers and patriarchs. Rape and forced impregnation is the inverse expression of this common logic, in which sexual violence is used to craft a transgressive but superior masculine subject position for perpetrators. Bergoffen (2005) describes the ways in which, during the Bosnian war, the use of rape by the Serbian forces routinely involved multiple perpetrators and they were staged in front of family members of the victims and other detainees. 'As publicly performed, they engage the power of the spectacle of violence to construct and formalize subject positions' (2005: 74). Participants described a similar patriarchal logic at work within sexually abusive groups, however in this instance rape was an instrument in a private war against women and children; a war against the threatening 'Others' that featured as objects of derision and hate. Through their destruction (literal or symbolic) the fiction of a transcendental, supreme masculine self was established.

Whilst participants reported that atrocities stimulated grandiose delusions of power amongst perpetrators, the impact of this violence upon victims was far from illusory. Through acts of reproductive harm, participants' reproductive capacities were turned against them. Non-consensual pregnancies conceived through rape served as a form of physiological and symbolic colonisation. The subsequent terminations and infanticides were horrifying ordeals that left many participants mute with grief, shock and terror. In organised and ritualistic abuse, it may be that the historically contingent configuration of masculinity in terms of sexuality, supremacy and domination has found one of its most extreme and violent expressions. Through this lens, we can see the logical progression of organised abuse from objectification to abjection and finally to desecration. From participants' accounts, it is clear that the impact of atrocity, as a gender strategy, upon the children and women that survive it is devastating. The adaptations that participants were forced to make in order to ameliorate the constant threat of death in abusive groups that practised atrocity stayed with them throughout their lives, in the form of ongoing fear, terror and the guilt borne by all those that survive campaigns of atrocity and terror whilst those around them fell victim to it.

Conclusion

The debates over allegations of organised, sadistic and ritualistic abuse have been based on a distinction between 'reality' and 'fantasy' of questionable utility, with various parties struggling over whether organised abuse is 'real' or just the product of imagination and memory error. This simplistic dichotomy between reality and fantasy has in many respects obscured the common ground shared by all sides in the disagreement, which is that fantasies of extreme sexual abuse exist and have a significant impact on the people that are affected by them. The point of disagreement is on how and where these fantasies are 'acted out'. Sceptics argue that they are manifest in 'false memories' and 'mass hysteria' that are then projected onto innocent men, leading to false allegations, prosecutions and so forth. Therapists, social workers and people who allege to have been victimised in organised abuse do not necessarily discount this possibility. Their contention is that such fantasies are also embodied in abusive group practices. Both arguments describe a process whereby psychological fantasy gives rise to particular kinds of harmful social behaviour: false allegations on one hand, and sexual violence against children and women on the other hand. The question is not how to distinguish 'reality' from 'fantasy' but instead how psychological and cultural forces shape individual and collective behaviour and vice versa.

Survivors of organised abuse have described abusive behaviours of such severity that social workers and therapists have struggled to account for such crimes using the usual vocabulary of 'child abuse' or 'domestic violence'. At times this has given rise to partial, unlikely or even irrational explanations but the sceptical position has also proven to be somewhat incoherent. It is not logical to argue that fantasies of sadistic and ritualistic abuse are so pervasive and powerful that they animate 'mass hysteria' and epidemics of 'false memories' and 'witch-hunting' but they have no influence of note over the behaviour of child sexual abusers. This position has won admirers despite its shortcomings because the alternative – that allegations of organised abuse are accurate descriptions of criminal conduct – is incongruous with 'commonsense' understandings of contemporary society. However, the widespread assumption that physical and sexual violence in Western countries is a limited phenomenon is, as Walklate (2008) put it, a product of the collective 'imaginary'. The majority of incidents of gendered violence go undetected, and victims often struggle to find care and support. Severe and repeated incidents of abuse tend to occur in situations in which the perpetrator has considerable control of his victim(s) and hence the most serious cases of sexual abuse frequently do not come to the attention of the authorities. Nonetheless, it is generally 'imagined' to be the case that physical and sexual violence is contained by the police and other agencies, that organised and coordinated sexual abuse only occur in faraway places, and survivors are adequately served by health and justice systems. This act of 'imagination' has also served as the basis for the misleading elaborations advanced by the 'false memory' movement and its allies, who have reaffirmed illusory but idyllic images of community and family life by characterising allegations of sexual and organised abuse as a conspiracy launched by malicious and hysterical women.

One of the reasons that accounts of organised abuse are so vulnerable to discrediting attacks is because they are replete with cultural clichés of evil and wrong-doing, such as rituals, witches and Satanists. Lauren felt that the behaviour of her abusive family was 'like the B-grade horror films', noting 'It's so pathetic, but of course, afterwards, it wasn't'. Her point was that the 'Vincent Price' aesthetic of some abusive group might appear garish or ridiculous to others, but to survivors such as herself it signified extremes of aggression and violence:

> With victims, what can appear to be really dorky or harmless – as a child, these things, they are connected to things that are absolutely terrifying. It might seem hammy, pretending to be vampires and witches and things, but, as a kid, you've seen them go through with it.

Upon reflection, it is perhaps unsurprising that symbols that are culturally associated with degradation and fear are not limited to fictional representations such as films and novels, but they also inform real acts of abuse, violence and torture. In the histories of participants, the use of these symbols was strategic as well as expressive, as costumes and rituals were integrated into simple but terrifying performances that communicated to young children as well as adults the consequences of disclosure and disobedience. The grandiose claims of magical powers and supernatural forces that often accompanied these performances could provoke considerable fear in victimised children although the pomposity of such behaviour had a demythologising effect over time for some. For example, Jane's abusers had forced her to call them 'Master' and claimed to have unlimited power and influence, but as she observed them over the years she came to see their behaviour as a deviant form of adolescent posturing.

> I have to remind myself of this, because of the brainwashing that's gone on that these are big powerful men, 'Jane, you are dealing with schoolboys.' That's it, basically.

Other participants had complex reasons for accepting and even exaggerating their abuser's claims to power and status. The life circumstances of many participants were challenging, characterised by poverty and physical and mental illness. For some, the belief that they were survivors of a mysterious, unspeakable evil bestowed a sense of dignity upon the problems that they had struggled with throughout their life. Each participant faced the question of how to create a sense of order and meaning from their abuse in their own way. I would suggest that the interviewees have undergone a doubled trauma: not only have they suffered severe sexual abuse but they have been failed and, in fact, silenced by prevailing cultural idealisations of 'childhood', 'family' and so forth. They lacked any collective representation of their suffering to console them or to provide a means through which they can communicate to others the enormity of their victimisation and survival. Hence their descriptions of finding hope and strength in the context of abuse and powerlessness were particularly moving. I am not a Christian but Kate's account of her discovery of the 'god who made the trees' can still bring a tear to my eye:

> When I was a little girl, I learnt that, if I was going to survive these horrendous things, I was going to have to find strength bigger than mine ... One time, when this [abuse] is going on, I looked at the trees, and I thought, 'Well, my father's useless, my mother's useless, and my sister is a kid. Everybody I know is pretty shitty. I'm going to take the god who made the trees.' And from that moment on, all day, every day and night, I made friends with the god who made the trees. And he was my strength, and he was my help, and I could withstand anything.
>
> ... Whether a person thinks that this exists, or does not exist, is probably immaterial inasmuch as it worked, and it kept me to goodness, to integrity, to a sense that one day, I would triumph, and I would transform all of this. And it's going to be alright. As a child, at three, I said to myself, 'I have to help these children' and I did. I was kind to them, even then. And I managed to do that later on, all the way through the years, and now my work is – of course – helping others who have been hurt in the same way. I've been very happy in the way I've been able to transform my childhood.

This book has described how children and women often feature as 'objects' in a symbolic order that is structured by masculine domination and gender polarity, in which recognition of the personhood of the 'Other' can become constrained in ways that conflates masculinity and subjectivity. This is a symbolic order that not only promotes and rationalises violence against women and children, but it shapes responses to this violence in ways that ultimately reaffirm the symbolic order from which it emerges. The proliferation of sceptical literature on organised abuse has staged, at a social and cultural level, the same effacement of the subjectivity of victims that underpins organised abuse itself.

However, the accounts of survival provided by participants in this project are a testament to their active agency and resistance. Through their own words, they are revealed as people with needs that must be addressed and voices that should be heard, rather than as passive victims of abuse or 'objects' of therapeutic malpractice that can be spoken for, and spoken over, by others.

Sexual abuse is mostly practised by solitary offenders but it is always social to the extent that it is a practice that reinforces structures of gender and age (Cossins 2000). The testimony of survivors suggests that the objectification of children and women through collective sexual violence is a strategy through which abusive groups construct and shape a shared sense of belonging and identity. For its 'raw material', this subculture draws on cultural associations between authentic masculinity, sexual aggression and control of children and women that are common in a range of contexts. As children, participants were confronted with the institutional power available to their abusers through their roles as fathers, grandfathers, priests, teachers, doctors and other patriarchal figures of authority. This power was given terrifying form through the practice of ritualistic abuse, as abusers adopted the ritualistic traditions of masculine domination and integrated them into organised abuse. The power that their abusers held over them as adults and as men was only the precursor to the long shadow they cast as representatives of a network of abusers who had co-opted the symbolic and functional power of larger institutions. This was a shadow that followed some participants well into adulthood as their victimisation continued and, for some women, came to include their own children. These years and decades of abuse and violence were not only symptomatic of the obsessive control exerted by the abusive groups, but they also illustrate the disinterest shown by a range of agencies in the plight of abused children and women.

It is clear that survivors of organised abuse face a number of systemic barriers to disclosure and help-seeking. In abusive groups, victims are subject to intensive manipulation by perpetrators in order to inhibit disclosure, including the induction of fear and pain of such a degree as to profoundly dysregulate memory and emotional processes. Those who have been victimized over a prolonged period of time have typically been forced into acts of perpetration, and they often harbor a genuine fear that, should they report their abuse to others, then they will also face criminal prosecution alongside those that abused them. Despite these barriers, many victims and survivors of organised abuse do seek a better life for themselves by contacting health and welfare services or the police and disclosing their abuse. However, at present these agencies often have limited capacity to marshal an appropriate response, and the needs of victims and survivors typically go unmet. As a covert and secretive form of sexual violence, organised abuse often evades detection and identification. Where sexual abuse is investigated, the possibility of an organised dimension often goes unexamined, whilst action taken against organised crime rarely addresses the plight of children and women trapped in physically and sexually abusive groups (Kelly 1996, Cooper 2004). Policing strategies in relation to organised abuse appear to be highly reactive and developed in response to community concerns or media scandals rather than through scrutinising the evidence. There is a clear need to raise the profile of organised abuse amongst those likely to encounter sexual abuse cases.

There is a heaviness in the heart that comes from prolonged exposure to graphic descriptions of abuse of the kind contained in this book, whether as author or reader. Books that parody or trivialise accounts of severe trauma have sold, and sold well, in bookstores and airports because they offer a brief foray into a controversial issue before restoring and affirming the reader's pre-existing assumptions about the nature and order of their society. In contrast, the lives that have been documented in this book are deeply troubling and they raise questions without simple or reassuring answers. They point to a hidden strata within society in which children and women experience irreversible injury and loss at the hands of abusers who have ordered their lives around the pursuit of harming others. This strata flourishes between the cracks of the 'public' and 'private' divide, drawing on the spaces and opportunities offered by normative arrangements of gender, age and power to craft a zone of impunity for serious physical and sexual violence. Lacan (1949) used the term 'body in bits and pieces' to describe the experience of the body as a fragmented assemblage of flesh, organs and bone, in comparison to the ideal image of the body as a perfect whole. Such an archaic experience of 'lack' or absence, I would suggest, is also present in the experience of society offered by organised abuse. Rather than a society purged of barbaric inclinations that offers unfailing protection to the vulnerable and never wavers in its execution of justice, we are confronted with a 'society in bits and pieces': a complex and imperfect place containing contradictions and hypocrisies from which we cannot neatly extricate ourselves. It is within these contradictions that organised abuse and other forms of gendered violence flourish but they also generate the impulses of denial, disbelief and minimisation that serve to mask the excesses of the gender order and preserve illusory but idealised images of society.

Recent allegations of organised, sadistic and even ritualistic abuse have received relatively limited media coverage in comparison to the controversies of the 1980s and 1990s. On the face of it, the diminished public profile of organised abuse may be interpreted as a negative consequence of these controversies, but it may also reflect a number of positive developments. It may be that the culture of news production is less hostile to such allegations and that kneejerk scepticism is a less common response to allegations of sexual abuse than it once was. It also appears that investigative practices by the police and child protection authorites with complex cases of sexual abuse have advanced to the point where allegations of organised abuse can no longer be dismissed outright as the product of professional malpractice or incompetence. The organised abuse 'scandals' of the 1980s and 1990s promoted the development of more integrated and standardised investigatory arrangements in relation to allegations of sexual abuse, which, rather than eliminating allegations of organised abuse, have increasingly resulted in their substantiation. Ongoing revelations of cultures of sexual abuse in religious organisations has lent further credibility to allegations of organised abuse (Keenan 2012). Importantly, organised abuse is now a subject with a substantial (although somewhat dispersed) evidence base from which to formulate and generate best practice models, whether in relation to child protection practice, mental health care or investigation and prosecution. The challenge is to integrate this evidence into policy and practice in spite of widespread resistance to the recognition of the extremes of gendered violence that occur in 'first world' countries that pride themselves on being too modern and progressive to harbour such inclinations.

Appendix
Research methodology

The qualitative research drawn on in this book began in 1997 as part of a Doctorate in Philosophy in public health, which was awarded in 2010 by the University of New South Wales. Recruitment notes were circulated through networks of mental health services and relevant community-based organisations in the fields of child abuse, sexual assault and child protection inviting adults with histories of organised abuse ('forms of sexual abuse involving multiple perpetrators and multiple victims') to contact the researcher if they were interested in being interviewed about their experiences. Potential participants were first sent a short questionnaire asking (a) if they had received or were receiving mental health care in relation to their history of abuse, and (b) whether they had friends or other supportive people in their life who knew about their abuse. Participants were also asked about their willingness to be interviewed and what they would like the outcome of the project to be.

Questionnaire respondents were considered for the project if they indicated via the questionnaire that they were currently accessing mental health services or if they had supportive people in their life that knew about their history of organised abuse. If this was the case, the participant would be contacted to initiate formal consent procedures and to establish a time and date for interview. If participants did not have current access to care and support of any kind, or if they showed *prima facie* indicators of severe distress or untreated mental illness, then they would be declined from the project and referred to a local mental health agency or sexual assault service if need be. Since no potential participant indicated that they were without support or demonstrated evidence of serious mental illness or distress and were therefore ineligible for the project, it did not prove necessary to screen any participant from the project or make any referrals during the recruitment phase. This supports the proposition of Becker-Blease and Freyd (2006) that adult survivors of child sexual abuse can self-select accurately for qualitative research.

After I had received a completed questionnaire, I contacted each potential participant via the phone, email or mail, depending on the mode they had elected to be contacted by, in order to discuss the research process further. In the pre-interview phase, I established whether they would like to have a support person present for the interview, and discussed with them the potentially traumatic nature of the interview and the steps we could take to maximise their comfort and security. I outlined the aims of the research and the planned conduct of the interview, and invited participants to ask questions of me. The most common of these was 'Why have you chosen this research project?' which provided me with an opportunity to provide a truncated history of my experiences as a carer. Participants frequently found this reassuring; my impression was that they were worried that, if I was a survivor, I would be traumatised by what they had to say, or that I was potentially a perpetrator. Conversely, if I was a dispassionate 'outsider', they knew from experience that it would be unlikely I would be able to grasp the full range of their experiences.

The interviews

Over the course of this project, 21 adults with histories of sexual abuse by multiple perpetrators shared their life histories with me. Sixteen participants were women and five were men. Prior to the interview, participants had often experienced years, if not decades, of grief and disability, as they struggled to construct a coherent life story from a maelstrom of amnesia, invasive flashbacks and overwhelming distress. My role as an interviewer was to provide a context in which participants felt safe engaging in the exposition of these histories with me. The literature on qualitative research heralds 'the interview' as the site of the construction of knowledge between researcher and participant, yet the focus on 'the interview' as the site of the emergence of knowledge in qualitative research runs the risk of trivialising the significance and durability of the life histories and self-identities that participants bring to the interview. Whilst participants readily recognised (and were intimately familiar with) the vagaries and ambiguities of memory, they came to the interview with a robust sense of their history and identity. Underlying their stories was a firm conviction that, although they might not always have got the details right, the stories they were recounting were sadly based in fact.

The semi-structured nature of the interview process in this project was designed to trace the life history of the participant and to explore the manner in which their recollections of organised abuse were embedded in their larger narratives of childhood, adolescence and development to the present day. Interviews were conducted within an open framework to allow for focused, conversational, two-way communication. I initially brought a prompt sheet to the interview but this proved unnecessary. Each interview had its own pace and style, since participants felt free to raise the issues and events that they felt were significant, and there was no need to impose a preconceived structure or chronology on the discussion. Interviews typically lasted three or four hours, although some interviews went for as long as eight hours (in multiple sessions). Face-to-face interviews were carried out through fieldwork in Tasmania, Victoria and New South Wales, and telephone interviews were carried out for participants in Western Australia, South Australia and Queensland. A telephone interview was also used for one participant who lived in New Zealand.

Whilst interviews did not necessarily proceed in a linear fashion, they generally began with a focus on the participant's early childhood and the family environment. I usually opened with a question such as 'Can you tell me about your childhood and your family when you were a young child?' and the interview proceeded from there. In this initial phase of the interview, establishing a rapport with the participant was just as important as the data that was being generated. My questions focused on generic childhood experiences, such as:

> **Starting primary school:** 'How did you feel starting school?', 'What were your impressions of starting school?'
>
> **Familial environment:** 'What are the words you would use to describe your mother/father?', 'Did you get along with your brothers/sisters?', 'What was your parents' relationship like?'

These questions enabled the participants to relax and paint a general picture of their early life. Once the participant felt comfortable with me, they would generally begin to speak about the circumstances in which their organised abuse took place, eg at home, at school, at church. I sometimes prompted participants with questions such as: 'Was home/school a safe space for you? If not, why not?' Conducting an interview that was safe and comfortable for participants involved identifying their strengths early in the interview and building on those strengths, rather than pressing them for information regarding experiences that were unclear or frightening.

Transcription and analysis

All interviews were personally transcribed by me, and identifying data was anonymised in the process of transcription. Each participant was provided with two copies of the interview transcript: one to make changes to and return, and another to keep for their own records. The transcripts were sent to participants with a letter in which I explained that they could make any changes that they wished to the transcript, including removing or adding material for any reason they saw fit. They were also free to withdraw from the project during this period. Once they returned the transcript to me, I explained that they were giving me permission to proceed with analysis, at which point I would begin to incorporate their interview into the project. My copy of the audio file of their interview was then destroyed, although participants were sent a copy if they wished. This ensured that no identifying data was being held at the university.

Once transcribed, interview data was imported into the qualitative analysis programme, NVivo, which enables users to assign a code to specific lines or segments of text, and I began to develop a preliminary coding 'matrix' of common themes emerging from the data. This process was based on the principles of grounded theory to create coded categories and to develop concepts that emerge from the data. This approach is defined by Strauss and Corbin (1998) as the breaking down, naming, comparing and categorising of data, a process in which hypotheses or theories are generated directly from the data, rather than through *a priori* assumptions or existing theoretical frameworks. In grounded theory, data collection, analysis and theoretical development are iterative processes that often occur alongside and impact upon one another. This was certainly the case throughout this project. Throughout coding and analysis, I adopted and tested a range of theoretical approaches in an effort to identify fruitful conceptual approaches to the data, which affected the kinds of questions I asked of participants in interview.

Over time, the coding of the data moved from a focus on generating categories and determining their dimensions and relationships to one another towards the more systematic development and linking of themes and issues. This phase coincided with a general shift in analysis from description to conceptualisation, as I considered the findings of the research in light of existing theoretical and empirical literature on sexual violence. Whereas the initial focus of analysis had been on identifying common themes and issues across the data, as analysis developed I increasingly turned back to the narrative form of the life history interviews to contextualise these issues and to consider, in more depth, the role that they played in the histories of individual participants. I also began to consider, in a more systematic way, the role of 'outliers' or those participants whose life stories ran counter to a particular theme or argument I was developing. In this way, I was able to review the emerging theoretical insights for internal consistency and logic. Once the coding categories specific to each chapter had reached 'saturation' point (that is, no significant new information seemed to emerge from coding (Strauss and Corbin 1998: 136)) the remaining task was to ensure that they were logically presented, the relationship between them properly explained and articulated, and the theoretical implications of each chapter, and the thesis as a whole, compellingly presented.

Taking reports of organised abuse seriously, in my view, involves subjecting them to a degree of analysis commensurate to the seriousness of the crimes. It is a mistake, however, to presume that self-reflexivity is the sole province of the researcher. Throughout this project, participants demonstrated a high degree of awareness of the manner in which they have constructed their autobiographies over time. In the lives of survivors of organised abuse, memory is often a force to be reckoned with, assaultive and elusive in equal measure. Survivors often endure extensive amnesia for their childhood *as well as* the intrusion of vivid recollections of dehumanisation and shame into their everyday life. Autobiographical coherence is a goal that many survivors have to work proactively towards, often over years of torturous reality-testing and corroboration. Some participants brought an extraordinary high index of suspicion to their own recollections, refusing to introduce new recollections into their life history before they had rigorously tested them for accuracy. Participants were, in a very real sense, the ethnographers of their own lives, with an unusual level of insight into the process by which they constructed their stories, their identities and their social positions.

Bibliography

Abel, G. G., Becker, J. V., Mittelman, M., Cunningham-Rathner, J., Rouleau, J. L. and Murphy, W. D. (1987) 'Self-reported sex crimes of nonincarcerated paraphiliacs', *Journal of Interpersonal Violence*, 2: 3–25.

Airaksinen, T. (1995) *The Philosophy of the Marquis de Sade*, London and New York: Routledge.

Allen, J. G. (2006) 'Mentalizing in practice', in J. G. Allen and P. Fonagy (eds) *Handbook of Mentalization-Based Treatment*, Chicester: John Wiley & Sons.

Atmore, C. (1997) 'Rethinking moral panic and child abuse for 2000', in J. Bessant and R. Hill (eds) *Youth Crime and the Media*, Hobart: National Clearinghouse for Youth Studies.

Bader, C. D. (2003) 'Supernatural support groups: who are the UFO abductees and ritual-abuse survivors?', *Journal for the Scientific Study of Religion*, 42: 669–78.

Bagley, C. and Pritchard, C. (2000) 'Criminality and violence in intra- and extra-familial child sex abusers in a 2-year cohort of convicted perpetrators', *Child Abuse Review*, 9: 264–74.

Beauregard, E. and Proulx, J. (2000) 'Profiles in the offending process of nonserial sexual murderers', *International Journal of Offender Therapy and Comparative Criminology*, 46: 386–99.

Becker-Blease, K. A. and Freyd, J. F. (2006) 'Research participants telling the truth about their lives: the ethics of asking and not asking about abuse', *American Psychologist*, 61: 218–26.

Becker, T., Karriker, W., Overkamp, B. and Rutz, C. (2008) 'The Extreme Abuse Surveys: preliminary findings regarding dissociative identity disorder', in A. Sachs and G. Galton (eds) *Forensic Aspects of Dissociative Identity Disorder*, London: Karnac Books.

Beckett, K. (1996) 'Culture and the politics of signification: the case of child sexual abuse', *Social Problems*, 43: 57–76.

Bell, V., Maiden, C., Munoz-Solomando, A. and Reddy, V. (2004) '"Mind control" experiences on the internet: implications for the psychiatric diagnosis of delusions', *Psychopathology*, 39: 87–91.

Benjamin, J. (1990) *The Bonds of Love: Psychoanalysis, Feminism and the Problem of Domination*. London: Virago Press.

—— (1995) *Like Subjects, Love Objects: Essays on Recognition and Sexual Difference*, New Havin & London: Yale University Press.

Bennetts, L. (1993) 'Nightmares on Main Street', *Vanity Fair*, 56: 42–62.

Bentovim, A. and Tranter, M. (1994) 'A systemic approach', in V. Sinason (ed.) *Treating Survivors of Satanist Abuse*, London and New York: Routledge.

Bergoffen, D. B. (2005) 'How rape became a crime against humanity: history of an error', in A. D. Schrift (ed.) *Modernity and the Problem of Evil*, Bloomington, IN: Indiana University Press.

Bibby, P. (1996a) 'Definitions and recent history', in P. Bibby (ed.) *Organised Abuse: The Current Debate*, London: Arena.

—— (ed.) (1996b) *Organised Abuse: The Current Debate*, London: Arena.

Bibby, P. (2011) 'Rot in jail, says mother as husband who tortured her gets 10 years', *Sydney Morning Herald*, 29 October, 3.

Bohleber, W. (2010) *Destructiveness, Intersubjectivity and Trauma: The Identity Crisis of Modern Psychoanalysis*, London: Karnac.

Bourdieu, P. (1977) *Outline of a Theory of Practice*, Cambridge and New York: Cambridge University Press.

—— (2001) *Masculine Domination*, Oxford: Polity Press.

Bourgois, P. (1996) 'In search of masculinity: violence, respect and sexuality among Puerto Rican crack dealers in East Harlem', *British Journal of Criminology*, 36: 412–27.

Brady, I. (2001) *The Gates of Janus: Serial Killing and its Analysis*, London: Feral House.

Brady, N. S. (2005) 'Charges shed light on church: Eastside "cult" is likely hiding members accused of sexual abuse, police say', *King County Journal*, 25 November, http://www.religionnewsblog.com/12910/charges-shed-light-on-church.

Brewer, G. and Bullough, V. (2005) Women, pornography, and prostitution in eighteenth-century Britain, *Sexuality & Culture*, 9: 14–27.

Briere, J. and Conte, J. (1993) 'Self-report amnesia for abuse in adults molested as children', *Journal of Traumatic Stress*, 6: 21–31.

Bromley, D. G. (1991) 'Satanism: the new cult scare', in J. T. Richardson, J. Best and D. G. Bromley (eds) *The Satanism Scare*, New York: Aldine Transaction.

Brooks, I. (2001) 'Multi-perpetrator abuse of children: Mothers of the victims tell their story', in S. Richardson and H. Bacon (eds) *Creative Responses to Child Sexual Abuse: Challenges and Dilemmas*, London and Philadelphia: Jessica Kingsley.

Brown, A. and Brown, N. J. (2007) 'The Northern Territory intervention: voices from the centre of the fringe', *Medical Journal of Australia*, 187: 621–3.

Brownmiller, S. (1975) *Against Our Will: Men, Women and Rape*, New York: Simon and Schuster.

Buck, S. (2008) 'The RAINS network in the UK (Ritual Abuse Information Network and Support)', in P. Perskin and R. Noblitt (eds) *Ritual Abuse in the Twenty-First Century: Psychological, Forensic, Social and Political Considerations*, Brandon, OR: Robert D. Reed Publishing.

Bulte, A. and de Conick, D. (1998) 'Interview with Regina Louf, witness XI at Neufchateau', *De Morgan*, 10 January, http://old.radicalparty.org/belgium/x1_eng7.htm.

Burgess, A. W., Hartman, C. R., McCausland, M. P. and Powers, P. (1984) 'Response patterns in children and adolescents exploited through sex rings and pornography', *American Journal of Psychiatry*, 141: 656–62.

Burgess, A. W. and Lindeqvist Clark, M. (eds) (1984) *Child Pornography and Sex Rings*, Lexington and Toronto: Lexington Books.

Burman, E. (1994) *Deconstructing Developmental Psychology*, London: Routledge.

Butler, J. (1990) *Gender Trouble: Feminism and the Subversion of Identity*, New York: Routledge.

Calof, D. (1998) 'Notes from a practice under siege: harassment, defamation and intimidation in the name of science', *Ethics & Behavior*, 8: 161–87.

Cameron, D. and Frazer, E. (1987) *The Lust to Kill: A Feminist Investigation of Sexual Murder*, Oxford: Polity Press.

Campbell, B. (1988) *Unofficial Secrets: Child Sexual Abuse – The Cleveland Case*, London: Virago Press.

Cann, J., Friendship, C. and Gozna, L. (2007) 'Assessing crossover in a sample of sexual offenders with multiple victims', *Legal and Criminological Psychology*, 12: 149–63.

Caputi, J. (1988) *The Age of Sex Crime*, London: The Women's Press.

Card, C. (2002) *The Atrocity Paradigm: A Theory of Evil*, New York: Oxford University Press.

Carli (1998) 'An Almost Unbreakable Circle', in J. Lorena and P. Levy (eds) *Breaking Ritual Silence: An Anthology of Ritual Abuse Survivor Stories*, Gardenville, NY: Trout and Sons.

Carrigan, T., Connell, R. and Lee, J. (1985) 'Towards a new sociology of masculinity', *Theory and Society*, 14: 551–604.

Carter, A. (1979) *The Sadeian Woman: An Exercise in Cultural History*, London: Virago.

Chodorow, N. (1978) *The Reproduction of Mothering: Psychoanalysis and the Sociology of Gender*, Berkeley: University of California Press.

Chu, J., Frey, L., Ganzel, B. and Matthews, J. (1999) 'Memories of childhood abuse: dissociation, amnesia and corroboration', *American Journal of Psychiatry*, 156: 749–55.

Chu, J. A. (2011) *Rebuilding Shattered Lives: Treating Complex PTSD and Dissociative Disorders*, Hoboken: John Wiley & Sons.

Clapton, G. (1993) *The Satanic Abuse Controversy: Social Workers and the Social Work Press*, London: University of North London Press.

Cleaver, H. and Freeman, P. (1996) 'Child abuse which involves wider kin and family friends', in P. Bibby (ed.) *Organised Abuse: The Current Debate*, London: Arena.

Cohen, M. (1999) 'Manliness, effeminacy and the French: Gender and the construction of national character in Eighteenth Century England', in T. Hitchcock and M. Cohen (eds) *English Masculinities 1660–1800*, London: Longman.

Coleman, J. (1994) 'Presenting features in adult victims of satanist ritual abuse', *Child Abuse Review*, 3: 83–92.

—— (2008) 'Satanist ritual abuse and the problem of credibility', in A. Sachs and G. Galton (eds) *Forensic Aspects of Dissociative Identity Disorder*, London: Karnac.

Colton, M., Roberts, S. and Vanstone, M. (2010) 'Sexual abuse by men who work with children', *Journal of Child Sexual Abuse*, 19: 345–64.

Colton, M. and Vanstone, M. (1996) *Betrayal of Trust: Sexual Abuse by Men who Work with Children,* London, Free Association Books.

Commission of Inquiry (2004) *Children in State Care: Allegations of Sexual Abuse and Death from Criminal Conduct,* Adelaide: Children in State Care Commission of Inquiry, http://www.sa.gov.au/subject/Crime%2C+justice+and+the+law/Mullighan+ Inquiry/Children+in+State+Care.

Connell, R. (1987) *Gender and Power: Society, the Person and Sexual Politics*, Sydney: Allen & Unwin.

—— (1995) *Masculinities*, Sydney: Allen & Unwin.

—— (2007) *Southern Theory: The Global Dynamics of Knowledge in Social Science*, Cambridge: Polity Press.

Connell, R. and Messerschmidt, J. W. (2005) 'Hegemonic masculinity: rethinking the concept', *Gender & Society*, 19: 829–59.

Cook, C. (1991) 'Understanding ritual abuse: a study of thirty-three ritual abuse survivors', *Treating Abuse Today*, 1: 14–18.

Cooper, L. (2004) *Dilemmas in Working with Women with Complex Needs, Canberra*: Department of Family and Community Services, http://www.fahcsia.gov.au/sa/housing/pubs/homelessness/saap_er_publications/dilemmas_women_complex/Pages/default.aspx.

Cooper, L., Anaf, J. and Bowden, M. (2006) 'Contested concepts in violence against women: "intimate", "domestic" or "torture"', *Australian Social Work*, 59: 314–27.

—— (2008) 'Can social workers and police be partners when dealing with bikie-gang related domestic violence and sexual assault?', *European Journal of Social Work*, 11: 295–311.

Corby, B., Doig, A. and Roberts, V. (2001) *Public Inquiries into Residential Abuse of Children*, London & Philadelphia: Jessica Kingsley.

Cossins, A. (2000) *Masculinities, Sexualities and Child Sexual Abuse*, The Hague: Kluwer Law International.

Cowburn, M. and Dominelli, L. (2001) 'Masking hegemonic masculinity: reconstructing the paedophile as the dangerous stranger', *British Journal of Social Work*, 31: 399–415.

Cozolino, L. J. (1989) 'The ritual abuse of children: Implications for clinical research', *The Journal of Sex Research*, 26: 131–8.

Creighton, S. J. (1993) 'Organized abuse: NSPCC experience', *Child Abuse Review*, 2: 232–42.

Crossley, N. (2004) 'Ritual, body technique and (inter)subjectivity', in K. Schilbrack (ed.) *Thinking Through Rituals: Philosophical Perspectives*, New York: Routledge.

Crowley, M. and Seery, B. (2001) 'Exploring the multiplicity of child sexual abuse with a focus on polyincestuous contexts of abuse', *Journal of Child Sexual Abuse*, 10: 91–110.

Daly, G. (1999) 'Ideology and its paradoxes: dimensions of fantasy and enjoyment', *Journal of Political Ideologies*, 4: 219–38.

Davies, N. (1998) 'Lives that were beyond belief', *Guardian*, 1 August, 12.

de Bruxelles, S. (2011) 'Leader of child-sex cult may die in jail for the suffering in "sick little kingdom"', *The Times*, 12 March, 32.

deMause, L. (1990) 'The history of child assault', *Journal of Psychohistory*, 18: 1–29.

Deneys, A. (1991) 'The political economy of the body in the *Liaisons dangereuses* of Choderlos de Laclos', in L. Hunt (ed.) *Eroticism and the Body Politic*, Baltimore: John Hopkins University Press.

Dietz, P. E., Hazelwood, R. R. and Warren, J. (1990) 'The sexually sadistic criminal and his offenses', *The Bulletin of the American Academy of Psychiatry and the Law*, 18: 163–78.

Dinnerstein, D. (1978) *The Rocking of the Cradle, and the Ruling of the World*, London: Souvenir.

Dobash, R. E. and Dobash, R. (1979) *Violence Against Wives*, New York: Free Press.

Donaldson, M. (1993) 'What is hegemonic masculinity?', *Theory and Society*, 22: 643–57.

Doran, C. and Brannan, C. (1996) 'Institutional abuse', in P. Bibby (ed.) *Organised Abuse: The Current Debate*, London: Arena.

Douglas, M. (1966) *Purity and Danger: An Analysis of Concepts of Pollution and Taboo*, London: Routledge & Kegan Paul.

Driscoll, L. and Wright, C. (1991) 'Survivors of childhood ritual abuse: multi-generational satanic cult involvement', *Treating Abuse Today*, 1: 5–13.

Elaine, C. and June, S. (2005) 'Commercial and sexual exploitation of children and young people in the UK – a review', *Child Abuse Review*, 14: 4–25.

Elliott, M., Browne, K. and Kilcoyne, J. (1995) 'Child sexual abuse prevention: what offenders tell us', *Child Abuse & Neglect*, 19: 579–94.

Ellzey, D. (2007) 'Agents graphically describe abuse', *Hammond Star*, 20 November, http://www.hammondstar.com/articles/2007/12/03/top_stories/9453.txt.

Epstein, O. B., Schwartz, J. and Wingfield Schwartz, R. (2011) *Ritual Abuse and Mind Control: The Manipulation of Attachment Needs*, London: Karnac.

Faller, K. C. (1987) 'Women who sexually abuse children', *Violence and Victims*, 2: 263–76.

—— (1988) 'The spectrum of sexual abuse in daycare: an exploratory study', *Journal of Family Violence*, 3: 283–98.

—— (1991) 'Poly-incestuous families: an exploratory study', *Journal of Interpersonal Violence*, 6: 310–22.

—— (1995) A clinical sample of women who have sexually abused children, *Journal of Child Sexual Abuse*, 4: 13–28.

Fejes, F. (2000) 'Murder, perversion and moral panic: the 1954 media campaign against Miami's homosexuals and the discourse of civic betterment', *Journal of the History of Sexuality*, 9: 305–47.

Ferrell, J. (1997) 'Criminological verstehen: inside the immediacy of crime', *Justice Quarterly*, 14: 3–23.

Finkelhor, D. and Williams, L. M. (1988) *Nursery Crimes: Sexual Abuse in Day Care*, Newbury Park: Sage.

Foucault, M. (1964) *Madness and Civilization: A History of Insanity in the Age of Reason*, New York: Pantheon.

—— (1967) *Madness and Civilisation*, London: Tavistock.

—— (1979) *The History of Sexuality: 1, The Will to Knowledge*, London: Allen Lane.

Fowley, D. (2010) *How Could She?*, London: Arrow.

Frankel, A. S. and O'Hearn, T. C. (1996) 'Similarities in response to extreme and unremitting stress: cultures of communities under siege', *Psychotherapy: Theory, Research, Practice, Training*, 33: 485–502.

Frankfurter, D. (1994) 'Religious studies and claims of satanic ritual abuse: a rejoinder to Stephen Kent', *Religion*, 24: 353–60.

—— (2001) 'Ritual as accusation and atrocity: satanic ritual abuse, gnostic libertinism and primal murders', *History of Religions*, 40: 352–80.

Franklin, K. (2004) 'Enacting masculinity: antigay violence and group rape as participatory theatre', *Sexuality Research and Social Theory*, 1: 25–40.

Fraser, G. (1990) 'Satanic ritual abuse: a cause of multiple personality disorder', *Journal of Child and Youth Care*, 55–65.

—— (1997) 'Introduction', in G. Fraser (ed) *The Dilemma of Ritual Abuse: Cautions and Guides for Therapists*, Washington: American Psychiatric Press.

Freyd, J. J. (1996) *Betrayal Trauma: The Logic of Forgetting Child Abuse*, Cambridge: Harvard University Press.

Frosh, S. (2002) *After Words: The Personal in Gender, Culture and Psychotherapy*, Basingstoke: Palgrave.

Gallagher, B. (1998) *Grappling with Smoke: Investigating and Managing Organised Child Sexual Abuse – A Good Practice Guide*, London: National Society for the Prevention of Cruelty to Children.

—— (1999) 'The abuse of children in public care', *Child Abuse Review*, 8: 357–65.

—— (2000a) 'The extent and nature of known cases of institutional child sexual abuse', *British Journal of Social Work*, 30: 795–817.

—— (2000b) 'Ritual, and child sexual abuse, but not ritual child sexual abuse', *Child Abuse Review*, 9: 321–7.

Gallagher, B., Hughes, B. and Parker, H. (1996) 'The nature and extent of known cases of organised child sexual abuse in England and Wales', in P. Bibby (ed.) *Organised Abuse: The Current Debate*, London: Arena.

Gaspar, R. (1996) 'Organising a response', in P. Bibby (ed.) *Organised Abuse: The Current Debate*, London: Arena.

Gaspar, R. and Bibby, P. (1996) 'How rings work', in P. Bibby (ed.) *Organised Abuse: The Current Debate*, London: Arena.

Gilgun, J. F. and McLeod, L. (1999) 'Gendering violence', *Studies in Symbolic Interactionism*, 22: 167–93.

Gitta, S. (1984) *The Invisible Children: Child Prostitution in America, West Germany and Great Britain*, London: A. Deutsch.

Glaser, B. G. and Strauss, A. L. (1967) *The Discovery of Grounded Theory: Strategies for Qualitative Research*, Hawthorne: Aldine De Gruyter.

Glaser, D. and Frosh, S. (1993) *Child Sexual Abuse*, Basingstoke: Macmillan.

Goddard, C. R. (1994) 'The organised abuse of children in rural England: the response of social services: Part one', *Children Australia*, 19: 37–40.

Goffman, E. (1961) *Asylums: Essays on the Social Situation of Mental Patients and Other Inmates*, New York: Anchor Books.

Gold, S. N. (2000) *Not Trauma Alone: Therapy for Child Abuse Survivors in Family and Social Context*, Lillington: Taylor & Francis.

Gold, S. N., Hyman, S. M. and Andrés-Hyman, R. C. (2004) 'Family of origin environments in two clinical samples of survivors of intra-familial, extra-familial, and both types of sexual abuse', *Child Abuse & Neglect*, 28: 1199–212.

Golston, J. C. (1993a) 'Ritual abuse: raising hell in psychotherapy. Creation of cruelty: the political military and multi-generational training of torturers. Violent initiation and the role of traumatic dissociation', *Treating Abuse Today*, 2: 5–16.

—— (1993b) 'Raising hell in psychotherapy. Part II. Comparative abuse: Shedding light on ritual abuse through the study of torture methods in political repression, sexual sadism, and genocide', *Treating Abuse Today*, 3: 12–19.

Goodwin, J. M. (1994a) 'Credibility problems in sadistic abuse', *The Journal of Psychohistory*, 21: 479–96.

—— (1994b) 'Sadistic abuse: definition, recognition and treatment', in V. Sinason (ed.) *Treating Survivors of Satanist Abuse*, London and New York: Routledge.

Gough, D. (1996) 'An overview of the literature', in P. Bibby (ed.) *Organised Abuse: The Current Debate*, London: Arena.

Gould, C. (1987) 'Satanic ritual abuse: child victims, adult survivors, system response', *California Psychologist*, 22: 1.

Grant, D. (2005) 'The Lynch affair: hypnosis as a pathway to abuse', *Sensorium*, 8: 8–9.

Green, L. (2001) 'Analysing the sexual abuse of children by workers in residential care homes: characteristics, dynamics and contributory factors', *Journal of Sexual Aggression*, 7: 5–24.

Griffith, G. and Simon, K. (2008) 'Child pornography law', *Briefing Paper No 9/08*. NSW Parliamentary Library, http://www.parliament.nsw.gov.au/prod/parlment/publications.nsf/0/289c584b88554bcbca2574b400125787/$file/child%20pornography%20law%20and%20index.pdf.

Guilliat, R. (1995) 'Demons from the past', *Sydney Morning Herald*, 1 February, 13.

—— (1996) *Talk of the Devil: Repressed Memory & the Ritual Abuse Witch-Hunt*, Melbourne: Text Publishing Co.

Habermas, J. (1989) *The Structural Transformation of the Public Sphere: An Inquiry into a Category of Bourgeois Society*, Cambridge: Polity Press.

Hacking, I. (1995) *Rewriting the Soul: Multiple Personality and the Sciences of Memory*, Princeton: Princeton University Press.

Hague, E. (2007) 'Rape, power and masculinity: the construction of gender and national identities in the war in Bosnia-Herzegovina', in R. Lentin (ed.) *Gender and Catastrophe*, London and New York: Zen Books.

Harkins, L. and Dixon, L. (2010) 'Sexual offending in groups: an evaluation', *Aggression and Violent Behavior*, 15: 87–99.

Harvey, K. (2004) *Reading Sex in the Eighteenth Century: Bodies and Gender in English Erotic Culture*, Cambridge: Cambridge University Press.

Hastings, D. (2009) 'Abuse in Louisiana ritualistic child sex case involving fundamentalist-cult church', *Associated Press,* 8 August.

Hawkins, R. and Briggs, F. (1997) 'The institutional abuse of children in Australia: past and present', *Early Child Development and Care*, 133: 41–55.

Hayden, T. (1991) *Ghost Girl: The True Story of a Child in Desperate Peril and the Teacher who Saved Her*, London: Macmillan.

Healey, C. (2008) 'Unsolved: investigating allegations of ritual abuse', in A. Sachs and G. Galton (eds) *Forensic Aspects of Dissociative Identity Disorder*, London: Karnac.

Hechler, D. (1988) *The Battle and the Backlash: The Child Sexual Abuse War*, Lexington and Toronto: Lexington Books.

Heil, P., Ahlmeyer, S. and Simons, D. (2003) 'Crossover sexual offenses', *Sexual Abuse: A Journal of Research and Treatment*, 15: 221–36.

Herman, J. L. (1981) *Father-Daughter Incest*, Cambridge and London: Harvard University Press.

—— (1992) *Trauma and Recovery*, New York: Basic Books.

Hitchcock, T. (1996) 'Redefining sex in eighteenth-century England', *History Workshop Journal*, 41: 73–90.

Hobbs, G. F., Hobbs, C. J. and Wynne, J. M. (1999) 'Abuse of children in foster and residential care', *Child Abuse & Neglect*, 23: 1239–52.

Hochschild, A. R. (1979) 'Emotion work, feeling rules, and social structure', *American Journal of Sociology*, 85: 551–75.

—— (1989) *The Second Shift: Working Parents and the Revolution at Home*, New York: Viking.

hooks, b. (1989) *Talking Back: Thinking Feminist, Thinking Black*, Boston: South End.

Hudson, P. (1990) 'Ritual child abuse: a survey of symptoms and allegations', *Journal of Child and Youth Care*, Special Issue: 27–53.

—— (1991) *Ritual Abuse: Discovery, Diagnosis and Treatment*, Saratoga: R&E Publishers.

Hunt, P. and Baird, M. (1990) 'Children of sex rings', *Child Welfare*, 69: 195–207.

Ignatieff, M. (1998) 'The stories we tell: television and humanitarian aid', in J. Moore (ed.) *Hard Choices: Moral Dilemmas in Humanitarian Intervention*, Lanham: Rowman & Littlefield.

Incardi, J. (1984) 'Little girls and sex: A glimpse at the world of the "baby pro"', *Deviant Behaviour*, 5: 71–8.

International Society for the Study of Trauma and Dissociation (2011) 'Guidelines for treating dissociative identity disorder in adults, third revision', *Journal of Trauma & Dissociation*, 12: 115–87.

Itzin, C. (1997) 'Pornography and the organization of intrafamilial and extrafamilial child sexual abuse: developing a conceptual model', *Child Abuse Review*, 6: 94–106.

—— (2001) 'Incest, paedophilia, pornography and prostitution: making familial abusers more visible as the abusers', *Child Abuse Review*, 10: 35–48.

James, A., Jenks, C. and Prout, A. (1998) *Theorizing Childhood*, Oxford: Polity Press.

Janus, S. S. and Heid Bracey, D. H. (1986) 'Runaways – pornography and prostitution', in J. Ennew (ed.) *The Sexual Exploitation of Children*, Cambridge: Polity Press.

Jefferson, T. (1994) 'Theorising masculine subjectivity', in T. Newburn and E. A. Stanko (eds) *Just Boys Doing Business? Men, Masculinities and Crime*, London and New York: Routledge.

—— (2002) 'Subordinating hegemonic masculinity', *Theoretical Criminology*, 6: 63–88.

Jenkins, P. (1998) *Moral Panic: Changing Concepts of the Child Molester in Modern America*, New Haven: Yale University Press.

Jenks, C. (1996) *Childhood*, London and New York: Routledge.

Jones, J. (1995) 'Institutional abuse: understanding domination from the inside looking out', *Early Child Development and Care*, 113: 85–92.

Jonker, F. and Jonker-Bakker, P. (1991) 'Experiences with ritualistic child sexual abuse: a case study from the Netherlands', *Child Abuse & Neglect*, 15: 191–6.

Judah, T. (2004) 'Child soldiers, sex slaves, and cannibalism at gunpoint: the horrors of Uganda's north', *The Independent*, 23 October, 31.

Katz, J. (1988) *Seductions of Crime: A Chilling Exploration of the Criminal Mind – From Juvenile Delinquency to Cold-Blooded Murder*, New York: Basic Books.

Keenan, M. (2012) *Child Sexual Abuse and the Catholic Church*, Oxford and New York: Oxford University Press.

Kelley, S. (1989) 'Stress responses of children to sexual abuse and ritualistic abuse in day care settings', *Journal of Interpersonal Violence*, 4: 502–13.

Kelly, L. (1996) 'Weasel words: pedophiles and the cycle of abuse', *Trouble and Strife*, 33: 44–9.

—— (1998) 'Confronting an atrocity: the Dutroux case', *Trouble and Strife*, 36: 16–22.

—— (2000) 'Wars against women: sexual violence, sexual politics and the militarised state', in S. Jacobs, R. Jacobson and J. Marchbank (eds) *States of Conflict: Gender, Violence and Resistance*, London and New York: Zed Books.

Kelly, L. and Regan, L. (2000) *Rhetoric and Realities: Sexual Exploitation of Children in Europe*, London: Child and Woman Abuse Studies Unit, University of North London, http://www.cwasu.org/filedown.asp?file=Rhetorics_Realities(1).pdf.

Kelly, L., Wingfield, R., Burton, S. and Regan, L. (1995) 'Splintered lives: sexual exploitation of children in the context of children's rights and child protection', Ilford: Barnardo's, http://www.barnardos.org.uk/splintered_lives_report.pdf

Kelly, L. and Scott, S. (1993) 'Literature review: the current literature about organized abuse of children', *Child Abuse Review*, 2: 281–7.

Kent, S. A. (1993a) 'Deviant scripturalism and ritual satanic abuse part one: possible Judeo-Christian influences', *Religion*, 23: 229–41.

—— (1993b) 'Deviant scripturalism and ritual satanic abuse part two: possible Masonic, Mormon, magick and pagan influences', *Religion*, 23: 355–67.

Kimmel, M. S., Hearn, J. and Connell, R. (eds) (2005) *Handbook of Studies on Men and Masculinities*, Thousand Oaks and London: Sage.

Kincaid, J. (1998) *Erotic Innocence: The Culture of Child Molesting*, Durham: Duke University Press.

Kinscherff, R. and Barnum, R. (1992) 'Child forensic evaluation and claims of ritual abuse or satanic cult activity: a critical analysis', in D. K. Sakheim and S. E. Divine (eds) *Out of Darkness: Exploring Satanism and Ritual Abuse*, New York: Lexington Books.

Kitzinger, J. (1998) 'The gender-politics of news production: silenced voices and false memories', in C. Carter, G. Branston and S. Allan (eds) *News, Gender and Power*, London: Routledge.

—— (2004) *Framing Abuse: Media Influence and Public Understanding of Sexual Violence Against Children*, London: Pluto Press.

Kluft, R. (1989) 'Reflections on allegations of ritual abuse', *Dissociation*, 11: 191–3.

—— (1995) 'Six completed suicides in dissociative identity disorder patients: clinical observations', *Dissociation*, 8: 104–11.

—— (1997) 'Overview of the treatment of patients alleging that they have suffered ritualized or sadistic abuse', in G. Fraser (ed.) *The Dilemma of Ritual Abuse: Cautions and Guides for Therapists*, Washington and London: American Psychiatric Press.

Koselleck, R. (1988) *Critique and Crisis: Enlightenment and the Pathogenesis of Modern Society*, Cambridge: MIT Press.

Kramer, L. (1997) *After the Lovedeath: Sexual Violence and the Making of Culture*, Berkeley: University of California Press.

Kristeva, J. (1982) *Approaching Abjection: An Essay on Abjection*, New York: Columbia University Press.

La Fontaine, J. S. (1993) 'Defining organized sexual abuse', *Child Abuse Review*, 2: 223–31.

—— (1998) *Speak of the Devil: Tales of Satanic Abuse in Contemporary England*, Cambridge and New York, Cambridge University Press.

Lacan, J. (1949) *Écrits*, New York: W. W. Norton.

Lacter, E. and Lehman, K. (2008) 'Guidelines to differential diagnosis between schizophrenia and ritual abuse/mind control traumatic stress', in P. Perskin and R. Noblitt (eds) *Ritual Abuse in the Twenty-First Century: Psychological, Forensic, Social and Political Considerations*, Brandon: Robert D. Reed Publishing.

Laing, L. (1999) 'A different balance altogether? Incest offenders in treatment', in J. Breckenridge and L. Laing (eds) *Challenging Silence: Innovative Responses to Sexual and Domestic Violence*, St Leonards: Allen & Unwin.

Lanning, K. (1992) *Investigator's Guide to Allegations of 'Ritual' Child Abuse*, Quantico: National Center for the Analysis of Violent Crime.

LeGates, M. (1976) 'The cult of womanhood in eighteenth-century thought', *Eighteenth-Century Studies*, 10: 21–39.

Lerner, M. (1980) *The Belief in a Just World: A Fundamental Delusion*, New York: Plenum Press.

Levi, P. (1986) *The Drowned and the Saved*, New York: Summit Books.

Levin, J. and Fox, J. (1985) *Mass Murder: America's Growing Menace*, New York: Plenum.

Liddle, A. M. (1993) 'Gender, desire and child sexual abuse: accounting for the male majority', *Theory, Culture and Society*, 10: 103–26.

—— (1996) 'State, masculinities and law: some comments on gender and English state-formation', *British Journal of Criminology*, 36: 361–80.

Lief, H. and Fetkewicz, J. (1997) 'The construction of false memory syndrome: a transactional model', *Psychological Inquiry*, 8: 303–6.

Loewenstein, R. J. (1996) 'Dissociative amnesia and dissociative fugue', in L. K. Michelson, and W. J. Ray (eds) *Handbook of Dissociation: Theoretical, Empirical and Clinical Perspectives*, New York: Plenum Press.

Loftus, E. F. (1993) 'Reality of repressed memory', *American Psychologist*, 48: 518–37.

Loftus, E. F. and Ketcham, K. (1994) *The Myth of Repressed Memory: False Memories and Allegations of Sexual Abuse*, New York: St Martin's Griffin.

Lord, E. (2008) *The Hell-Fire Clubs: Sex, Satanism and Secret Societies*, New Haven: Yale University Press.

Lorena, J. M. and Levy, P. (1998) *Breaking Ritual Silence: An Anthology of Ritual Abuse Survivors' Stories*, Gardnerville: Trout and Sons.

Lyng, S. (1990) 'Edgework: a social psychological analysis of voluntary risk-taking', *American Journal of Sociology*, 95: 851–86.

MacKinnon, C. (1989) *Toward a Feminist Theory of the State*, Cambridge and London: Harvard University Press.

Masson, J. M. (ed.) (1984) *The Assault on Truth: Freud's Suppression of the Seduction Theory*, Toronto, Collins Publishers.

—— (1985) *The Complete Letters of Sigmund Freud to Wilhelm Fliess 1887– 1904*, Cambridge and London: Belknap Press/Harvard University Press.

Matza, D. and Sykes, G. M. (1961) 'Juvenile delinquency and subterranean values', *American Sociological Review*, 26: 712–19.

Mauss, M. (2000) *The Gift: The Form and Reason of Exchange in Archaic Societies*, New York and London: W.W. Norton & Co.

McAlinden, A. M. (2006) '"Setting 'em up"': personal, familial and institutional grooming in the sexual abuse of children', *Social and Legal Studies*, 15: 339–62.

McFadyen, A., Hanks, H. and James, C. (1993) 'Ritual abuse: a definition', *Child Abuse Review*, 2: 35–41.

McKeon, M. (1995) 'Historicizing patriarchy: the emergence of gender difference in England, 1660–1760', *Eighteenth-Century Studies*, 28: 295–322.

Medeiros, E. (2007) 'Integrating mental health into post-conflict rehabilation: the case of Sierra Leonean and Liberian "child soldiers"', *Journal of Health Psychology*, 12: 498–504.

Meloy, J. R. (1988) *The Psychopathic Mind: Origins, Dynamics and Treatment*, Northvale: Jason Aronson.

—— (2000) 'The nature and dynamics of sexual homicide: an integrative review', *Aggression and Violent Behaviour*, 5: 1–22.

Meloy, J. R., Gacono, C. B. and Kenney, L. (1994) 'A Rorschach investigation of sexual homicide', *Journal of Personality Assessment*, 62: 58–67.

Messerschmidt, J. W. (1993) *Masculinities and Crime: Critique and Reconceptualization of Theory*, Lanham: Rowman and Littlefield.

—— (1999) 'Making bodies matter: adolescent sexualities, the body and varieties of violence', *Theoretical Criminology*, 3: 197–220.

—— (2000) 'Becoming "real men": adolescent masculinity challenges and sexual violence', *Men and Masculinities*, 2: 286–307.

Metcalf, C. (2008) 'The Establishment paedophile: how a monster hid in high society', *The Spectator*, 12 July, http://www.spectator.co.uk/essays/all/826056/the-establishment-paedophile-how-a-monster-hid-in-high-society.thtml.

Middleton, W. (2005) 'Owning the past, claiming the present: perspectives on the treatment of dissociative patients', *Australasian Psychiatry*, 13: 40–9.

Middleton, W. and Butler, J. (1998) 'Dissociative identity disorder: an Australian series', *Australian and New Zealand Journal of Psychiatry*, 2: 794–804.

Miller, A. (2012) *Healing the Unimaginable: Treating Ritual Abuse and Mind Control*, London: Karnac.

Miller, E., Decker, M. R., McCauley, H. L., Tancredi, D. J., Levenson, R. R., Waldman, J., Schoenwald, P. and Silverman, J. G. (2010) 'Pregnancy coercion, intimate partner violence and unintended pregnancy', *Contraception*, 81: 316–22.

Millett, K. (1971) *Sexual Politics*, London: Hart-Davis.

Misztal, B. (2003) *Theories of Social Remembering*, Buckingham: Open University Press.

Mollon, P. (1994) 'The impact of evil', in V. Sinason (ed.) *Treating Survivors of Satanist Abuse*, London and New York: Routledge.

—— (1996) *Multiple Selves, Multiple Voices: Working with Trauma, Violation and Dissociation*, West Sussex: John Wiley & Sons.

—— (2001) *Releasing the Self: The Healing Legacy of Heinz Kohut*, London: Whurr.

—— (2008) 'When the Imaginary becomes the Real', in A. Sachs and G. Galton (eds) *Forensic Aspects of Dissociative Identity Disorder*, London: Karnac.

Morris, A. (2009) 'Gendered dynamics of abuse and violence in families: considering the abusive household gender regime', *Child Abuse Review*, 18: 414–27.

Morris, S. (2009) 'Child abuser George admits her crimes were disgusting and vile: police interview tape with nursery workers released: fourth person charged in connection with case', *Guardian*, 13 October, 12.

—— (2011) 'Colin Blanchard could spend life in jail for role in paedophile ring', *Guardian.co.uk*, 10 January, http://www.guardian.co.uk/uk/2011/jan/10/colin-blanchard-jail-paedophile-ring.

Motz, A. (2008) *The Psychology of Female Violence*, Hove and New York: Routledge.

NCA Joint Committee Report (1995) 'Organised Criminal Paedophile Activity', Canberra: Parliamentary Joint Committee on the National Crime Authority, http://www.aph.gov.au/Parliamentary_Business/Committees/Custom_Contents/SenateCommittees/accctte/completedinquiries/pre1996/ncapedo/report.

Nelson, S. (2008) 'The Orkney "satanic abuse case": who cared about the children?', in R. Noblitt and P. Perskin (eds) *Ritual Abuse in the Twenty-First Century: Psychological, Forensic, Social and Political Considerations*, Brandon: Robert D. Reed Publishing.

Noblitt, J. R. and Perskin, P. S. (2000) *Cult and Ritual Abuse: Its History, Anthropology and Recent Discovery in Contemporary America*, Westport: Praeger.

Norfolk, A. (2012d) How children's home failed to protect its only resident from sex abuse by 25 men. *thetimes.co.uk*, May: no.

O'Connell Davidson, J. (2005) *Children in the Global Sex Trade*, Cambridge: Polity Press.

O'Neill, M. (2009) 'Stop my daughter having babies', *The Sunday Telegraph*, 30 August, http://www.dailytelegraph.com.au/news/stop-my-daughter-having-babies/story-e6frewt0-1225767344587.

O'Sullivan, C. (1998) 'Ladykillers: similarities and divergences of masculinities in gang rape and wife battery', in L. H. Bowker (ed.) *Masculinities and Violence*, Thousand Oaks and London: Sage.

Ofshe, R. and Watters, E. (1993) 'Making monsters', *Society*, 35: 364–76.

—— (1996) *Making Monsters: False Memories, Psychotherapy, and Sexual Hysteria*, California: University of California Press.

Ogden, E. 1993. 'Satanic cults: ritual crime allegations and the false memory syndrome', unpublished thesis, University of Melbourne.

Olio, K. A. and Cornell, W. F. (1998) 'The facade of scientific documentation: a case study of Richard Ofshe's analysis of the Paul Ingram case', *Psychology, Public Policy, and Law*, 4: 1182–97.

Otnow, D., Yeager, C. A., Swica, Y., Pincus, J. H. and Lewis, M. (1997) 'Objective documentation of child abuse and dissociation in 12 murderers with dissociative identity disorder', *American Journal of Psychiatry*, 154: 1703–10.

Owen, C. (2010) *Living with Evil*, London: Headline Review.

Parkin, W. and Green, L. (1997) 'Cultures of abuse within residential child care', *Early Child Development and Care*, 133: 73–86.

Pateman, C. (1988) *The Sexual Contract*, Oxford: Polity Press.

Peter, T. (2006) 'Mad, bad or victim? Making sense of mother-daughter sexual abuse', *Feminist Criminology*, 1: 283–302.

Petraitis, V. and O'Connor, C. (1999) *Rockspider: The Danger of Paedophiles – Untold Stories*, Melbourne: Hybrid Publishers.

Philadelphoff-Puren, N. (2004) 'Dereliction: women, rape and football', *Australian Feminist Law Journal*, 21: 35–51.

Pierce, R. L. (1984) 'Child pornography: a hidden dimension of child abuse', *Child Abuse & Neglect*, 8: 483–93.

Plummer, K. (2010) 'Generational sexualities, subterranean traditions, and the hauntings of the sexual world: some preliminary remarks', *Symbolic Interaction*, 33: 163–90.

Pope, K. S. (1996) 'Memory, abuse and science: questioning claims about the false memory syndrome epidemic', *American Psychologist*, 51: 957–74.

Pratt, J. (2009) 'From abusive families to internet predators?', *Current Sociology*, 57: 69–88.

Rafferty, J. (1997) 'Ritual denial', *The Guardian*, 22 March, 26.

Reid, S. (2010) 'Predatory gangs, middle class girls forced into the sex trade – and a very troubling taboo', *Daily Mail*, 7 August, 54.

Rendall, J. (1999) 'Women and the public sphere', *Gender & History*, 11: 475–88.

Renold, E. and Creighton, S. J. (2003) *Images of Abuse: A Review of the Evidence on Child Pornography.*, London: National Society for the Prevention of Cruelty to Children,

http://www.nspcc.org.uk/Inform/research/findings/imagesofabuse_wda48280.
html.

Revitch, E. and Schlesinger, L. (1981) *The Psychopathology of Homicide*, Springfield:
Charles C. Thomas.

Richardson, J. T., Best, J. and Bromley, D. G. (eds) (1991) *The Satanism Scare*, New
York: Aldine Transaction.

Robinson, A. L., Koester, G. A. and Kaufman, A. (1994) 'Striae vs scars of ritual abuse
in a male adolescent', *Archives of Family Medicine*, 3: 398.

Rogers, N. (1999) 'Mad mothers, over-zealous therapists and the paedophile inquiry',
Southern Cross Law Review, 3: 115–35.

Rose, N. (1989) *Governing the Soul*, London: Routledge.

Ross, C. A. (1995) *Satanic Ritual Abuse: Principles of Treatment*, Toronto: University of
Toronto.

—— (1997) *Dissociative Identity Disorder: Diagnosis, Clinical Features, and Treatment of
Multiple Personality*, New York: Wiley.

—— (2009) 'Errors of logic and scholarship concerning dissociative identity disorder', *Journal of Child Sexual Abuse*, 18: 221–31.

Rousseau, G. S. and Porter, R. (1987) 'Introduction', in G. S. Rousseau, and R. Porter
(eds) *Sexual Underworlds of the Enlightenment*, Manchester: Manchester University
Press.

Rust, M. E. (1985–86) 'The nightmare is real', *Student Law*, 13–19.

Rutz, C., Becker, T., Overkamp, B. and Karriker, W. (2008) 'Exploring commonalities reported by adult survivors of extreme abuse: preliminary empirical findings',
in P. Perskin and R. Noblitt (eds) *Ritual Abuse in the Twenty-First Century:
Psychological, Forensic, Social and Political Considerations*, Brandon, OR: Robert D.
Reed Publishing.

Sachs, A. and Galton, G. (eds) (2008) *Forensic Aspects of Dissociative Identity Disorder*,
London: Karnac.

Sagan, E. (1988) *Freud, Woman and Morality: The Psychology of Good and Evil*, New
York: Basic Books.

Sahakyan, L. and Kelley, C. M. (2002) 'A contextual change account of the directed
forgetting effect', *Journal of Experimental Psychology: Learning, Memory and Cognition*,
28: 1064–72.

Sakheim, D. K. and Devine, S. E. (1992) 'Introduction', in D. K. Sakheim and S. E.
Devine (eds) *Out of Darkness: Exploring Satanism and Ritual Abuse*, New York:
Lexington Books.

Salter, A. (1998) 'Confessions of whistle-blower: lessons learnt', *Ethics & Behavior*, 8:
115–24.

Salter, M. (2008) 'Organised abuse and the politics of disbelief', in C. Cunneen and
M. Salter (eds) *Proceedings of the 2nd Australian and New Zealand Critical Criminology
Conference*, Sydney: Crime and Justice Research Network and the Australian and
New Zealand Critical Criminology Network, http://pandora.nla.gov.au/pan/93325/
20090123-1412/www.unsw.edu.au/gen/pad/critcrimproceedings2008.pdf.

—— (2011) 'Organised abuse and testimonial legitimacy', in M. Lee, G. Mason and
S. Milivojevic (eds) *ANZCCC: The Australian and New Zealand Critical Criminology
Conference 2010, Proceedings*, Institute of Criminology, Sydney Law School, The
University of Sydney, http://ses.library.usyd.edu.au/handle/2123/7372.

Salter, M. and Richters, J. (forthcoming) 'Organised abuse: a neglected category of sexual abuse with significant lifetime mental health care sequelae', *Journal of Mental Health*.

Salter, M. and Tomsen, S. (2012) 'Violence and carceral masculinities in Felony Fights', *British Journal of Criminology*, 52: 309–23.

Sanday, P. R. (1996) *A Woman Scorned: Acquaintance Rape on Trial*, Berkeley: University of California Press.

—— (2007) *Fraternity Gang Rape: Sex, Brotherhood, and Privilege on Campus*, New York, New York University Press.

Sarson, J. and McDonald, L. (2007) 'Ritual abuse-torture in families', in N. Jackson (ed.) *Encyclopedia of Domestic Violence*, New York and Oxon: Routledge.

—— (2008) 'Ritual abuse-torture within families/groups', *Journal of Aggression, Maltreatment and Trauma*, 16: 419–38.

Sax, R. (2011) 'Fox 11 legal analyst Robin Sax weights in on Sandusky interview', Myfoxla.com, 16 November, http://www.myfoxla.com/dpp/news/robin-sax-jerry-sandusky-interview-20111115.

Scarry, E. (1985) *The Body in Pain: The Making and Unmaking of the World*, Stanford: Stanford University Press.

Schoettle, U. C. (1980) 'Child exploitation: a study of child pornography', *Journal of the American Academy of Child and Adolescent Psychiatry*, 19: 289–99.

Schultz, T., Passmore, J. L. and Yoder, C. Y. (2003) 'Emotional closeness with perpetrators and amnesia for child sexual abuse', *Journal of Child Sexual Abuse*, 12: 67–88.

Scott, S. (1993) 'Beyond belief: beyond help? Report on a helpline advertised after the transmission of a Channel 4 film on ritual abuse', *Child Abuse Review*, 2: 243–50.

—— (1998) 'Counselling survivors of ritual abuse', in Z. Bear (ed.) *Good Practice in Counselling People Who Have Been Abused*, London: Jessica Kingsley.

—— (2001) *Beyond Disbelief: The Politics and Experience of Ritual Abuse*, Buckingham, Open University Press.

Scully, D. (1988) 'Convicted rapists' perceptions of self and victim', *Gender & Society*, 2: 200–13.

Sedgwick, E. K. (1994) *Tendencies*, London: Routledge.

Seenan, G. (2005) 'Social workers blamed for continued abuse of three daughters in remote island community', *The Guardian*, 8 October, 4.

Segrave, M., Milivojevic, S. and Pickering, S. (2009) *Sex Trafficking: International Context and Response*, Portland: Willan.

Shaffer, R. E. and Cozolino, L. J. (1992) 'Adults who report childhood ritualistic abuse', *Journal of Psychology and Theology*, 2: 188–93.

Shakeshaft, C. (2003) 'Educator sexual abuse', *Hofstra Horizons*, Spring, 10–13.

Sheehan, P. (2011) 'Only multiple, credible accusers dent progress of sexual predators', *Sydney Morning Herald*, 7 July, http://www.smh.com.au/opinion/society-and-culture/only-multiple-credible-accusers-dent-progress-of-sexual-predators-20110706-1h2d7.html.

Shengold, L. L. (1979) 'Child abuse and deprivation: soul murder', *Journal of the American Psychoanalytic Association*, 27: 533–59.

Showalter, E. (1997) *Hystories: Hysterical Epidemics and Modern Culture*, London: Picador.

Silbert, M. H. and Pines, A. M. (1985) 'Early sexual exploitation as an influence in prostitution', *Social Work*, 28: 285–9.

Simpson, A. E. (1987) 'Vulnerability and the age of female consent: legal innovation and its effect on prosecution for rape in eighteenth-century London', in G. S. Rousseau and R. Porter (eds) *Sexual Underworlds of the Enlightenment*, Manchester: Manchester University Press.

Sinason, V. (ed.) (2002) *Attachment, Trauma and Multiplicity: Working with Dissociative Identity Disorder*, London: Brunner-Routledge.

Sivers, H., Schooler, J. and Freyd, J. (2002) 'Recovered memories', in V. S. Ramachandran (ed.) *Encyclopedia of the Human Brain*, San Diego, CA: Academic Press.

Smart, C. (1991) *Feminism and the Power of Law*, London and New York: Routlege.

—— (2007) *Personal Life*, Cambridge and Malden: Polity Press.

Smith, M. (1993) *Ritual Abuse: What It Is, Why It Happens, How To Help*, New York: HarperCollins.

Snow, B. and Sorenson, T. (1990) 'Ritualistic child abuse in a neighborhood setting', *Journal of Interpersonal Violence*, 5: 474–87.

Socarides, C. W. (2004) 'A psychoanalytic classification of the paedophilias: two clinical illustrations', in C. W. Socarides and L. R. Loeb (eds) *The Mind of the Paedophile: Psychoanalytic Perspectives*, London: Karnac.

South Australian Ombudsman (2004) *Annual Report 2003–2004: Report of the Ombudsman Concerning an Alleged Failure by the Department for Human Services (Family and Youth Services) to Acknowledge and Deal with a Conflict of Interest Arising from the Placement of a Child into Foster Care*, Adelaide: South Australian Ombudsman.

Spanos, N., Burgess, C. and Burgess, M. (1994) 'Past life identities, UFO abductions and satanic ritual abuse: the social construction of memories', *The International Journal of Clinical and Experimental Hypnosis*, 42: 433–46.

Stanley, L. (1993) 'The knowing because experiencing subject: narratives, lives and autobiography', *Women's Studies International Forum*, 16: 205–15.

Stein, M. (2006) 'Missing years of abuse in children's homes', *Child and Family Social Work*, 11: 11–21.

Strauss, A. and Corbin, J. (1998) *Basics of Qualitative Research: Techniques and Procedures for Developing Grounded Theory*, Thousand Oaks: Sage.

Summers, A. (1975) *Damned Whores and God's Police*, Sydney: Allen Lane.

Summit, R. C. (1983) 'The child sexual abuse accomodation syndrome', *Child Abuse & Neglect*, 7: 177–93.

—— (1994) *Ritualistic Child Abuse: A Report on the Seminar Presented by Professor Roland Summit for the New South Wales Child Protection Council, Sydney*, Sydney: NSW Child Protection Council.

Svedin, C. G. and Back, K. (1996) *Children Who Don't Speak Out: About Children being Used in Child Pornography*, Stockholm Raüdda Barnen: Swedish Save the Children.

Swann, S. (1999) 'A model for understanding abuse through prostitution', in Barnardo's (ed.) *Whose Daughter Next: Children Abused Through Prostitution*, London: Barnado's.

Tamarkin, C. (1994a) 'Investigative issues in ritual abuse cases, Part I', *Treating Abuse Today*, 4: 5–9.

—— (1994b) 'Investigative issues in ritual abuse cases, Part II', *Treating Abuse Today*, 4: 14–23.

Tate, T. (1990) *Child Pornography: An Investigation*, London: Methuen.

Taylor, J. (2010) 'Guilty after six-year trial, Portugal's high-society paedophile ring', *The Indepedent*, 4 September, 26.

Taylor, M., Holland, G. and Quayle, E. (2001) 'Typology of paedophile picture collections', *The Police Journal*, 74: 97–102.

Taylor, M., (2012) Muslim leaders warn of far right exploitation of Rochdale child sex case, *Guardian.co.uk*, 12 May.

Terr, L. C. (2003) '"Wild child": how three principles of healing organized 12 years of psychotherapy', *Journal of the American Academy of Child & Adolescent Psychiatry*, 42: 1401–9.

Thornton, M. (1990) *The Liberal Promise: Anti-discrimination Legislation in Australia*, Melbourne: Oxford University Press.

Tomison, A. (1995) 'Update on child sexual abuse', *Issues in Child Abuse Prevention*, 5, http://www.aifs.gov.au/nch/pubs/issues/issues5/issues5.html.

Tomsen, S. (2008) 'Masculinity, crime and criminalisation', in C. Cunneen and T. Anthony (eds) *The Critical Criminology Companion*, Sydney: Federation Press.

Tremlett, G. (2010) 'Portuguese TV star guilty with five others of abusing boys at state-run orphanages: ambassador, doctor and ombudsman convicted', *Guardian*, 4 September, 24.

Turner, J. G. (1987) 'The properties of libertinism', in R. Purks Maccubin (ed.) *'Tis Nature's Fault: Unauthorized Sexuality during the Enlightenment*, Cambridge: Cambridge University Press.

Tyler, R. P. and Stone, L. E. (1985) 'Child pornography: perpetuating the sexual victimization of children', *Child Abuse and Neglect*, 9: 313–18.

Vandiver, D. M. (2006) 'Female sex offenders: a comparison of solo offenders and co-offenders', *Violence and Victims*, 21: 339–54.

Victor, J. S. (1993) *Satanic Panic: The Creation of a Contemporary Legend*, Chicago: Open Court.

—— (1998) 'Moral panics and the social construction of deviant behavior: a theory and application to the case of ritual child abuse', *Sociological Perspectives*, 41: 541–65.

Vigarello, G. (2001) *A History of Rape: Sexual Violence in France from the 16th to the 20th Century*, Cambridge: Polity.

Wakefield, H. and Underwager, R. (1994) *Return of the Furies: An Investigation into Recovered Memory Therapy*, Chicago and La Salle: Open Court.

Walker, K. and Brown, S. J. (2011) 'Non-sex offenders display distorted thinking and have empathy deficits too: a thematic analysis of cognitions and the application of empathy', *Journal of Sexual Aggression*, 1–21.

Walklate, S. (2008) 'What is to be done about violence against women?', *British Journal of Criminology*, 48: 39–54.

Walt, V. (2005) 'A town called Angers', *Time*, 165: 12–15.

Warren, J., Hazelwood, R. R. and Dietz, P. E. (1996) 'The sexually sadistic serial killer', *Journal of Forensic Sciences*, 41: 970–4.

Waterman, J., Kelly, R. J., Olivieri, M. K. and McCord, J. (1993) *Beyond the Playground Walls: Sexual Abuse in Preschools*, New York: Guilford.

Weisberg, D. K. (1985) *Children of the Night: A Study of Adolescent Prostitution*, Lexington: Lexington Books.

West, C. and Zimmerman, D. H. (1987) 'Doing gender', *Gender & Society*, 1: 125–51.

Whitfield, C. L. (2001) 'The "false memory" defense: using disinformation and junk science in and out of court', *The Journal of Child Sexual Abuse*, 9: 53–78.

Wild, N. J. (1989) Prevalence of child sex rings. *Pediatrics,* 83, 553–8.

Wild, N. J. and Wynne, J. M. (1986) 'Child sex rings', *British Medical Journal*, 293: 183–5.

Williams, L. and Finkelhor, D. (1990) 'The characteristics of incestuous fathers: a review of recent studies', in W. L. Marshall, D. R. Laws and H. E. Barbaree (eds) *Handbook of Sexual Assault: Issues, Theories and Treatment of the Offender*, New York: Plenum Press.

Winnicott, D. W. (1960) 'The theory of the parent-infant relationship', *International Journal of Psycho-Analysis*, 41: 585–595.

Wolff, L. (2005) 'Depraved inclinations: libertines and children in Casanova's Venice', *Eighteenth-Century Studies*, 38: 417–40.

Wood Report (1997) *Final Report. Vol IV: The Paedophile Inquiry, Sydney*: The Government of the State of New South Wales, Royal Commission into the New South Wales Police Service, http://www.pic.nsw.gov.au/files/reports/RCPS%20 Report%20Volume%204.pdf.

Wright, S. A. (2006) 'Satanic cults, ritual abuse and moral panic: deconstructing a modern witch-hunt', in H. A. Berger (ed.) *Witchcraft and Magic: Contemporary North America*, Philadelphia: University of Pennsylvania Press.

Wyre, R. (1996) 'The mind of the paedophile', in P. Bibby (ed.) *Organised Abuse: The Current Debate*, Aldershot: Ashgate.

Yama, M. F., Tovey, S. L. and Fogas, B. S. (1993) 'Childhood family environment and sexual abuse as predictors of anxiety and depression in adult women', *American Journal of Orthopsychiatry*, 63: 136–41.

Young, W. C., Sachs, R. G., Braun, B. G. and Watkins, R. T. (1991) 'Patients reporting ritual abuse in childhood: a clinical syndrome, Report of 37 cases', *Child Abuse & Neglect*, 15: 181–9.

Youngson, S. C. (1994) 'Ritual abuse: the personal and professional costs for workers', in V. Sinason (ed.) *Treating Survivors of Satanist Abuse*, London and New York: Routledge.

Žižek, S. (1991) *For They Know Not What They Do: Enjoyment as a Political Factor*, London and New York: Verso.

—— (1993) *Tarrying with the Negative*, Durham: Duke University Press.

—— (1994) *The Metastases of Enjoyment: Six Essays on Women and Causality*, London and New York: Verso.

—— (1996) 'Invisible ideology: political violence between fiction and fantasy', *Journal of Political Ideologies*, 1: 15–32.

Index